Classic
American Cooking
FROM • THE • ACADEMY

BRUCE AIDELLS
JOHN PHILLIP CARROLL
MICHAEL GOODWIN
JAY HARLOW
CYNTHIA SCHEER
NAOMI WISE
Writers

SALLY W. SMITH
PEGGY WALDMAN
Editors

CALIFORNIA CULINARY ACADEMY

Bruce Aidells *(top right)* gained a reputation for lively and innovative cuisine as a restaurant chef in Berkeley, California. His interest in Cajun specialties led him to make Louisiana-style sausages, which he sells nationwide. **John Phillip Carroll** *(bottom right)* began his food career in California as a restaurant chef and cooking teacher. He has collaborated on three cookbooks including the *Fannie Farmer Baking Book* and the California Culinary Academy series book *Breads,* and he serves on the board of directors of the San Francisco Professional Food Society. **Jay Harlow** *(top left)* is a freelance writer and cooking teacher living in Oakland, California. A food columnist for the *San Francisco Chronicle,* he has worked as a restaurant chef and has written three cookbooks, including the California Culinary Academy book *Enjoying American Wines.* **Cynthia Scheer** *(bottom center)* is a Bay Area food writer and home economist. She has been a magazine food editor and has written 15 cookbooks. Other books by Cynthia Scheer in the California Culinary Academy series are *Affordable Elegant Meals, Breads, Breakfasts & Brunches, Salads,* and *Soups & Stews.* **Naomi Wise** *(bottom left)* and **Michael Goodwin** *(top center),* San Francisco-based freelance writers, have traveled extensively through the Americas collecting recipes and foodstuffs. They are co-authors (with Charles Perry) of *Totally Hot! The Ultimate Hot Pepper Cookbook,* and together they write restaurant reviews for a weekly newspaper.

The California Culinary Academy In the forefront of American institutions leading the culinary renaissance in this country, the California Culinary Academy in San Francisco has gained a reputation as one of the most outstanding professional chef training schools in the world. With a teaching staff recruited from the best restaurants of Western Europe, the Academy educates students from around the globe in the preparation of classical cuisine. The recipes in this book were created in consultation with the chefs of the Academy. For information about the Academy, write the Office of the Dean, California Culinary Academy, 625 Polk Street, San Francisco, CA 94102.

Front Cover Louisiana's Boiled Seafood Dinner showcases the abundance of succulent shellfish found in local waters (page 78).

Title Page The addition of shrimp and rice transforms stewed vegetables into a hearty Southern-style main dish—Shrimp Okra Pilau (page 36).

Back Cover
Upper Flavorful toppings all but smother Tucson Chimichangas, a crispy burrito filled with chicken, cheese, chiles, and spices (page 89).
Lower The Pacific States' bounty from both land and sea combines in this easy menu of Barbecued Oysters and Alder-Grilled Salmon with fresh vegetable salad and dessert fruit plate (page 122).

Contributors

Photographer
Michael Lamotte

Additional Photographers
Alan Copeland, Academy photography; Marshall Gordon, pages 31, 77, and 108; Kit Morris, authors and chefs, at left; Jackson Vereen, page 10

Photographic Stylist
Sara Slavin

Food Stylists
Sandra Cook, Amy Nathan, Cynthia Scheer

Additional Food Stylists
M. Susan Broussard, page 10
Doug Warne, pages 31, 77, and 108

Calligraphers
Keith Carlson
Chuck Wertman

Illustrators
Edith Allgood, page 96
Ron Hildebrand, pages 6, 26, 46, 66, 86, and 106

Copyeditor
Toni Murray

Proofreader
Andrea Y. Connolly

Designers
Linda Hinrichs
Carol Kramer

Printed in Hong Kong through Mandarin Offset.

Acknowledgments appear on page 128.

The California Culinary Academy series is published by the staff of Cole Group.

Publisher
Brete C. Harrison

VP and Director of Operations
Linda Hauck

VP Marketing and Business Development
John A. Morris

Associate Publisher
James Connolly

Director of Production
Steve Lux

Senior Editor
Annette Gooch

Production Assistant
Dotti Hydue

Address all inquiries to
Cole Group
4415 Sonoma Highway/ PO Box 4089
Santa Rosa, CA 95402-4089
(800) 959-2717   (707) 538-0492
FAX (707) 538-0497

Distributed to the book trade by
Publishers Group West.

C O N T E N T S

NEW ENGLAND   **5**
by John Phillip Carroll
Main Dishes   7
Vegetables and Side Dishes   10
Relishes   12
Family Supper Menu   14
Breads   16
Desserts   18
Boston Dinner Menu   20

LOUISIANA   **65**
by Bruce Aidells
Appetizers and Soups   68
Vegetables and Side Dishes   71
Main Dishes   73
Backyard Seafood Dinner
   Menu   78
Desserts   81
Fais Dodo Menu   82

THE SOUTH   **25**
*by Naomi Wise and
   Michael Goodwin*
Main Dishes   27
Soul Food Dinner Menu   32
Soups, Vegetables, and
   Side Dishes   34
Breads   37
Church Social Menu   38
Desserts   41

THE SOUTHWEST   **85**
*by Naomi Wise and
   Michael Goodwin*
Main Dishes   87
Noche Buena Feast Menu   90
Sauces   95
Soups, Side Dishes, and
   Vegetables   96
Breads   98
Texas Barbecue Menu   100
Desserts   102

THE HEARTLAND   **45**
by Cynthia Scheer
Sunday Breakfast Menu   47
Substantial Soups   48
Main Dishes   50
Side Dishes and Salads   57
Fourth of July Picnic Menu   58
Desserts   61

THE PACIFIC STATES   **105**
by Jay Harlow
Appetizers and First Courses   107
Soups, Salads, and
   Side Dishes   110
Breads   112
Gold Miner's Brunch Menu   114
Main Dishes   117
Desserts   120
Seashore Barbecue Menu   122

Index   124
Metric Chart and
   Acknowledgments   128

This Family Supper is so appealing that it's worth taking the time to arrange the meat and vegetables on your best platter. Recipes start on page 14.

New England

The food we call American has many roots—the cooking of the Indians living here when Europeans first arrived; the bounty of the land, sea, and fresh water; and the cuisines of the homelands left behind by those who immigrated to these shores. From its roots the richness and diversity of American food has developed in distinct, regional patterns. This book celebrates the classic cooking of regional America, starting with New England in the days of the Pilgrims. This chapter is particularly rich in fish and shellfish dishes, along with traditional standards such as Boston Baked Beans (see page 21) and Boston Brown Bread (see page 22).

THE TRADITIONS OF NEW ENGLAND

Although the British were the earliest colonial force in New England, the present-day states of Vermont, Connecticut, New Hampshire, Maine, Massachusetts, and Rhode Island also were settled by later waves of German, Irish, Swedish, and Dutch immigrants. All contributed to the bounty of New England cooking, as did the sea trade that brought many more exotic elements into the cuisine. Foreign sailors mixed with the colonists, most of whom were Northern European. The Portuguese and Italian sailors, for example, taught new ways of preparing the bounty of the sea in tomatoey stews and garlicky dishes.

While Native American Indians had shown the early settlers how to cultivate corn and grind it for corn breads, the sailors introduced new ways to use it—in rich sweet breads and hearty cornmeal puddings like polenta. Trade with India brought curried dishes to America (see Kedgeree, page 7) as well as the ginger used in chutneys, gingerbreads, and Indian pudding.

The recipes included here represent early New England. There is evidence of the Indian influence (see Succotash, page 11), the flavors of India trade (see Gingerbread, page 16), and the "waste not, want not" ethic of the Puritans. These recipes use resources the colonists found on hand—fish, corn, maple syrup—as well as early imports like molasses, and foods they learned to preserve, such as the salted cod used in Scalloped Codfish (page 7).

Early New England cooking was done on a wood fire, usually in a big iron caldron slung over the embers. Breads were often baked in heavy covered kettles set right among the coals or on a flat metal surface in front of the fire.

In most cooking and baking, molasses, maple syrup, or maple sugar was used instead of costly granulated sugar. Some dishes—like fish chowders and fish cakes, baked beans, brown bread, and Indian pudding—were known as standing dishes, in the sense that they were traditional, time-honored favorites.

When food was plentiful there were long periods of feasting. The best known feast is Thanksgiving, first celebrated by the Pilgrims and their Indian friends in 1621. Probably more like a clambake than the traditional dinner we know today, it would have featured venison, shellfish and fish, fowl (duck, goose, and eagle, but probably no turkey), corn bread, succotash, and beach plums (which grow on the coast from Nova Scotia to Virginia).

The settlers generally had two meals a day—a big dinner around noontime and supper in early evening. Supper often brought out leftovers from dinner, which could be chopped, combined, and hashed together in one big skillet for reheating. This dinner-and-supper pattern is still common in many parts of the country, especially where farmers must rise before dawn to do their chores, working up quite an appetite by midday.

Early New England cooking, with its fragrant earthiness, is thrifty and sturdy—dishes that let you cook at leisure, that won't be harmed if kept warm for an hour or two, and that often taste better reheated the next day. Many of these recipes can easily be made with what you have on hand, and they take well to substitutions and variations. Meals were created in response to what was available from the sea, farms, and forests, and this is the type of informal American home cooking that's popular again today.

MAIN DISHES

Main dishes in New England cookery are sturdy and fragrant. Produced by leisurely cooking, they make pleasant family meals for weekends. The recipes lean heavily on fresh ocean fish, as well as on the salted and preserved meats and fish that have long been New England staples.

SCALLOPED CODFISH

Dried, salted cod was as much a New England staple as cornmeal, and it was frequently used in savory pies, chowders, and fish hash. It was so common, in fact, that it became a source of wealth for many who produced it in quantity. Today it is available in many supermarkets, packed in 1-pound wooden boxes. It can also be found in Italian markets and specialty stores in whole, dried fillets, 2 to 3 feet long. However purchased, dried, salted cod must be soaked in several changes of cold water to soften, revive, and desalt it. Small fillets, like those in the wooden cartons, need about 24 hours of soaking, and whole fillets might take up to 2 or 3 days. After soaking, it looks and feels like fresh fish and is just as perishable, so use it within a day or freeze it. Try Scalloped Codfish as a main dish for a winter dinner or for breakfast or brunch.

> 1 pound salted cod fillets, soaked and drained (see introduction)
> ¼ cup butter
> 1 medium onion, chopped
> 1 cup toasted bread crumbs
> 2 tablespoons flour
> 1¾ cups milk
> ¼ cup dry sherry
> ¼ teaspoon freshly ground pepper
> Salt, to taste

1. Preheat oven to 400° F. Place fish in a medium saucepan with water to cover. Simmer gently for 10 minutes. Drain well. Either shred fish with 2 forks or chop coarsely in a food processor. Set aside.

2. In a small skillet over medium-low heat, melt 2 tablespoons of butter. Add onion and cook gently for 10 minutes, until softened. Add bread crumbs and toss. Set aside.

3. In a small saucepan over medium heat, melt remaining butter. Add flour and cook, stirring, for 2 minutes. Whisk in milk and cook over medium heat, stirring almost constantly, until thickened. Add chopped fish, sherry, and pepper; blend well. Taste and add salt if necessary.

4. Spread half the fish mixture in a buttered 1½-quart baking dish and sprinkle with half the crumbs. Spoon on remaining fish and top with remaining crumbs. Prepared baking dish can sit for an hour or two if desired; refrigerate it if the day is especially hot. Bake until bubbly and lightly browned, about 20 to 30 minutes.

Serves 4.

KEDGEREE

This unusually named dish of curried rice flecked with fish probably has East Indian roots; indeed, it goes well with traditional curry condiments like chutney. Just about any cooked or smoked firm-fleshed fish is good for kedgeree, including turbot, halibut, cod, salmon, and canned tuna. With sliced tomatoes and biscuits, it makes a fine breakfast or supper dish.

> ⅓ cup butter, melted
> 3 cups cooked rice
> 2 cups cooked fish
> 4 hard-cooked eggs, chopped
> ¾ cup heavy cream
> ¼ cup chopped parsley
> 2 teaspoons curry powder
> ¼ teaspoon each salt and freshly ground pepper

1. Preheat oven to 350° F. In a large bowl combine butter, rice, fish, eggs, cream, parsley, curry, salt, and pepper. Stir and toss until all ingredients are moistened and thoroughly mixed.

2. Turn into a buttered 1½-quart baking dish and bake until heated through, about 20 to 25 minutes.

Serves 4 to 6.

CLAM PIE

The English have many examples of savory meat pies and pasties, but the colonists made theirs using the ocean's bounty. This pie—a hearty mixture of clams, potatoes, and onions in a creamy sauce—is a thick, flavorful chowder in a crust.

> 3 cans (6½ oz each) minced clams or 1½ cups chopped fresh clams
> Bottled clam juice, if needed
> ¼ cup butter
> 1 small onion, finely chopped
> 5 tablespoons flour
> 1½ cups milk
> 1 large boiled potato, peeled and diced
> ¼ teaspoon ground pepper
> Salt, to taste
> Basic pastry for a 2-crust 9-inch pie (see page 63)

1. Drain clams well and reserve liquid. If necessary, add bottled clam juice to make ½ cup liquid. Set aside.

2. In a medium saucepan over medium heat, melt butter. Add onion and cook gently for about 10 minutes, until softened but not browned.

3. Add flour; cook, stirring, for 2 minutes. Slowly add milk, whisking constantly, then whisk in reserved clam liquid. Stir in clams and diced potato, then season with pepper and salt (if you have used canned clams, you probably will not need to add salt). Simmer about 5 minutes, stirring frequently, then set aside.

4. On a lightly floured smooth surface, roll out half the pastry for a bottom crust and fit it into a 9-inch pie pan. Spread clam mixture evenly in dough-lined pan. Roll out remaining pastry for a top crust and drape over the pie. Trim and crimp the edges and cut several vents in the top for steam to escape.

5. Bake until well browned, about 40 minutes. If crust begins to puff up during baking, just puncture gently with a knife and it will deflate. Remove from oven and let rest a few minutes before serving.

Serves 4 to 6.

PARSNIP STEW

The cream-colored parsnip is a familiar and respected root in New England cookery. Related to and resembling the carrot, parsnips are nourishing and substantial, with a faint sweetness. They are a fine addition to soups and stews; they are delicious boiled, buttered, and served with meat or poultry; and they can even be substituted for pumpkin to make a pie. Recipes for this old-fashioned vegetable stew always use parsnips, potatoes, onions, and salt pork, in varying amounts. It is hearty and economical and makes a good simple dinner along with corn bread or steamed brown bread and a salad. It is even more delicious reheated after a day or two.

- ¼ pound salt pork, cut in ¼-inch dice
- 2 onions, peeled and thinly sliced
- 4 to 5 medium parsnips (about 1¼ pounds), peeled and cut in ½-inch dice
- 3 medium potatoes, peeled and cut in ½-inch dice
- 2 tablespoons flour
- 2½ cups (approximately) water
- 2½ cups milk
  Salt and freshly ground pepper, to taste

1. Place diced salt pork in a 4- to 5-quart pan and brown it over moderate heat, stirring frequently, until golden (about 10 minutes).

2. Add onion and continue cooking, stirring occasionally, until lightly browned, about 10 minutes more.

3. Add parsnips and potatoes. Sprinkle flour over the top, then cook and stir for about 2 more minutes.

4. Stir in the water and 1½ cups of the milk. If necessary add a little more water, so vegetables are just covered. Cover and simmer gently over low heat for about 20 minutes, stirring occasionally, until vegetables are tender when pierced. Season with salt and freshly ground pepper. Remove from heat and stir in the remaining cup of milk.

Makes about 10 cups, 6 servings.

CORNED-BEEF HASH

Corned-beef hash fills the kitchen with a wonderful, almost spicy aroma that fully justifies adding extra potatoes and meat to New England Boiled Dinner (see page 14) so you'll have leftovers for this hearty dish. Allow a good 30 to 40 minutes to cook hash, since it must crust on the bottom twice before a final crust is formed and the hash turned out onto a platter. The meat and potatoes should be coarsely chopped; if you use a food processor, take care not to chop them too fine. Serve with a green salad or coleslaw (see page 60), and catsup at the table. For breakfast, place a hot poached egg on each serving if you wish.

- 2 to 3 cups chopped cooked corned beef
- 2 to 3 cups chopped boiled potatoes
- 1 onion, finely chopped
- ¼ teaspoon freshly ground pepper
- 4 tablespoons butter or shortening
- ⅓ cup heavy cream

1. In a large bowl, mix beef, potatoes, onion, and pepper.

2. In a 10-inch skillet (preferably well-seasoned cast iron) over medium-low heat, melt butter. Spread meat-and-potato mixture evenly over the bottom, forming a thick cake. Press down firmly all over with the back of a spatula. Cook about 10 minutes, giving pan a sharp jerk now and then to prevent sticking.

3. Scrape all over the bottom of the pan with a spatula to loosen the crust, and stir it into the hash. Press down firmly all over to make a flat cake, and cook about 10 minutes more, giving pan a sharp jerk now and then to prevent sticking.

4. Pour cream over hash, then scrape up crust again and stir to incorporate it. Flatten hash with a spatula and cook another 10 minutes, giving pan a few sharp jerks now and then to keep hash from sticking.

5. To serve, you may cut into wedges, flipping each piece over on a plate, crusted side up. Or you may unmold the whole hash by flipping the skillet upside down onto a platter. While this looks impressive, remember the skillet is hot and heavy, and you must work fast, so unmolding is a little tricky. It is easier if you get a friend to help you.

Serves 4 to 6.

Red-Flannel Hash Add 2 cups diced cooked beets to the hash mixture and fry as directed.

SCALLOPED OYSTERS

In colonial times oysters were as common as muffins are today. By the mid-1800s they were even being shipped by train to the Midwest. This simple dish of tender oysters surrounded by buttery, crisp crumbs is one of the best ways to enjoy them hot and is ideal for a family supper.

- 1 pint shucked oysters, with their liquid
- ½ cup melted butter
- 1 cup fresh cracker crumbs (plain ones such as soda crackers or pilot biscuits)
- ½ cup fresh bread crumbs
- ¼ teaspoon each salt and freshly ground pepper
- 2 tablespoons cream
- 2 teaspoons Worcestershire sauce
  Several drops hot pepper sauce (optional)

1. Preheat oven to 425° F. Drain oysters well, reserving their liquid.

2. In a medium bowl toss together butter, cracker crumbs, and bread crumbs. Spread half of the crumbs over the bottom of a buttered 8-inch square baking dish. Arrange oysters in a single layer over crumbs; sprinkle with salt and pepper.

3. In a small cup, stir together cream, Worcestershire, hot pepper sauce (if used), and 3 tablespoons of the reserved oyster liquid. Spoon over oysters.

4. Spread remaining crumbs over the top and bake for 25 minutes.

Serves 4.

FISH CHOWDER

The English word *chowder* comes from the French *chaudière*, meaning a big iron kettle—the kind that hung over glowing coals in the fireplace and was used for all types of cooking. But you'll need neither an iron pot nor a fireplace to make the chowder that follows. This is the type of cooking in which proportions aren't too important. You can use more or less of anything, as long as you have the essential salt pork, onions, potatoes, and milk. This hearty dish can be the centerpiece of dinner, accompanied by a crusty loaf of bread and a salad.

> *4 to 6 ounces salt pork, cut in small dice*
>
> *2 large onions, peeled and thinly sliced*
>
> *4 medium potatoes, peeled and cut in ½-inch dice*
>
> *4 cups fish stock or 2 cups bottled clam juice plus 2 cups water*
>
> *2 pounds boneless, skinless, firm white fish fillets (such as cod, haddock, sea bass, hake, or snapper), cut in 1-inch chunks*
>
> *2 cups milk, half-and-half, or whipping cream, depending on desired richness*
> *Salt and freshly ground black pepper, to taste*
>
> *2 to 4 tablespoons butter, softened*
> *Soda crackers, pilot biscuits, or any other plain cracker*

1. In a Dutch oven or soup kettle, cook salt pork slowly until the fat has been rendered and the tiny bits are well browned. Use a slotted spoon to lift out browned bits and drain on paper towels. Remove and discard all but about 3 tablespoons of fat (enough to film pan).

2. To fat remaining in pan, add onions and cook slowly for 15 minutes. Add potatoes and cook gently 5 minutes more, tossing once or twice.

3. Pour in fish stock, cover, and simmer gently until potatoes are just tender when pierced (15 to 20 minutes).

4. Add fish and reserved pork bits to pot and simmer, partially covered, just until fish is cooked through (about 5 minutes).

5. Stir in milk and gently heat to a simmer without boiling. Season with salt and pepper (because of the salt pork, you will need little, if any, additional salt).

6. Ladle into heated soup plates and top each with a dab of butter. Serve with crackers.

Makes about 12 cups, about 6 servings.

A time-honored chowder with salt pork, onions, potatoes, and chunks of fish is a soup for all seasons. Fresh ingredients and creamy broth provide a light, summery quality, but the soup also has enough heft to warm you on crisp fall and winter days. Complete it ahead through step 3 if you wish, then reheat to a simmer, add the fish and salt pork bits, and finish as directed.

OPENING BIVALVES

Purchase live oysters, clams, and mussels. The shells will be tightly closed or will snap shut when tapped. Scrub the shells thoroughly with a stiff brush under cold water. Soft-shell clams are fragile; take care not to break them. Now the bivalves are ready to be opened. The process, shown here with oysters, is the same for all types. However, opening oysters often takes strength. Wear a heavy glove or use a towel to protect your hand, and use an oyster knife with a short, strong blade and hand guard. Bivalves are easier to open when cold.

1. Hold oyster with deep cup facing down. Insert tip of oyster knife into the hinge and twist it to open shell.

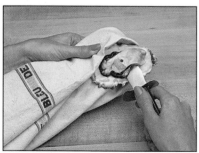

2. Slide knife along inside of upper shell to sever the muscle that attaches it to flesh. Discard upper shell. Slide knife under flesh to sever bottom muscle.

CLAM FRITTERS

Tender, puffy fritters of chopped clams in an egg batter, deep-fried until golden, were once quite popular at roadside diners in coastal areas, especially in New England and the Pacific Northwest. They were often called clamburgers. Canned clams work well in this recipe, which you might serve with French fries and a fresh vegetable or salad.

> 3 cans (6½ oz each) *minced clams* or 1½ cups chopped *fresh clams*
> Bottled *clam juice,* if needed
> 1 egg
> Dash *hot pepper sauce*
> 2 tablespoons *butter,* melted
> ½ cup *milk*
> 1 cup *flour*
> 2 teaspoons *baking powder*
> ¼ teaspoon *salt*
> *Salad oil* or *shortening,* for frying
> *Tartar sauce* and *lemon wedges,* or *catsup*

1. Drain clams well, reserving liquid. If necessary, add bottled clam juice to make ½ cup liquid.

2. In a medium bowl combine clams, reserved liquid, egg, hot pepper sauce, butter, and milk.

3. In another bowl stir and toss together flour, baking powder, and salt. Add to the clam mixture and beat with a fork until blended.

4. Heat ¼ inch oil in a large skillet over medium-high heat. When it is almost smoking, drop batter into fat by tablespoons. Fry, turning once, until golden on both sides, about 2 to 3 minutes. Fry only as many at one time as will fit comfortably without crowding. Drain briefly on paper towels and serve as soon as possible on warm plates. Accompany with tartar sauce and lemon wedges or with catsup.

Makes about 25 fritters, 6 servings.

VEGETABLES AND SIDE DISHES

In New England, vegetable mixtures are often as hearty as the main courses they accompany, and indeed many of them can be served alone as lighter, meatless main dishes. They are also good for Sunday breakfast, with biscuits, ham or bacon, and eggs prepared as you like.

MAPLE-GLAZED SWEET POTATOES

Here is a recipe that makes use of two common and compatible colonial ingredients—maple syrup and sweet potatoes (or yams). The potatoes are subtle enough not to overpower the delicate syrup. The crusty brown slices, just slightly sweet, are good for breakfast with bacon and eggs or as a vegetable accompaniment to either poultry or ham.

> 3 to 4 medium *sweet potatoes* (about 2 lbs)
> 6 tablespoons *butter*
> ¼ teaspoon each *salt and freshly ground pepper*
> ¼ cup *maple syrup*

1. Peel sweet potatoes, quarter them lengthwise, then cut crosswise with a sharp knife or food processor into ⅛-inch-thick slices.

2. In a large skillet over medium heat, melt butter. Add potatoes and season with salt and pepper. Toss for a minute or so to thoroughly coat potatoes.

3. Lower heat and cover pan (use a makeshift cover of foil or a baking sheet if necessary) for about 10 minutes. Toss occasionally to prevent sticking. Potatoes should be just tender when pierced; if not, cook a few minutes longer.

4. Add maple syrup and raise heat to medium. Cook uncovered for 5 to 10 minutes more, tossing or stirring occasionally, until potatoes are thoroughly glazed.

Serves 4 to 6.

CORN PUDDING

The flavor and texture of corn pudding made with canned creamed corn is never as smooth as when made from freshly grated corn. Although extracting the pulp from the kernel is a chore, it's worth it. The job can be done with a knife, but there are also handy gadgets known as "corn scrapers," available in cookware shops, country stores, and through mail-order outlets. A corn scraper is worth purchasing, they are inexpensive and do the task in a fraction of the time.

> 8 to 10 ears fresh corn
> 3 eggs
> 1 cup milk
> ½ cup heavy cream
> ½ teaspoon salt
> ¼ teaspoon freshly ground pepper
> 2 tablespoons melted butter
> ¼ cup cornmeal

1. One ear of corn at a time, slide the point of a small, very sharp knife down the center of each row of kernels. Although it is tedious, be sure to work slowly and carefully, cutting all the way down to the cob. Now hold each ear over a large bowl, and with the blunt edge of the blade scrape down all around, depressing the kernels and pressing out the corn pulp. You should have about 2 cups.

2. Preheat oven to 350° F. To corn pulp add eggs, milk, cream, salt, pepper, butter, and cornmeal. Beat with a whisk or fork until thoroughly blended; pour into a buttered 1½-quart baking dish.

3. Set the pudding-filled dish into a larger dish; set on oven rack. Pour boiling water into the larger dish to come about two thirds up the sides of the smaller one. Bake until pudding no longer trembles when dish is jiggled slightly and a skewer inserted in the center comes out clean, about 1 hour to 1 hour and 15 minutes. Pudding can sit in the oven, with door slightly ajar, for up to 20 minutes. It will slowly sink a bit, which is okay.

Serves 6.

CORN OYSTERS

These little fritters are named for their shape; when the small blobs of corn-kernel batter are fried to a golden hue, they resemble real oysters. They have a good corn flavor and a slightly chewy texture. Serve them for breakfast with maple syrup; or to accompany meat or chicken, topped with butter if you wish.

> 2 cups corn kernels, fresh or canned
> ¼ cup milk
> 2 eggs, separated
> ¼ cup flour
> 1 teaspoon baking powder
> ¼ teaspoon each salt and freshly ground pepper
> 3 to 6 tablespoons bacon drippings or shortening
> Butter or maple syrup (optional)

1. In a medium bowl combine corn kernels, milk, and egg yolks.

2. In a small cup stir and toss together flour, baking powder, salt, and pepper. Add to corn mixture and blend well.

3. In medium bowl of electric mixer, beat egg whites until they stand in soft peaks (do not overbeat), then fold into corn mixture.

4. Heat 3 tablespoons bacon drippings in a large skillet over medium-high heat until the fat almost smokes and a bit of batter sizzles when dropped into it. Drop the batter by rounded tablespoons into hot pan and cook the "oysters" until golden brown, turning once, about 4 minutes in all. Drain well on paper towels and keep warm in a 200° F oven. Continue until all batter is used, adding more fat to the pan as necessary.

5. Serve hot, with butter or maple syrup, if desired.

Makes about 20 "oysters," 6 servings.

SUCCOTASH

The name *succotash* is a derivation of an Indian word, *m'sickquatash,* meaning "corn not crushed or ground." Colonists learned from Indians the land-saving practice of planting corn and beans together, then training the bean vines up the corn stalks. At the harvest they simply combined the two in cooking. Today we usually make succotash with corn and lima beans, but many New England cooks prefer cranberry beans, and the Pennsylvania Dutch often add green peppers, tomatoes, and other vegetables. Some early recipes also called for fowl or meat plus potatoes or turnips, thus making more of a stew. This modern recipe is simple, colorful, and delicious, and it is very good made with frozen vegetables.

> ¼ cup butter
> 2 cups fresh corn kernels or frozen corn kernels, thawed
> 2 cups cooked lima beans
> ¼ teaspoon salt
> ¼ teaspoon freshly ground pepper
> ½ cup heavy cream
> 2 tablespoons chopped parsley

1. In a medium saucepan over medium heat, melt butter. Add corn, beans, salt, and pepper; stir to combine.

2. Add cream and simmer gently, uncovered, for about 5 minutes.

3. Stir in parsley and serve.

Serves 6.

RELISHES

Among the charms of New England cooking are its many traditional condiments and relishes. Their colors, textures, and spicy flavors perk up plain meats and poultry—and they embellish the table as well, glistening in glass serving dishes.

MUSTARD PICKLES

For as far back as my grandmother can remember, in her family this dish has been called winter salad. The name makes great sense, since pickling is a way of preserving an abundance of summer vegetables to have on hand in the wintertime. It's a sweet, spicy, colorful vegetable relish strongly flavored with mustard, and it's a dandy accompaniment to roast meats and chicken.

        3 medium red bell peppers
        3 medium green bell peppers
        3 large cucumbers
        4 large onions
        4 medium green tomatoes
        6 large stalks celery
        1 head cauliflower
        1 cup un-iodized salt
        4 quarts cold water
        6 tablespoons dry mustard
        1 tablespoon powdered tumeric
        2 teaspoons celery seed
      2½ cups sugar
        1 cup flour
        8 cups cider vinegar

1. Wash all vegetables well to remove any dirt. Cut peppers and cucumbers in half and scrape out their seeds. Peel and halve onions. Slice peppers and onions ½ inch thick. Cut cucumbers in 1-inch cubes. Cut stem end from each tomato, then cut tomatoes into cubes about ¾ inch to a side. Cut celery into ½-inch pieces. Break cauliflower into florets.

2. Toss all vegetables together in a very large bowl or enameled pot. Mix salt with the water and stir until salt dissolves. Pour over vegetables, cover, and let stand 8 hours or overnight.

3. Drain vegetables and rinse well under cold running water. Place them in a large pot, cover with fresh cold water, and bring just to a boil. Drain well in a colander.

4. Dry the pot, and in it combine mustard, tumeric, celery seed, sugar, and flour. Stir until thoroughly mixed. Gradually pour in vinegar, whisking constantly to prevent lumps. Bring to a boil, stirring almost constantly, and boil gently until thick and smooth (about 5 minutes). Add vegetables to hot mixture and cook, stirring until heated through (about 5 minutes).

5. Spoon boiling mixture into hot, sterilized jars, leaving ½-inch headspace. Wipe rim of each jar with a clean, dampened cloth, and seal with metal lids and rings.

6. *Process in a boiling water bath as follows:* Place jars on a rack in a deep pot or kettle with enough boiling water to cover jars by at least 1 inch. Cover pot and bring water back to a full boil, then boil 10 minutes.

7. Lift jars from water and set on a towel or rack to cool completely before storing.

Makes about 8 pints.

WATERMELON PICKLES

Here's another example of Yankee thrift and a good way to make use of watermelon rind, which is usually thrown away. These pickles are often prepared on July 5, with the remains of watermelon from the Fourth. They are sweet, spicy, and good at a backyard barbecue or as a condiment with corned-beef hash or a boiled dinner.

        Rind from 1 very large
          watermelon
      2 quarts water
      ½ cup un-iodized salt
      3 cups sugar
    2½ cups cider vinegar
      1 lemon, thinly sliced
        Small cinnamon sticks
      1 tablespoon whole allspice
        Whole cloves
      2 tablespoons chopped candied
        ginger (optional)

1. Trim the green skin and inner pink pulp from watermelon rind. Cut rind into 1-inch squares.

2. In a large bowl combine the water and salt, stirring until salt dissolves. Place rind in salt solution, weight down with a plate, and let stand in a cool place for about 8 hours (or overnight).

3. Drain thoroughly and rinse under cold running water, then drain well again. Place rind in a large saucepan or Dutch oven and cover with cold water. Bring to a simmer and cook very gently just until tender (about 10 minutes). Drain and set rind aside.

4. In the same pan in which you cooked rind, combine sugar, vinegar, and lemon. Smash 2 cinnamon sticks with a hammer or rolling pin to break them into coarse pieces. Add to pan, along with allspice, 1 teaspoon cloves, and ginger (if used). Bring to a simmer, stirring occasionally, and cook gently until liquid clears and sugar dissolves (about 10 minutes).

5. Add the drained rind and simmer until rind is translucent (about 10 minutes).

6. Spoon rind into hot, sterilized jars, including a few cloves and pieces of cinnamon stick in each. Fill with the boiling syrup, leaving ½-inch headspace. Wipe rim of each jar with a clean, dampened cloth and seal with metal lids and rings.

7. *Process in a boiling water bath as follows:* Place on a rack in a deep pot or kettle with enough boiling water to cover jars by at least 1 inch. Cover pot and bring water back to a full boil, then boil 10 minutes.

8. Lift jars from water and set on a towel or rack to cool completely. Pickles will be better if allowed to stand for several weeks.

Makes 3 to 4 pints.

CRANBERRY CHUTNEY

Pungent chutneys of fruit, sugar, vinegar and spices, like the curry dinners they often accompany, are native to India. But their spicy sweetness also makes them a perfect mate for slightly salty foods such as ham, corned beef, codfish cakes, and hash. Cranberries (which the colonists used to cook with maple syrup to make a dessert or relish) give this a New England flavor.

4 medium to large green or firm ripe tomatoes, finely chopped
¼ cup salt
1 quart cider vinegar
3½ cups firmly packed brown sugar
8 large tart apples, peeled, cored, and chopped
4 cups cranberries
2 red onions, peeled and chopped
2 cups dried currants
½ cup finely chopped, peeled ginger root or 2 tablespoons powdered ginger

1. In a medium bowl toss chopped tomatoes with 2 tablespoons of the salt, cover, and let stand for about 12 hours, or overnight.

2. Drain tomatoes well and soak in fresh cold water for 15 minutes, then drain again.

3. In a large pot combine vinegar, brown sugar, and the remaining salt. Add apples, cranberries, onions, currants, ginger, and drained tomatoes. Bring just to a boil and simmer for 5 minutes, stirring frequently.

4. Remove from heat and cool for an hour or two, so the raisins plump and the flavors blend.

5. Bring back to a simmer and cook uncovered over low heat for about 30 minutes, stirring frequently, until apples and onions are very tender and chutney has thickened slightly.

6. Spoon into hot, sterilized jars, leaving ½-inch headspace. Wipe rim of each jar with a dampened, clean cloth and seal with metal lids and rings.

7. *Process in a boiling water bath as follows:* Place filled jars on a rack in a deep kettle with enough boiling water to cover jars by at least 1 inch. Cover pot and bring back to a full boil, then boil 10 minutes.

8. Lift jars from water and set on a towel or rack to cool completely before storing.

Makes about 7 pints.

Years ago it was necessary for families to preserve much of what they grew in their gardens and on their farms. Today we do it not so much out of necessity, but because it's fun and prideful, and even the youngest cooks can participate. You'll find that your own pickles, relishes, and chutneys glisten so brightly in clear glass jars—and look so satisfying on the pantry shelf—it's worth reviving the nearly lost art of home canning.

13

FAMILY SUPPER

*New England
Boiled Dinner*

Parker House Rolls

*Apple Dumplings
With Nutmeg Sauce*

Beer, Cider

This is an old-fashioned family meal composed of classic New England dishes. It makes a good midday Sunday dinner, with Horseradish Sauce or Mustard Pickles (see page 12), and beer or cider to drink, followed by an afternoon stroll. Be sure to boil up plenty of extra meat and potatoes, so you can have a traditional hash a day or two later (see page 8).

NEW ENGLAND BOILED DINNER

Just about every culture has its boiled dinner, dating back to the days when most cooking was done in a single pot slung over the fire. This is slow, relaxed cooking, which can take care of itself while you go attend to other things. Once done, the meat can be kept warm for a couple of hours, or it can be reheated. The vegetables can be trimmed ahead of time, but should be cooked just before serving, so they retain their fresh color and shape. This recipe calls for a generous amount of corned beef, since it's worth having leftovers for sandwiches or corned-beef hash.

    5 to 6 pounds corned-beef
      brisket
    8 to 12 small beets, tops
      removed
    8 to 12 small boiling potatoes,
      peeled
    8 to 12 small boiling onions,
      peeled
    8 to 12 carrots, scraped
    6 small turnips, peeled
    1 head green cabbage,
      quartered and cored
      Mustard

Horseradish Sauce

    1 cup chilled whipping cream
    4 to 5 tablespoons prepared
      horseradish
    3 tablespoons cider vinegar
      Salt and freshly ground
      pepper, to taste

1. Rinse corned beef under running water and place in a large, deep pot. Cover with cold water and bring just to a boil over high heat; skim off any scum that rises to the surface. Reduce heat to low, partially cover pot, and let simmer gently for 3 hours. (At this point meat may sit in the hot cooking liquid for another hour or two if you wish to delay serving. Bring back to a simmer before continuing with the vegetables.)

2. About an hour or so before you wish to serve, place beets in a medium saucepan, cover with water, and boil until tender when pierced (about 30 to 40 minutes). Drain; peel when cool enough to handle. Return peeled beets to saucepan, add a few ladlefuls of the corned-beef broth, and keep warm over low heat.

3. While beets are boiling, drop potatoes into simmering corned-beef pot and cook for 10 minutes. Drop in onions, carrots, and turnips, and simmer until vegetables are quite tender when pierced (about 30 minutes more). Add cabbage wedges and simmer exactly 3 minutes.

4. Remove meat from pot, slice thinly, and arrange on a large warm platter. Surround meat with vegetables. Drain beets, and place in another serving bowl.

5. Serve with mustard and Horseradish Sauce.

Serves 6 to 8.

Horseradish Sauce Whip cream until it stands in stiff peaks. Fold in horseradish and vinegar, and season with salt and pepper.

PARKER HOUSE ROLLS

These small, folded, semicircular rolls originated at Harvey Parker's Parker House hotel in Boston. Soft, white, and just slightly sweet, they are often served with meats and poultry. When you fold the circles of dough in half (step 6), be sure to press firmly, or they will fly open during baking. This dough, which is easy to prepare and shape, also makes good cinnamon rolls and coffee cakes. To reheat rolls, place them in a plain brown paper bag, sprinkle with a few drops of water, close the bag, and set in a 350° F oven for about 10 minutes.

    1 package active dry yeast
    1¼ cups warm (105° to 115° F)
      milk
    2 tablespoons sugar
    ¼ cup butter, softened, or
      vegetable shortening
    1 teaspoon salt
    3¼ to 3½ cups flour
    ¼ cup melted butter

1. In a large bowl sprinkle yeast over milk. Add sugar, stir, and let sit about 5 minutes. Beat in butter and salt with a wooden spoon. Add 2 cups flour and beat until you have a smooth, heavy batter. Stir in enough remaining flour to make a soft, shaggy dough.

2. Turn out onto a smooth, lightly floured surface and knead for 2 minutes. Let rest 10 minutes. Resume kneading until dough is smooth and elastic, 8 to 10 minutes more, sprinkling on a little more flour when necessary to keep it from being too sticky.

3. Place dough in a greased bowl, turn to grease all sides, cover with plastic wrap, and let rise in a warm place until doubled in bulk (about 1½ hours).

4. Punch dough down and knead into a smooth ball. If possible, chill the dough for about 2 hours. Although not essential, this step will make it easier to form the rolls.

5. Divide dough in half. On a floured surface, shape each piece into a 12-inch rope. Cut each rope into twelve 1-inch pieces. Shape each piece into a round disk about 2½ to 3 inches across.

6. With a pencil or the handle of a wooden spoon, make a firm depression across the middle of each disk. Brush the dough on one side of the depression lightly with melted butter; fold the other side over, pressing firmly. Set rolls on greased baking sheets about 1 inch apart.

7. Cover with a clean towel and let dough rise until doubled in bulk (about 45 minutes, or longer if dough was chilled). Preheat oven to 375° F about 15 minutes before the end of rise time.

8. Brush lightly with remaining melted butter (reheat if it has solidified), and bake until lightly browned (15 to 18 minutes). Serve warm.

Makes 2 dozen rolls.

Make-Ahead Tip Dough can be completed through step 4 and refrigerated, tightly covered, for up to 3 days. If it rises a bit, just punch it down. When you are ready to proceed with step 5, you can work with the dough direct from the refrigerator (it will become more malleable as you work with it).

Seeded Parker House Rolls After brushing formed rolls with butter, sprinkle lightly with poppy seeds or sesame seeds. Rise and bake as directed.

APPLE DUMPLINGS WITH NUTMEG SAUCE

Early on, before ovens were common, dumplings were wrapped in cloth and steamed or boiled, making a rather soggy, heavy mass. Modern dumplings, which are baked, are crisp, brown, and delectable. Whole apples wrapped in rich biscuit dough, baked until tender and golden, and served with a creamy nutmeg sauce, are a perfect conclusion to a family dinner and a wonderfully homey dessert for guests. If you wish, omit the Nutmeg Sauce and serve with any remaining pan juices and a pitcher of cream or a scoop of vanilla ice cream. The amount of dough given here is generous, since it's far easier working with too much than too little.

> 6   *Golden Delicious apples*
> 2   *tablespoons each sugar and butter*
> 1½ *cups apple juice*

Biscuit Dough

> 3   *cups flour*
> 2   *tablespoons sugar*
> 4   *teaspoons baking powder*
> 1   *teaspoon salt*
> 1   *cup vegetable shortening*
> ¾   *cup milk*

Nutmeg Sauce

> 1   *cup apple juice*
> 1   *cup whipping cream*
> ½   *teaspoon ground nutmeg*
> 2   *tablespoons sugar*
> 4   *tablespoons butter*

1. Peel and core apples, leaving them whole; set aside.

2. On a smooth, lightly floured surface, push, pat, and roll Biscuit Dough to a rectangle 20 by 13 inches, keeping the sides as even as possible and lifting and flouring often to prevent sticking. Cut in half lengthwise, then in thirds crosswise, thus making six 6½-inch squares.

3. Preheat oven to 375° F. Place an apple in the center of each dough square. One at a time, bring the 4 corners of each square together at the top, to enclose the apple. Twist and pinch attached corners together to seal. If dough tears, just patch to your heart's content; don't worry if it looks a little ragged.

4. Place dumplings in a buttered 13- by 9-inch baking dish about 1 inch apart. Sprinkle with sugar and dot with butter; pour apple juice around dumplings. Bake until dough is golden brown and apples are tender when pierced with a toothpick or skewer (about 45 minutes). If they brown too much while baking, cover loosely with foil. While apples bake, prepare Nutmeg Sauce.

5. When apples are done, remove dumplings to a platter. Pour any juices remaining in the baking dish into the Nutmeg Sauce, reheat if necessary, and pass the sauce along with the dumplings.

Serves 6.

Biscuit Dough In a medium bowl stir and toss together flour, sugar, baking powder, and salt. Add shortening and blend with a pastry blender or your fingertips until mixture resembles bread crumbs. Pour in milk and stir with a fork just until dough holds together in a shaggy, cohesive mass. Turn onto a smooth, lightly floured surface and knead 10 times.

Nutmeg Sauce In a medium saucepan combine apple juice, whipping cream, nutmeg, and sugar. Bring to a boil and boil until reduced to about 1¼ cups (about 10 minutes). Swirl in butter and set aside.

BREADS

Bread baking is richly satisfying; for so little effort you are rewarded with handsome foods, tempting aromas, and wonderful flavors. Here are a few tried-and-true recipes to show how good—and often simple—homemade baked goods can be.

GINGERBREAD

There are few recipes with so many variations: Gingerbread ranges from mildly spicy to dark and pungent, from soft as cake to hard as rock. In colonial New England, the harder type was often carried on journeys as an energy-providing snack, and slices of gingerbread were sold by food peddlers on the street. The recipe given here produces gingerbread that is firm, cakelike, and not too sweet. It is as good with a meal of baked ham or roast chicken as it is for dessert with applesauce or ice cream.

2½ cups flour
 2 teaspoons baking soda
 ½ teaspoon salt
 1 tablespoon ground ginger
 ½ cup vegetable shortening
 ¼ cup firmly packed dark
    brown sugar
 2 eggs
 1 cup each *molasses and
    boiling water*

1. Preheat oven to 375° F. Generously grease and lightly flour an 8-inch square pan. In a medium bowl stir and toss together flour, baking soda, salt, and ginger.

2. In large bowl of an electric mixer, beat shortening and sugar together until well blended. Beat in eggs, then add molasses and blend well. Stir in the water. Immediately add flour mixture and stir until batter is smooth.

3. Spread batter evenly in prepared pan. Bake until a toothpick or skewer inserted in the center of the bread comes out clean, 35 to 40 minutes. Remove from oven and set on a rack to cool. Serve warm or cold.

Serves 6 to 8.

ANADAMA BREAD

Allegedly, Anadama Bread was named for a Yankee housewife whose husband, when forced to prepare his own food, grumbled, "Anna, damn her!"—which became, as years passed, "anadama." The bread is crusty, brown, and chewy; it makes delicious toast and sandwiches.

 2 cups cold water
 ½ cup cornmeal
 3 tablespoons butter
 ⅓ cup molasses
1½ teaspoons salt
 2 packages active dry yeast
 ⅓ cup warm (105° to 115° F)
    water
4½ to 5 cups flour

1. Bring cold water to a boil in a medium saucepan. Slowly pour in cornmeal, stirring briskly, and cook over medium heat, stirring constantly, until mixture is quite thick, about 5 minutes. Remove from heat and add butter, molasses, and salt. Set aside and let cool to lukewarm.

2. Sprinkle yeast over warm water in a small cup or bowl, stir, and let stand 5 minutes to dissolve.

3. Beat dissolved yeast into cooled cornmeal mixture. Add 2 cups flour and beat until thoroughly blended. Add enough of the remaining flour to make a soft but manageable dough.

4. Turn dough out onto a smooth, lightly floured surface and knead for 2 minutes. Let rest for 10 minutes.

5. Resume kneading until dough is smooth and elastic, about 8 minutes more, sprinkling on just enough additional flour to keep it from being too sticky.

6. Place dough in a large greased bowl, turn to grease all surfaces, cover with a towel, and let rise in a warm place until doubled in bulk (about 1½ to 2 hours).

7. Punch dough down, halve, and shape into 2 loaves. Place in greased 4½- by 8½-inch loaf pans. Let rise until dough is almost doubled in bulk and reaches the pan tops, about 45 minutes to 1 hour. Preheat oven to 350° F near the end of the rise.

8. Bake for 45 to 50 minutes. Remove from pans and cool on a rack.

Makes 2 loaves.

OATMEAL GEMS

These are blond, chewy, slightly sweet muffins, good with soups and stews. The name *gem* refers to the old-fashioned cast-iron pans, which produce a first-rate muffin with a crusty exterior and a pointy top. If you don't have cast-iron gem pans, use plain muffin tins. Leftover muffins are delicious split, toasted, and buttered.

 2 cups quick-cooking oatmeal
1½ cups buttermilk
 ¼ cup molasses
 2 tablespoons sugar
 2 eggs
 ½ teaspoon salt
 1 cup flour
 1 teaspoon baking soda

1. Preheat oven to 400° F. Grease 2½-inch muffin pans or line them with cupcake papers. Combine oatmeal and buttermilk in a medium bowl and let stand about 15 minutes.

2. Beat in molasses, sugar, eggs, and salt. Stir flour and baking soda together, then add to oatmeal mixture and mix just until dry ingredients are moistened.

3. Fill prepared pans two thirds full. Bake until a toothpick inserted in a muffin comes out clean, about 20 minutes. Serve warm.

Makes about 16 muffins.

JOHNNYCAKE

These fried cornmeal disks were originally called journey cakes because our forefathers took them on trips to eat cold. Fortunately, we have the luxury of enjoying them hot from the griddle, with butter and maple syrup for breakfast, or as an accompaniment to dinner. They may be made with either white cornmeal (as they are in Rhode Island) or yellow.

    1 cup yellow or white cornmeal
    ½ teaspoon salt
    1 tablespoon butter
    1 cup boiling water
    ¼ cup milk
       Bacon drippings or salad oil

1. Place cornmeal, salt, and butter in a medium bowl. Pour in the water, whisking briskly to prevent lumps. Stir in milk.

2. Set a large griddle or skillet over moderate heat and film with bacon drippings or oil. The fat should be quite hot for frying. To test, carefully drop in a tablespoon of batter; it should immediately spread and sizzle as it hits the hot griddle.

3. Drop batter by heaping tablespoons onto griddle, allowing room for cakes to spread. Cook 2 to 3 minutes, turning midway, until golden brown on both sides. Serve immediately. Continue cooking until all batter is used, adding more bacon drippings to the griddle as necessary.

Makes about twenty 3-inch cakes, 4 to 6 servings.

Homemade breads and muffins can be as simple or fancy as you wish—loaves and rolls made with yeast take more time and attention than those leavened with baking powder or baking soda. No matter which bread you choose, it will perk up even the plainest dinner, and leftovers are delicious reheated or toasted the next morning for breakfast.

17

Many of us have made savory dumplings—steamed biscuits floating on a simmering soup or stew. Just as easy to prepare, these dumplings simmer on bubbling butter and maple syrup and make a delicious dessert. You'll need to excuse yourself from the table for a few minutes to complete them, but guests who know what's coming shouldn't mind waiting. Be sure to use pure maple syrup—it will pay off in flavor.

DESSERTS

New England desserts are homey and old-fashioned. Some names may sound silly, but pandowdies, slumps, and dumplings are treasures that leave us feeling warm and satisfied.

BAKED RICE PUDDING

This rice pudding, effortless to make, appeals even to those who claim they don't like rice pudding. Long, slow baking results in a rich, sweet, golden cream, equally good warm or cold.

>   4 cups milk
> ½ cup sugar
> ¼ teaspoon salt
> ¼ teaspoon ground nutmeg
> ¼ cup long-grain rice
>   Whipping cream (optional)
>   Maple syrup (optional)

1. Preheat oven to 300° F. Combine milk, sugar, salt, nutmeg, and rice in a buttered 1½-quart baking dish about 4 inches deep; stir to blend.

2. Bake for about 3 hours, stirring every 30 minutes, until pudding is creamy and slightly thickened.

3. Serve warm or at room temperature; pass pitchers of cream and maple syrup at the table, if desired.

Serves 4 to 6.

Raisin Rice Pudding Add ½ cup raisins the last hour of baking.

GREEN-TOMATO PIE

Backyard gardeners are often left with green tomatoes at season's end, when the frost comes. This sweet, spicy, and almost forgotten pie is a good and unusual way to use some of them. You'll be surprised at the flavor, which is not at all tomatoey.

>   *Basic Pastry for a 2-crust 9-inch pie (see page 63)*
>   6 *large green tomatoes*
>   1 *cup sugar*
> ⅓ *cup flour*
>   1 *teaspoon ground cinnamon*
> ½ *teaspoon ground allspice*
> ¼ *cup dried currants*
>   2 *tablespoons cider vinegar*
>   2 *tablespoons butter*

1. Preheat oven to 400° F. Roll out half the pastry and fit it into a 9-inch pie pan to form the bottom crust. Roll out remaining dough for the top crust and set aside.

2. Cut stem end out of each tomato, then slice tomatoes ¼ inch thick. Place sugar, flour, cinnamon, allspice, and currants in a large bowl; stir and toss to mix.

3. Spread ⅓ of the tomato slices in the pastry-lined pan and sprinkle with ⅓ of the sugar mixture. Repeat layers 2 more times, ending with the sugar mixture. Drizzle with vinegar and dot with butter. Cover pie with top crust, then trim and crimp the edges. Cut several vents in top.

4. Bake until crust is well browned and the juices are bubbling (about 40 to 45 minutes). Serve warm or at room temperature.

Serves 8.

CARAMELIZED MAPLE DUMPLINGS

These fluffy maple dumplings cook slowly on a sauce of maple syrup and butter, gradually absorbing the sauce as they caramelize on the bottom, like a sticky bun. Serve them hot, and pass additional maple syrup and a pitcher of cream at the table.

- 1 cup butter, softened
- ¾ cup maple syrup
- 2 cups flour
- ½ teaspoon salt
- 1 tablespoon baking powder
- ¼ teaspoon baking soda
- ⅔ cup milk

1. Place ½ cup each butter and maple syrup in a 10-inch skillet with a tight-fitting lid (or other shallow pan about 10 inches across). Melt over low heat, then set aside.

2. In a medium bowl stir and toss together flour, salt, baking powder, and baking soda. Add the remaining butter and blend together with your fingertips or a pastry blender until mixture resembles coarse meal.

3. Stir the remaining maple syrup into milk. Add to flour mixture; stir briskly with a fork until it forms soft yet cohesive shaggy-looking dough.

4. Bring butter and maple syrup back to a boil, stirring constantly. Rapidly drop heaping-tablespoon blobs of dough into the boiling syrup, leaving about 1 inch between them—you should have about 12 dumplings.

5. Cover pan and turn heat to low. Cook for 15 minutes without lifting the cover, then peek: Dumplings should be puffed and fluffy, the syrup thick and caramelized, and a toothpick inserted in a dumpling should come out clean. Cover and cook a few minutes longer if necessary.

6. Serve immediately in soup plates, along with any syrup in the pan.

Serves 6.

ELECTION CAKE

Election cakes (also called March Meeting Cakes) were baked by housewives and peddled in villages, usually on town meeting or election days. The cake will be better if wrapped airtight and set aside overnight before slicing.

- 1 package active dry yeast
- 1 cup warm (105° to 115° F) milk
- 1 teaspoon salt
- 2 cups less 2 tablespoons flour
- 1 cup butter, softened
- 1 egg
- 1 cup firmly packed brown sugar
- ½ cup buttermilk
- 1½ teaspoons ground cinnamon
- ½ teaspoon each ground cloves and nutmeg
- ½ cup raisins
- 1 cup chopped dates or figs, or a mixture
- ½ teaspoon baking soda
- 1 tablespoon warm water

1. Sprinkle yeast over warm milk in a large bowl, stir in salt, and let stand 5 minutes to dissolve.

2. Add ½ cup of the flour and beat with a wooden spoon until smooth. Add butter and beat again until smooth. Beat in egg, sugar, buttermilk, cinnamon, cloves, and nutmeg.

3. Add remaining flour in 2 parts, beating well after both additions. Stir in raisins and dates.

4. Dissolve baking soda in the water and mix into batter.

5. Scrape batter into a greased 9- by 5- by 3-inch loaf pan and smooth the top with your wet fingertips. Cover loosely with a towel and let rest for 1½ hours. Preheat oven to 350° F near the end of the rest.

6. Bake until a thin wooden skewer inserted in center of loaf comes out clean, about 1 hour to 1 hour and 10 minutes. Cool in pan 5 minutes, then turn out onto a rack to cool completely.

Makes 1 loaf.

INDIAN PUDDING

As Imogene Wolcott says in her *Yankee Cook Book,* "There are as many variations to this basic recipe as there are days of the year." Few things are as basic or delicious as Indian pudding. It's a prime example of the driving Puritan thriftiness, and making the best of what was available. This thick cornmeal porridge, baked for hours, heady and dark with molasses and spices, was a staple of the English settlers, similar to their hasty pudding (also made with cornmeal), and likely served as a snack or starchy vegetable with a meal. Today we enjoy it for dessert, either hot, warm, or cold. It is equally good plain, with vanilla ice cream, or with a pitcher of whipping cream to be poured over each serving.

- 4 cups milk
- ⅔ cup molasses
- ⅓ cup cornmeal
- 2 teaspoons ground ginger
- ½ teaspoon ground cinnamon
- ½ teaspoon salt
- 2 tablespoons butter

1. Preheat oven to 350° F. In a medium saucepan heat 3 cups of milk and the molasses until very hot. Slowly pour in cornmeal, whisking constantly. Stir in ginger, cinnamon, salt, and butter. Bring to a boil, reduce heat, and boil gently for 15 minutes, stirring frequently.

2. Scrape mixture into a buttered 1½-quart baking dish about 4 inches deep; bake for 20 to 30 minutes, until bubbling. Stir in ½ cup of the remaining milk and return dish to the oven for another 20 minutes.

3. Remove from the oven and pour last ½ cup milk on top, but do not stir it in. Reduce heat to 250° F. Return to oven and bake for 2 to 2½ hours longer; top of pudding will glaze over as it bakes.

Serves 6.

APPLE PANDOWDY

Pandowdy is similar to cobbler, deep-dish pie, slump, and betty (which has a bread-crumb topping). The sliced apples, flavored with spices and molasses and covered with a buttermilk-biscuit crust, are delicious warm with ice cream or whipping cream and seem only to gain in flavor when reheated.

> 7 large baking apples, preferably Golden Delicious
> ⅓ cup sugar
> ¼ cup molasses
> 1 teaspoon cinnamon
> ½ teaspoon nutmeg
> 2 tablespoons butter

Biscuit Topping

> 1 cup flour
> 1 teaspoon baking powder
> ¼ teaspoon each baking soda and salt
> 2 tablespoons sugar
> ¼ cup vegetable shortening
> ⅓ cup buttermilk

1. Preheat oven to 425° F. Peel, halve, and core apples. Cut lengthwise into slices ¼ inch thick.

2. In a large bowl toss slices with sugar, molasses, cinnamon, and nutmeg. Spread evenly in a buttered baking dish of about 3-quart capacity and about 9 to 10 inches in diameter. Dot with butter.

3. Cover with foil; poke 6 small holes in the foil for steam to escape. Bake until apples are tender when pierced (about 40 minutes).

4. While apples bake, prepare Biscuit Topping. Then, on a smooth, lightly floured surface, pat and roll dough to match the shape of the baking dish, about ⅛ inch thick (like pie crust).

5. When apples are tender remove dish from the oven and discard foil. Carefully drape dough over apples, tucking in edges all around the dish—be careful with the hot dish. Return to oven until top is well browned (15 to 20 minutes).

Serves 6 to 8.

Biscuit Topping In a medium bowl stir and toss together flour, baking powder, baking soda, salt, and sugar. Add shortening and blend into flour with a pastry blender or your fingertips until mixture looks like coarse crumbs. Add buttermilk and stir with a fork until dough comes together in a rough mass. Turn onto a lightly floured surface and knead 10 times.

BLUEBERRY SLUMP

Desserts with odd names such as *slump* or *grunt* involve cooked fruit with a topping. Here, hot blueberries are covered with mounds of biscuit dough. Serve warm or at room temperature with whipped cream or vanilla ice cream.

> 4 cups blueberries
> ⅓ cup sugar
> 2 tablespoons water
> 1 cup flour
> 2 teaspoons baking powder
> ¼ teaspoon each cream of tartar and salt
> ¼ cup vegetable shortening
> ⅓ cup milk

1. Preheat oven to 375° F. Place blueberries, sugar, and the water in a 1½-quart baking dish; stir to combine.

2. Bake until blueberries have begun to soften and exude their juices (10 to 15 minutes). Remove from oven and increase heat to 425° F.

3. Meanwhile, in medium bowl stir and toss together flour, baking powder, cream of tartar, and salt. Add shortening and blend with your fingertips or a pastry blender until mixture resembles coarse meal.

4. Pour in milk all at one time and stir briskly with a fork until dough forms a shaggy mass that comes away from the side of the bowl; it will be quite damp and sticky.

5. Drop dough randomly in 6 heaping-tablespoon blobs over the hot berries. Return dish to oven; bake until topping is puffy and golden brown, about 15 to 20 minutes.

Serves 4 to 6.

Boston has produced a number of memorable dishes, some of which are collected here in a tribute to the city. This dinner gives a cook latitude and yields many dividends. The dinner can be as informal or as dressy as you like. Serve the chowder first, and follow with the beans and salad; have warm brown bread on the table. The hot dishes get better if reheated once or twice and will fill the kitchen with wonderful aromas every time. The chowder, beans, brown bread, and pie all can be prepared in advance.

CLAM CHOWDER

Clam chowder has stimulated many disagreements over what makes an "honest" version. The authenticity of any recipe is uncertain, and today we have two distinct versions: New England chowder—made with clams, salt pork, milk, and potatoes—and Manhattan chowder, a tomatoey vegetable soup with clams. About the latter, Eleanor Early writes in her charming *New England Cookbook*, "Some people make vegetable soup with a bivalve drawn through it and have the audacity to call it clam chowder." The following recipe is a rich, creamy Yankee chowder, which, with crusty bread and a salad, makes a whole meal—or it can be served in cups as a first course. Fresh steamed clams are definitely best, but if they aren't available, canned clams and bottled clam juice make a very acceptable chowder.

    3 to 4 pounds littleneck or
       steamer clams, in the shell, or
       4 cans (6½ oz each) minced
       clams
    ¼ pound (one 2-inch cube) salt
       pork, finely diced
    1 onion, finely chopped
    2 tablespoons flour
    3 to 4 medium potatoes, peeled
       and cut in ½-inch dice (about
       3 to 4 cups)
       Bottled clam juice, if necessary
    3 cups milk
       Salt and freshly ground
       pepper, to taste

1. If you are using fresh clams, scrub them well under running water, then soak for 1 hour in 2 changes of cold water. Place in a large kettle with ½ inch cold water, set over high heat, cover the pan, and let steam until clams are open (about 5 minutes). Discard any that do not open. Drain well, reserving liquid. Pick meat from clamshells and chop meat finely by hand or in a food processor. If you are using canned clams, drain well, reserving the liquid. Set clams aside.

2. In a 3- to 4-quart heavy-bottomed saucepan, cook salt pork slowly until the fat has been rendered and the bits are brown. With a slotted spoon, lift out browned bits and drain on paper towels.

3. To fat remaining in the pan, add onion and cook gently for about 5 minutes. Sprinkle flour on top and cook, stirring, for 2 more minutes. Add diced potatoes and cook 2 minutes longer.

4. To reserved clam liquid, add bottled clam juice if necessary to make 2½ cups. Add to potato mixture and stir well. Add enough water so ingredients are just covered. Cover and simmer 15 minutes.

5. Add drained clams and salt pork bits and simmer until potatoes are tender (about 10 minutes more). Stir in milk, season with salt and pepper, and bring just to a simmer.

Makes about 10 cups, 6 servings.

BOSTON BAKED BEANS

It's likely the first settlers in the New World knew some sort of baked beans in England, but here they found the Indians cooking beans in deep fire pits. Baked beans have since found their way all across America in one version or another. Recipes vary, but the basic ingredients—beans, salt pork, and sweetener—are the same. In colonial times, when the Sabbath began Saturday night and was a solemn day of rest, baked beans were a traditional Sabbath dish. It was customary to begin cooking early Saturday, so they would simmer quietly all day and evening and be ready for an effortless Saturday supper, Sunday breakfast, or noontime dinner. Today, beans are more secular and good to eat anytime (although they still take all day to cook). The recipe given below is less sweet than some. If you wish, add a little catsup; it's not traditional, but it makes the dish a bit darker and tangier. Otherwise, pass catsup at the table.

    2 cups (1 lb) dry small white
       beans
       Salt
    3 tablespoons each molasses
       and brown sugar
    1 tablespoon dry mustard
    ¼ cup catsup (optional)
    1 onion, peeled and left whole
    ¼ pound salt pork

1. Pick over beans to remove any pebbles or bits of dirt, then rinse well in a colander. Place in a large pan, add 1 teaspoon salt and enough water to cover beans by about 3 inches. Bring to a rolling boil over high heat, and boil for 2 minutes. Remove from heat, cover pan, and let stand 1 hour.

2. Uncover pan, bring back to a boil, reduce heat and simmer until beans are tender, about 1 to 1½ hours. Add more water if necessary to keep beans well covered.

3. Drain well, reserving the liquid. In a bean pot or casserole of about 2½-quart capacity, combine molasses, brown sugar, mustard, catsup (if desired), and ½ teaspoon salt. Add drained beans, and stir in enough reserved cooking liquid to just cover beans; mix well. Push whole onion down in one side of beans. Cut several gashes in salt pork and bury it on the other side.

4. Cover pot, place in oven, and turn heat to 350° F. Bake until beans are bubbling (about 1 hour). Reduce heat to 250° F and bake for 6 to 8 hours more, stirring every hour or so. As the beans cook, they will absorb liquid; continue adding reserved cooking liquid (or water) a little at a time, to keep them moist but not soupy. Baked beans are done when thick, fragrant, and a deep brownish red. They can remain in a 200° F oven for an hour or two longer if you wish; just remember to add liquid occasionally so they do not dry out. They also reheat beautifully the next day. Remove and discard onion before serving. Serve with sliced salt pork if you wish.

Serves 4 to 6.

BOSTON BROWN BREAD

Steamed brown bread, like the baked beans it traditionally accompanies, gets its characteristic reddish brown color from molasses, which was often used in colonial times to replace more costly sugar. Studded with raisins and dark with molasses, it is customarily served with a big pot of baked beans on Saturday or Sunday night. Since it predates the common use of ovens, it is steamed; therefore it remains quite moist and dense. Boston Brown Bread is also dandy spread with softened cream cheese and served with afternoon coffee or tea. To make it you will need a cylindrical mold such as an empty 1-pound coffee can or two empty 1-pound fruit or vegetable cans.

  ½ cup each *rye flour, whole-wheat flour, and cornmeal*
  1¼ teaspoons baking soda
  ½ teaspoon salt
  1 cup buttermilk
  ⅓ cup molasses
  ½ cup raisins

1. Have ready several quarts of water boiling on the stove and a deep kettle with a tight-fitting lid. In a medium bowl stir and toss together flours, cornmeal, baking soda, and salt.

2. Stir buttermilk and molasses together, add to dry ingredients along with raisins, and stir until completely mixed.

3. Pour batter into a buttered 1-pound coffee can or divide it equally between two 1-pound fruit or vegetable cans about 3 inches in diameter and 4 to 5 inches high. Cover tightly with foil.

4. Place can(s) in kettle on a rack and pour in boiling water to come halfway up the sides. Cover kettle and set over low heat. Regulate the temperature so the water barely bubbles. Cook for about 2 hours if using the larger mold, about 1½ hours if using the smaller ones. A wooden skewer plunged into the middle of a loaf should come out clean.

5. Remove mold(s) from water, let stand about 5 minutes, then unmold onto a rack to cool completely.

Makes 1 large or 2 small cylindrical loaves.

BOSTON CREAM PIE

It's uncertain why this cream-filled, chocolate-topped sponge cake is called a pie, although it has been served by this name at Boston's famous old Parker House hotel since 1856. If you wish, you may use any small, round yellow or sponge cake layers, even store-bought, although the cake given here is especially good and easy to make.

  3 eggs
  1 cup sugar
  1¼ cups cake flour
  1½ teaspoons baking powder
  ½ teaspoon salt
  ⅔ cup milk
  2 tablespoons butter
  1 teaspoon vanilla extract

Cream Filling

  ¼ cup sugar
  3 tablespoons flour
     Pinch of salt
  1 cup milk, heated
  2 egg yolks
  2 tablespoons butter
  1 teaspoon vanilla extract

Chocolate Frosting

  1 square (1 oz) unsweetened chocolate, melted
  2 tablespoons butter, softened
  1 cup confectioners' sugar
  2 to 3 tablespoons milk or cream

1. Preheat oven to 350° F. Grease and flour two round 8-inch cake pans. Crack eggs into a medium bowl and beat with electric mixer for 1 minute at high speed. Gradually add sugar and continue beating until mixture is light and fluffy, about 3 minutes.

2. In another medium bowl combine flour, baking powder, and salt, and sift together 3 times; set aside.

3. Combine milk and butter in a small pan and heat just to a boil. Slowly add to egg mixture, stirring constantly or beating on lowest speed. Stir in vanilla. Fold in combined dry ingredients just until you see no drifts of unblended flour.

4. Divide batter evenly between prepared cake pans. Bake until a toothpick inserted in cake comes out clean, about 20 minutes. Let cool 5 minutes, then turn out onto a rack to cool completely before continuing. In the meantime prepare filling and frosting.

5. Cut each layer in half horizontally, making 4 layers in all. Spread a generous ⅓ cup of cooled filling on top of one layer. Add a second layer and top with ⅓ cup of filling. Add a third layer and top with remaining filling. Add the fourth layer. Spread top of cake only with Chocolate Frosting—the sides are left plain.

Serves 8.

Cream Filling Combine sugar, flour, and salt in a small saucepan. Gradually add milk, whisking constantly. Cook over medium heat, stirring constantly, until mixture thickens and boils. Remove from heat, beat in egg yolks, and boil 1 minute more. Remove from heat and stir in butter. Let cool completely, then stir in vanilla.

Chocolate Frosting In a small bowl combine chocolate, butter, sugar, and 2 tablespoons milk. Beat vigorously with an electric mixer until smooth. If frosting is too thick, beat in more milk by drops until it is of spreading consistency.

Washington Pie Omit cream filling and chocolate frosting. Instead, spread ¼ cup raspberry jam on top of each of first three layers and dust top of cake generously with confectioners' sugar.

The wonderful aromas of hot clam chowder and baked beans will set any guest's mouth watering for this Boston Dinner. Recipes start on page 20.

Greens and puffs of mashed potatoes complement pork chops smothered with onions in a satisfying Soul Food Dinner. Recipes start on page 32.

The South

Guests anywhere will appreciate the hospitality that real southern cooking offers. Many of the most impressive dishes—such as spicy Maryland Crab Cakes (see page 27) and Key-Lime Pie (see page 42)—are quick and easy to prepare. A complete discussion of Southern Hams (see page 28) offers all the information needed to buy and prepare this favorite regional specialty. For southern dinners, two complete menus are presented: a satisfying Soul Food Dinner (see page 32) of Smothered Pork Chops, Country-Style Greens, and Sweet-Potato Pie and a Church Social potluck (see page 38) serving Fried Chicken With Cream Gravy and luscious Pecan Pie.

SOUTHERN HOSPITALITY

When Yankees talk about southern hospitality, they usually have visions of an extravagant plantation society, which never existed outside Hollywood. But southerners know what real southern hospitality is, and it can be found in households of any income. What's more, that hospitality extends to table fare just as much as to guests. Even in the earliest days of the American colonies, pragmatic southerners welcomed foreign foodstuffs into their kitchens and gardens.

Much of what we think of as traditional southern cooking is really an Americanized version of West African cuisine. For centuries, black cooks ran the style-setting plantation kitchens of the South—first as slaves, later as servants—and in the process mingled African flavors and techniques with local ingredients and tastes.

Many familiar "southern" ingredients—such as yams, okra, and collardlike greens—are native to Africa. Others such as tomatoes, corn, and hot peppers (brought to West Africa by Portuguese slavers in the sixteenth century) and rice (brought by Arab

slavers at about the same time) were West African staples by the early nineteenth century, at the height of the slave trade.

These ingredients found their way into southern dishes ranging from the spicy crab cakes of Maryland (see page 27) and the okra stews of the coastal lowlands (see page 36) to the yam pone (see page 34) and country-style greens of the Deep South (see page 33). Only in the mountain areas of the Appalachians and the Ozarks, where hill-country farmers were generally too poor to buy slaves, did African cookery fail to take root.

Whether their kitchens stand on stony mountaintops or rich bottomlands, the cooks of the South are unifed by one culinary concept: "Fussy" cooking is almost always the exception rather than the rule. When a southerner tells an unexpected guest, "I'll just whip up a little something," she can probably do just that since many of the South's tastiest dishes are quick and easy, "whipped up" from stores found in nearly every larder.

The South is decidedly the land of the floury kitchen; most cupboards hold several types of flour (cornmeal, all-purpose, cake, and self-rising). The special trick that gives extra

lightness to both fried and baked dishes is buttermilk, which contributes additional leavening to batters—and keeps about twice as long as does whole milk. Most frying is done in lard; this not only provides a wonderfully crisp coating but also furnishes another use for the adaptable hog, flourishing in areas where beef cattle would founder from heat prostration.

Pork is not only favored in its natural state, but southern smokehouses produce the country's finest hams and deep-smoked bacons (see page 28). Supplementing pork are chicken, small game (rabbits, squirrels, possums), coastal seafood, and fresh-water fish—especially the accommodating catfish. Fruit and pecan trees flourish in the southern climate, inspiring delectable pies, cobblers, and puddings—all of which turn out to be surprisingly easy in the making. And finally, the area turns a generous portion of its corn harvest into Kentucky bourbon and "Tennessee sippin' whiskey," which flavor the South's "tipsy" cakes.

Best of all, the tradition of southern hospitality continues today. So y'all come on in the kitchen while we whip up a little something.

MAIN DISHES

Here are the fried and smothered skillet dishes so typical of the South, along with the spicy seafood cookery of the Atlantic coast, and a piquant Latin dish from Miami.

PAN-FRIED CATFISH

As a bottom feeder, the "wild" catfish has an uncertain culinary reputation, but the rolling green hills of Tennessee are studded with limpid freshwater ponds where catfish are carefully bred and raised. Typically, a catfish farm includes a ramshackle roadside restaurant, from which an irresistible aroma of crisp, cornmeal-coated fried catfish and new-made hush puppies wafts up and down the highway. One taste is enough to improve the catfish's reputation. Don't forget the hush puppies (see page 38).

> 4 to 6 small catfish (about 1 lb each) or 2 to 3 pounds thick fillets from larger catfish
> ½ cup flour
> 1 teaspoon salt
> ½ teaspoon coarsely ground black pepper
> 2 eggs
> 1 tablespoon water
> 1 cup white cornmeal
> Oil for frying

1. Rinse catfish in cold water and roll in paper towels to dry.

2. Mix flour, salt, and pepper. Dredge fish in the mixture and shake off excess. Place on waxed paper. Place eggs in a pie pan, add the water, and beat lightly to combine. Spread cornmeal on a large plate.

3. Heat ¼ inch oil in a large (12-inch) heavy skillet (or two skillets, to cook all the fish at once). While oil is heating, dip fish in egg mixture, then roll in cornmeal to coat thoroughly, gently pressing the cornmeal onto fish so that it will stick. Place each coated fish on waxed paper.

4. When oil is rippling and fragrant (350° F), gently add fish to skillet(s), using long tongs to protect against spattering oil. Fry until coating is browned and fish is cooked through, turning carefully midway through cooking. Whole fish takes about 3 minutes per side, fillets 2 minutes per side. (For fillets, check doneness by inserting a knife; flesh should flake easily. For whole fish, inspect the flesh at the opening. Catfish retains a slightly pink color when cooked, but the flesh turns opaque.) Drain fish on paper towels and keep in the oven at low heat until ready to serve.

Serves 4 to 6.

MARYLAND CRAB CAKES

Nothing can match the sweetness of Chesapeake Bay crab, but this dish is worth making with other types as well. The homemade Tartar Sauce that accompanies it is wholly different from the commercially bottled product.

> 1 pound crabmeat (preferably from Maryland blue crabs)
> 1 cup soft bread crumbs
> 1 large egg, lightly beaten
> ¼ cup mayonnaise
> 1 tablespoon mustard
> 1 teaspoon Worcestershire sauce
> 2 tablespoons minced parsley
> ¼ teaspoon white pepper
> Dash Tabasco sauce
> Oil for frying
> Lemon wedges

Tartar Sauce

> ½ cup mayonnaise
> ¼ cup sour cream
> 1 teaspoon lemon juice
> ¼ teaspoon Dijon mustard
> 1 tablespoon chopped shallots or green onions
> 1 tablespoon minced parsley
> 2 tablespoons minced chives or 1 tablespoon minced fresh dill
> Pinch tarragon
> 2 tablespoons capers, drained, or 2 cornichons (small pickles), chopped
> Cayenne pepper or Tabasco sauce, to taste

1. If you are using something other than Maryland blue crab, taste a pinch of it; if it is too salty, rinse briefly under cold running water.

2. Carefully pick over crabmeat, removing any shell and other inedible bits; leave crab in large lumps. Gently mix in bread crumbs.

3. Combine egg, mayonnaise, mustard, Worcestershire, parsley, pepper, and Tabasco. Gently blend this mixture with crabmeat.

4. Form crab mixture into six thick patties. Wrap individually in plastic wrap and refrigerate for half an hour to firm the mixture.

5. Pour ¼ inch of oil into a large skillet; heat until aromatic and rippling (about 350° F). Add crab cakes and fry, turning once, until golden on both sides (about 3 minutes per side). Serve immediately with lemon wedges and Tartar Sauce.

Serves 6.

Tartar Sauce Thoroughly mix mayonnaise, sour cream, lemon juice, mustard, shallots, parsley, chives, tarragon, and capers. Add cayenne or Tabasco, a little at a time, tasting carefully after each addition.

SOUTHERN HAMS

The main difference between southern country ham and commercial ham is in the processing: The country ham is slowly cured, smoked, and aged, using no artificial methods to speed up the process; commercial hams, in contrast, are injected with brine and steam-smoked. In addition the hogs used for country hams are usually specially selected and raised on special diets. (Smithfield hams, for instance, must be made from free-ranging hogs fed on acorns, hickory nuts, and peanuts.) As a result of these differences, country hams are denser, saltier, smokier, and more flavorful than commercial hams.

The famous Smithfield hams must, by law, have been cured and smoked in Smithfield, Virginia. The hams are dry-cured in salt (rather than brined) and coated with pepper; the flavor is magnificently intense. Other southern country hams may be cured with sugar as well as salt and occasionally with additional spices.

Keeping Country Hams

Dry-cured whole hams need not be refrigerated before cooking, but they should be hung in a cool, dry area. They may be kept for as long as desired. The skin of the ham may be covered with a mold. This is not a cause for alarm. The mold is harmless, and the skin will not be eaten. (Aged prime beef also develops a mold, which the butcher scrapes off before you ever see it.) Some country-ham suppliers furnish packages of sliced ham as well as whole hams. Although the packaging is sufficiently airtight that it is safe for several days for shipment at any time of the year, you should refrigerate or freeze slices until ready to use. After cooking, leftover ham, well wrapped, will keep about 3 weeks refrigerated and about 3 months frozen.

Cooking Country and Smithfield Hams

Dry-cured hams are extremely salty and are coated with pepper as well as any mold that develops during aging. To remove some of the salt and soften the coating, soak the ham at room temperature for 12 to 36 hours in several changes of water. Then scrub the outside of the ham with a stiff brush to remove the mold and coating.

Cover the ham with cold water and bring to a simmer (do not allow it to reach a boil). Simmer until the meat is partly tender but still firm, about 20 minutes per pound. Allow to cool enough to handle and carefully remove the skin, leaving a thick coating of fat on the ham. Score the fat in diamond shapes; glaze the ham with brown sugar, corn syrup, or maple syrup (thinned, if desired, with cider or pineapple juice); then bake in preheated 400° F oven for just long enough to set the glaze (about 15 minutes).

Alternatively, the simmering can be omitted, and the ham can be baked in a preheated 350° F oven, allowing 20 minutes per pound. Put water or cider in the pan. In this case, when ham is nearly done, remove it from the oven and let cool a little; remove the skin, score and glaze the fat, and continue to bake until the glaze is browned. If you prefer, soak the slices in water or milk for 1 hour, and pan-fry them.

Sources of Hams

Smithfield Hams:

Luter's Hams, Smithfield Packing Company, Smithfield, VA 23430 (804-357-4321). Hickory-smoked, pepper-coated, aged.

Southampton Supply Company, Box 419, Franklin, VA 23851 (804-562-5111). Wood-smoked, pepper-coated, aged.

Country Hams:

Early's Honey Stand, Rural Route 2, Spring Hill, TN 37174 (615-486-2230). Dry-cured, hickory-smoked, whole, and sliced. Also a source of hickory-smoked bacon.

B&B Food Products, Route 1, Cadiz, KY 42211 (502-235-5297). Short-shank hams, sugar-cured, hickory- and sassafras-smoked, aged.

CIDER-BAKED COUNTRY HAM

In this treatment the ham is baked with cider so that no simmering on the stovetop is needed.

1 Smithfield ham or country ham (12 to 14 lbs)
4 cups apple cider
½ cup bourbon
Brown sugar for glaze

1. Soak ham in several changes of cold water for at least 24 hours. Scrub under cold running water with a stiff brush and wipe dry.

2. Preheat oven to 350° F. Place a long sheet of heavy aluminum foil in the bottom of a shallow roasting pan (foil should be long enough to make a tent for the ham). Place ham on the foil, pour on cider, and seal foil around the ham. Bake for about 4 hours, until ham is cooked through and tender.

3. Remove ham from oven and allow to cool until it can be handled. Discard the aluminum foil. Remove drippings (save fat if desired). Gently and carefully remove skin, leaving a thick layer of fat. Score the fat in a diamond pattern with a sharp knife, and return ham to the oven for 15 minutes to heat the surface. Slide out oven shelf so that ham is fully exposed. Heat bourbon in a small saucepan, pour it over the ham and, using a long match *and great caution*, set bourbon alight. *Be sure* that nothing flammable is near the oven opening. When flames die down, spread brown sugar over the fat, and return it to the oven until sugar forms a dark melted glaze (about 15 minutes).

Serves 8 to 10.

COUNTRY HAM SLICES WITH RED-EYE GRAVY

All ham slices will be enlivened by this surprising sauce. The secret is black coffee.

  4 slices (½ inch thick) country ham or "old-fashioned" ham, cooked or uncooked
  4 tablespoons rendered drippings from baked ham, or vegetable oil
  ¼ cup light brown sugar
  ½ cup strong black brewed (not instant) coffee

1. Score through the fat at the edges of the ham slices to keep them from curling. Heat drippings in a large, heavy skillet. Add ham and sauté over medium heat, turning several times, until lightly browned on both sides (20 to 25 minutes if you are using uncooked slices, about 10 minutes if cooked).

2. Remove ham and keep warm. Stir sugar into pan juices and cook at low heat, stirring constantly, until sugar dissolves. Add coffee and simmer until gravy turns rich brown (about 5 minutes); do not boil. Pour gravy over the ham and serve.

Serves 4.

Note If you are using *uncooked* slices of a salty, dry-cured ham, add a cup of water to the skillet along with the ham. The ham will absorb all the water by the time it is cooked through; add more water if the original amount is absorbed too quickly.

COUNTRY-FRIED STEAK

The South claims the honor of producing the country's finest hickory-smoked bacon and hams (see opposite page). The exquisitely smoky, flavorful grease they render is never thrown away but is saved like a precious resource. Poured through a strainer into a heatproof container, then covered, bacon or ham grease will keep for about a week in a cool cupboard, about two months in the refrigerator, or almost indefinitely in the freezer. It provides the inimitable flavor in southern cream gravy. In the recipe that follows, the drippings flavor an inexpensive cut of beef, which is slowly sautéed until it's as tender as fillet and served with mashed potatoes to absorb the extra gravy. If southern smokehouse products are unavailable, buy the best bacon your butcher offers, enjoy it for breakfast, and save the drippings for this and other dishes.

  1½ pounds boneless round or Swiss steak, about ¾ inch thick, trimmed of excess fat
  ½ cup flour
  ½ teaspoon salt
  ¾ teaspoon black pepper
  2 teaspoons paprika
  3 tablespoons rendered bacon or ham fat
  1½ cups whole milk
     Additional salt and pepper, to taste
     Cayenne pepper, to taste

1. If possible, have the butcher run steak through a tenderizer. Otherwise, pound both sides of steak with the ridged side of a meat mallet (or with a heavy can held at an angle so the edge penetrates the meat) until the steak is striated on both sides.

2. In a small bowl, mix flour, ½ teaspoon salt, the ¾ teaspoon black pepper, and paprika. Remove 3 tablespoons of the mixture; reserve for the gravy. Rub half the remaining seasoned flour into one side of the steak. Place the steak between sheets of waxed paper (to keep the flour from flying) and pound the flour into the steak with the flat side of a meat mallet. Turn steak over and repeat.

3. Cut steak into serving pieces. Heat bacon fat in a large, heavy skillet over high heat. When it is fragrant add meat and brown on both sides at high heat (about 2 minutes per side). Lower heat to a simmer, cover pan, and cook meat about 45 minutes, until very tender, carefully turning steaks once about halfway through the cooking time.

4. Remove meat from skillet and keep warm. Stir reserved flour mixture into pan liquid. As soon as the aroma of raw flour disappears, slowly add milk, stirring constantly. Increase heat to medium-low and stir until the gravy is smooth, hot, and thickened. Correct seasoning and pour gravy over steaks. Accompany with Down-Home Mashed Potatoes (see page 33).

Serves 3 to 4.

Chicken-Fried Steak Use 3- or 4-portion-sized cube steaks instead of round steak. In a medium bowl, mix 1 cup flour with 1 teaspoon pepper and ½ teaspoon salt. Reserve 3 tablespoons for the gravy. In another medium bowl beat together 2 eggs and 1 cup milk. Dip steaks in this liquid, then dredge in the seasoned flour, shaking off the excess. (If a thick coating is desired, repeat.) Heat ½ inch oil (preferably peanut, corn, or sunflower) in a large, heavy skillet over high heat until it is hot and hazy at the surface (about 360° F). Fry steaks until browned, about 3 minutes per side. Remove from skillet and keep warm. Pour fat out of skillet and replace with 3 tablespoons rendered bacon or ham fat. Make cream gravy as directed in step 4.

Texas Chuck-wagon Country-Fried Steak After pounding round steak, soak it for 2 hours in a mixture of 1 tablespoon white vinegar and 2 teaspoons salt (this will tenderize it and give a tang to the gravy). Dredge steaks in a mixture of 1½ cups flour and 1½ teaspoons black pepper. Proceed with step 3.

The woodsy leanness of game from the forests makes an unexpected, exquisite marriage with succulent Atlantic Coast seafood in this spicy, sophisticated Rabbit and Oyster Gumbo from the Georgia Sea Islands. Serve with plain boiled rice and a tossed salad for a festive autumn dinner.

GEORGIA RABBIT AND OYSTER GUMBO

The word *gumbo* comes from West Africa, where it means okra and soups thickened with okra. African slaves brought the dish to America and, although it settled mainly on the Gulf Coast of Louisiana, gumbos can be found throughout the Deep South. This recipe, from the relatively inaccessible Georgia Sea Islands, is less Americanized than most. Like most West African cuisine, it's fairly peppery, so if hot food isn't your passion, you may want to reduce (or eliminate) the cayenne.

> 1 *rabbit, cut up in 6 to 8 pieces (see opposite page)*
> 2 *quarts chicken or fish stock*
> ¼ *cup oil (preferably peanut, corn, or sunflower)*
> ½ *cup flour*
> ½ *pound okra, ends trimmed, sliced into ½-inch rounds*
> 1 *large green bell pepper, chopped*
> 1 *large onion, chopped*
> 1 *stalk celery, chopped*
> ½ *teaspoon cayenne pepper*
> ¼ *teaspoon thyme*
> ¼ *teaspoon salt, or to taste*
> ¼ *teaspoon black pepper, or to taste*
> 1 *jar (1 pt) East Coast oysters, drained*
> *Tabasco sauce (optional)*

1. Trim and discard all visible fat from rabbit (see opposite page). Put rabbit and stock in a large pot and bring to a boil. Lower heat to medium, partially cover, and simmer for an hour, skimming occasionally. Remove rabbit pieces with a slotted spoon and let cool. Leave stock over low heat, covered, to keep hot. When rabbit pieces are cool enough to handle, bone rabbit and reserve meat.

2. Heat oil in a large, heavy skillet over medium-high heat until it is quite hot. Make a roux by stirring in flour a bit at a time, whisking vigorously with a wire whisk to break up any lumps. Cook until roux turns peanut-butter brown (see page 77), about 10 minutes, stirring constantly and whisking whenever necessary to break up any lumps. Do not stop stirring or the roux will burn.

3. When the roux is the right color, add okra, green pepper, onion, and celery, stirring vegetables in carefully, in small batches, so their moisture does not make the roux burn. Lower heat to medium and cook until vegetables are tender, about 13 minutes, stirring frequently.

4. Add contents of skillet to stockpot and raise heat to high. Add cayenne, thyme, salt, pepper, and rabbit meat; bring to a boil; lower heat; and simmer 5 minutes, skimming occasionally. Add oysters, remove from heat, cover, and let stand 10 minutes.

5. Serve in large soup bowls over boiled rice. Tabasco may be added at the table to raise the "heat" if desired.

Serves 4 to 5.

ROPA VIEJA
"Old clothes"—Cuban shredded beef

The American melting pot is still bubbling, and thanks to the large, long-standing Cuban community in Florida, this colorful fiesta dish is becoming an increasingly popular southern favorite. The preparation breaks into two days' work.

For Boiling

1½ pounds flank steak, trimmed of fat and cut into 1-inch cubes

1 turnip, scrubbed and quartered

1 large onion, chopped

¼ teaspoon salt

½ teaspoon black pepper

For Completing

¾ cup (approximately) peanut oil

2 tablespoons dried achiote seeds (see Note)

1 large onion, chopped

4 large cloves garlic, peeled and minced

1 large green bell pepper, chopped

1 small hot chile, seeded, deveined, and chopped

2 carrots, peeled and finely chopped

2 cans (1 lb each) tomatoes, drained and coarsely chopped

2 bay leaves

⅛ teaspoon ground cinnamon

⅛ teaspoon ground cloves

½ teaspoon sugar

½ teaspoon black pepper

¼ teaspoon salt

1 tablespoon capers, drained

6 slices of bread (crusts trimmed off), each cut into 2 triangles

1. *To boil the steak:* Place steak, turnip, onion, salt, and pepper in a heavy saucepan. Add water (enough to cover steak and vegetables), bring to a boil, cover, reduce heat to medium, and cook 3 hours. Add more water if needed. Remove meat with a slotted spoon and let cool.

2. Strain cooking water and reserve 1 cup. Discard vegetables.

3. When meat has cooled it should separate easily into strands. If it does not, hit it a few times with a meat mallet or the broad handle of a knife. Shredded meat can be stored in the refrigerator in a well-sealed plastic bag for up to 5 days; store reserved cooking liquid as well.

4. *To complete the Ropa Vieja:* In a small saucepan over medium-high heat, heat ¼ cup of the oil until it is fragrant, about 1 minute. Stir in achiote seeds, lower heat to a simmer, and cook 20 to 30 seconds, stirring, until the oil takes on a deep orange color. Strain oil and discard seeds.

5. Pour strained oil into a large, heavy saucepan. Raise heat to medium-high. Add onions, garlic, green pepper, chile, and carrots; sauté 10 minutes, stirring frequently.

6. Add tomatoes, bay leaves, cinnamon, cloves, sugar, pepper, and salt. Cook 10 minutes, stirring frequently, until most of the liquid evaporates.

7. Add reserved meat, capers, and reserved broth; stir, and cook 10 minutes more, stirring frequently.

8. Meanwhile, pour the remaining oil into a large skillet (adjust quantity so oil is ¼ inch deep) and heat over high heat until oil is fragrant and rippling. Fry bread triangles briefly (about 30 seconds per side) and carefully until golden brown, adding more oil if necessary; turn bread and brown other side. Drain on paper towels.

9. Serve Ropa Vieja garnished with fried bread triangles.

Serves 4 to 6.

<u>Note</u> Achiote (also called annatto) seeds are used primarily as a coloring agent, although they also release a mild but distinctive flavor when heated. They can be found in Latin and East Indian groceries. If unavailable, substitute paprika, frying it as directed for achiote and straining the oil through a fine sieve.

Step-by-Step

CUTTING UP A RABBIT

Cut a cleaned, skinned rabbit along center of breast from neck to tail. With a small, sharp knife, detach and remove all organs from the cavity. Trim away all tallowy fat in cavity, at leg joints, and along backbone. (It has an unpleasant taste.)

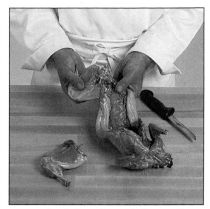

1. *Use both hands to dislocate front and hind leg joints by snapping them sharply away from body. Carefully sever with a knife or poultry shears.*

2. *With torso of rabbit held between both hands, cavity facing you, snap backbone between upper and lower back; finish by cutting along crack in bone. If desired, cut each torso piece in half by inserting knife along one side of backbone. If you wish, remove annoying small bones by snapping them away from breast bone. Use sharp yanks with fingers or needle-nose pliers to remove small bones from flesh.*

POOKIE'S LIVER AND ONIONS

Even if you hate liver and onions, you'll find this tender, soulful version a revelation. If you *like* liver and onions, you're about to see star bursts. This recipe is based on a dish by brilliant chef Pookie Turner.

- ½ pound beef liver, in one thin cut
- Salt
- Pepper
- Flour for dredging
- 2 tablespoons cooking oil (preferably peanut, corn, or sunflower)
- 2 tablespoons butter
- 2 green onions, minced
- 1 clove garlic, minced
- 1½ medium onions, sliced
- 1½ teaspoons flour
- 1½ cups beef broth
- ¾ teaspoon Kitchen Bouquet (seasoning sauce)

1. Season liver with salt and pepper, to taste. Dredge lightly in flour.

2. Heat lightly oiled heavy skillet over high heat until fragrant, about 1 minute. Add liver and fry until lightly browned, about 1 minute per side. Remove liver and reserve.

3. Clean skillet and return it to stove over medium heat until dry. Add butter, and heat until it is melted. Add green onions, garlic, and onions; fry, stirring, until onion is translucent (about 6 minutes).

4. Sprinkle the 1½ teaspoons flour over mixture and cook briefly—until the flour turns golden and loses its raw aroma (about 1 minute); do not let flour brown. Stir in broth, Kitchen Bouquet, ½ teaspoon salt, and ½ teaspoon pepper. Turn heat to medium-high and bring to a boil. Cook, stirring, until liquid thickens slightly, about 6 minutes. Adjust seasoning, if necessary.

5. Return liver to pan and cook on both sides for 30 seconds each. (If liver is thick, cook 90 seconds per side.) Remove from heat and serve immediately with boiled rice.

Serves 2.

SOUL FOOD DINNER

Smothered Pork Chops
Down-Home Mashed Potatoes
Country-Style Greens
Sweet-Potato Pie
Iced Tea

Soul food is satisfying, comforting, practical cuisine, an update of the Afro-American dishes the slaves ate before emancipation (and afterward, too). Pork was the least expensive meat before the Civil War (even cheaper than chicken), and slaves got the parts "low on the hog" that the plantation owners scorned. Wild greens could be foraged, and yams were cultivated in the tiny garden plots outside the slave quarters. Out of these conditions, there evolved such savory dishes as the ones included in this menu: the universally beloved smothered pork chops, along with mashed potatoes to soak up the rich gravy (mashed potatoes go with fried chicken, too); the bacon-flavored greens of Mississippi (in other menus, you can serve them with corn bread); and for dessert, what else but a sweet-potato pie.

SMOTHERED PORK CHOPS

No matter where they're served, smothered meat dishes are extremely popular (and remarkably similar) throughout the South: chops heaped high with sautéed onions and a spicy brown gravy. This Mississippi/Louisiana recipe borrows several New Orleans Creole techniques.

- 2 tablespoons butter
- 2 tablespoons flour
- 1½ cups rich beef broth
- Pinch sage leaves, crumbled
- 6 thick loin pork chops
- 1 cup flour for dredging
- Salt and pepper, to taste
- ½ cup lard
- 3 large onions, sliced
- 3 cloves garlic, minced
- ¼ cup celery, minced

1. In a small saucepan melt butter over medium-high heat, stir in the 2 tablespoons flour, and cook, stirring constantly with a wire whisk, until lightly browned. Stir in broth and sage, mix well, remove from heat, and set aside. This mixture will be the sauce.

2. Add salt and pepper to the 1 cup flour; dredge chops in the mixture. In a large, heavy skillet heat ¼ cup of the lard over medium-high heat. Add chops and cook until they are browned. Move browned chops to a large, ovenproof casserole with a cover. Preheat oven to 350° F.

3. Melt the remaining lard in skillet over high heat. Add onions, garlic, and celery; lower heat to medium, and cook, stirring frequently to avoid burning, until onions are golden (about 8 to 10 minutes). Remove vegetables with a slotted spoon and place over chops in the casserole.

4. Pour off all lard from the skillet. Add reserved sauce, raise heat to high, bring to a boil, and cook for 1 minute, stirring vigorously and scraping the bottom of the skillet. Pour sauce over chops in casserole, cover, and bake 30 minutes. Serve with mashed potatoes.

Serves 6.

DOWN-HOME MASHED POTATOES

Mashed potatoes need not be perfectly smooth; in fact, a few small lumps improve the texture. Nor should the milk be premeasured and heated: The quantity needed will depend on the type and age of the potatoes. (Mealy baking potatoes that have been stored for a long time take more milk than new potatoes.) Just pour milk in gradually, beating after every addition, until the potatoes are just right. A few minutes in the oven before serving will reheat and puff up the potatoes .

- 1 medium-large (about 11 oz) potato per person
- 1 tablespoon butter for each potato
  Milk as needed (¼ to ½ cup per potato)
  Salt and white pepper, to taste
  Paprika, for garnish

1. Bring a large pot of salted water to a boil. Meanwhile, peel potatoes and quarter or halve them (depending on size). Drop potatoes into the pot as they are peeled, even if water is not quite boiling yet. Cook potatoes over high heat until fork tender (about 25 minutes after water comes to a boil). Some pieces can be left a little underdone. Drain well.

2. Place potatoes and butter in a large bowl. Using a potato masher or fork, coarsely mash them together. Make a well in the center and pour in a small amount of milk.

3. With an electric mixer (*not* a blender or food processor, which will turn potatoes into a starchy goo) beat potatoes, adding more milk a little at a time as needed, until the desired texture is obtained. Tasting carefully, add salt and pepper. At this point, potatoes can be set aside, uncovered, until the rest of dinner is nearly ready. One half hour before serving time, preheat oven to 350° F.

4. Mound potatoes in an ovenproof casserole, sprinkle with paprika, and bake uncovered 20 minutes.

COUNTRY-STYLE GREENS

Contrary to rumor, greens do not need hours of boiling in a sea of liquid, as this Mississippi recipe proves. What they *do* need, however, is the flavor of smoked slab bacon or ham; if you must substitute ordinary bacon or ham, you'll need twice as much. Greens are the traditional accompaniment to pork or ham; they also pair up well with corn bread or candied yams.

- 2 bunches fresh collard, turnip, or mustard greens
- 1 tablespoon lard or rendered bacon fat
- 1 medium onion, minced
- ¼ pound good-quality smoked slab bacon or smoked ham, cut in ½-inch dices or ½ pound ordinary sliced bacon or ham
- 2 cups water
  Salt and freshly ground black pepper, to taste
  Dash of Louisiana-style hot sauce

1. Trim away and discard the tough stems of greens. To loosen grit, place the leaves and the remaining tender stems (you should have about 2 quarts) in a large bowl, cover with lukewarm water, and soak for 5 minutes. Rinse several times in lukewarm water to wash away any remaining sand.

2. Melt lard in a large, heavy, nonreactive pot with a lid. (Do not use an aluminum pot; if possible, use one with an enamel coating.) Add onions and bacon. Fry together over medium-high heat, stirring often, until onions wilt and bacon starts to brown (about 5 minutes).

3. Add greens and the water and bring to a boil over high heat. Cover, lower heat to medium, and cook until greens are tender, with just a little crunch (about 20 minutes).

4. Uncover, raise heat to high, and boil off some of the excess water (about 5 minutes). Add salt, pepper, and hot sauce to taste, and serve hot (dish should be slightly soupy).

Serves 6.

SWEET-POTATO PIE

In this very accommodating pie, the amount of sweet potato used need not be exact.

- 1 large or 2 small sweet potatoes (roughly 14 oz)
- 4 tablespoons butter
- ½ cup light brown sugar
- ½ cup milk
- 3 eggs, separated
- ¼ teaspoon salt, or to taste
- ⅛ teaspoon grated nutmeg, or to taste
- ½ teaspoon cinnamon, or to taste
- ¼ teaspoon ground cloves, or to taste
- ½ teaspoon vanilla extract
- 1 prepared pie crust (use ½ recipe Flaky Pastry, page 63)

1. Preheat oven to 375° F. Pare sweet potato, cut in half lengthwise, then cut each piece once crosswise, and drop into boiling water to cover. Boil until tender (15 to 20 minutes). Meanwhile, cut butter in small chunks and place in a medium mixing bowl with sugar.

2. Drain sweet potato and quickly mash with butter and sugar. While mixture is still hot, beat until smooth. Beat in milk and egg yolks. Add salt, nutmeg, cinnamon, cloves, and vanilla; carefully adjust spicing to taste.

3. Using an electric mixer with clean, dry beaters, beat egg whites in a small bowl until stiff. Gently fold beaten whites into sweet potatoes. Pour mixture into pie crust, place on a baking sheet, and bake 40 minutes. Lower heat to 350° F and bake until top is medium brown and crust is golden brown (an additional 5 to 10 minutes). Serve at room temperature or chilled.

Serves 8.

Variation For the more familiar, heavier pie filling, omit milk, and beat whole, unseparated eggs into the sweet potato mixture. Bake at 375° F for 40 minutes. Serve warm or at room temperature.

SOUPS, VEGETABLES, AND SIDE DISHES

The South's semitropical bounty of peanuts, okra, tomatoes, black-eyed peas, and yams appears in soups and side dishes; and the omnipresent hominy grits of the breakfast table reappear at dinner as a festive, creamy pudding.

VIRGINIA CREAM OF PEANUT SOUP

It's only natural that inhabitants of a peanut-growing area would find uses for peanuts beyond snacking. This rich, soothing soup is surprisingly elegant in flavor, despite the fact that it is based on the humble goober. Be sure to add enough lemon juice to cut the unctuousness of the nuts.

  3 tablespoons butter
  ½ medium onion, coarsely
      minced
  1 stalk celery, diced
  3 tablespoons flour
  1 quart chicken stock
  ¼ teaspoon celery salt
  1 cup smooth peanut butter
  1 cup half-and-half (or
      light cream)
  2 tablespoons lemon juice,
      or more to taste
      Salt and black pepper, to taste
  ¼ cup chopped peanuts, for
      garnish
  2 tablespoons chopped chives,
      for garnish
      Freshly ground black pepper

1. Melt butter in a heavy, deep saucepan (2-quart capacity). Add onion and celery and sauté over medium-low heat, stirring occasionally, until onion is soft but not brown (about 5 minutes). Sprinkle flour over vegetables and stir over low heat until very lightly browned (1 to 2 minutes). Add stock slowly, stirring constantly. Raise heat to high and continue stirring until mixture comes to a boil. Lower heat and add celery salt. Simmer for 30 minutes.

2. Remove soup from heat and pour it through a strainer, discarding the solids. Add peanut butter, half-and-half, lemon juice, and salt and pepper to taste. Soup can be made in advance to this point and refrigerated until ready to serve.

3. Reheat soup over low heat just until it reaches serving temperature (do not boil). Taste carefully for seasoning; add more lemon juice if desired. Just before serving, sprinkle with chopped peanuts, chopped chives, and a liberal grinding of pepper.

Makes about 6 cups.

YAM PONE

What is a "pone"? Originally, it was a flat cake made of cornmeal and water, baked on a wooden paddle or among hot coals by the Native Americans of the South. Today, though, a pone is just as likely to be a sweet, starchy casserole like the one that follows. Yam pone tastes somewhat like candied yams, but it is quicker to prepare, since the yams are shredded, then sweetened and cooked in a single operation. Choose cardamom for a subtle exotic flavor that accentuates the sweetness; choose thyme for a more savory, musky taste.

      Unsalted butter to grease dish
  3 medium yams or sweet pota-
      toes (about 1½ lb total)
  1 egg, lightly beaten
  ½ cup milk
  ¼ teaspoon ground nutmeg
  ½ teaspoon allspice
  ½ teaspoon cinnamon
  ¼ teaspoon salt
      Pinch ground cardamom
      or thyme
  ¼ cup brown sugar
  1 teaspoon molasses
  4 tablespoons unsalted butter,
      melted
      Whole pecans, for garnish

1. Preheat oven to 400° F. Grease a 1½- or 2-quart soufflé dish or ovenproof casserole with the unsalted butter. Peel yams and grate them (a food processor fitted with the perforated disk may be used). Place yams in a large mixing bowl.

2. Beat egg and milk together. Pour over grated yams. Add nutmeg, allspice, cinnamon, salt, cardamom, brown sugar, and molasses; stir well.

3. Turn yam mixture into the buttered baking dish. Dribble the 4 tablespoons melted butter over the top and bake for 30 minutes. Stud the top with pecans and continue baking until yams are tender and yield to a knife inserted in the center (15 to 30 minutes longer).

Serves 4 to 6.

BAKED GARLIC GRITS

Hominy grits, coarse cereal made from dried white corn, is decidedly a southern taste. Hospitable southerners who want to help their northern friends develop a taste for grits are likely to introduce them to this elaborate and delicate version, which resembles a fallen cheese soufflé. Serve baked grits for brunch (the batter can be mixed the night before) or at dinner; it is especially suited to accompany roasts or barbecues. Use Cheddar cheese if grits will accompany a hearty dish, Swiss cheese if accompanying a delicate main course.

  ½ cup milk
  3 eggs
  ½ pound grated sharp Cheddar
      cheese or Swiss cheese
  2 tablespoons freshly grated
      Parmesan cheese
  8 tablespoons unsalted butter,
      cut in small pieces
  2 medium cloves garlic, minced
  ¼ teaspoon black pepper
  1 tablespoon snipped chives
      or minced green onion tops
  4 cups water
  1 teaspoon salt
  1 cup quick-cooking grits
  1 teaspoon butter

1. Preheat oven to 325° F.

2. In a medium bowl beat together milk and eggs. Add cheeses, butter, garlic, pepper, and chives. Set aside.

3. Bring the water and salt to a boil. Add grits, stir, and return to a boil. Lower heat to medium and continue cooking, stirring often, until grits are thickened (about 5 minutes). Pour out any unabsorbed water. Off heat, immediately pour cheese mixture into the grits and stir until cheeses and butter melt. (Grits may be prepared in advance to this point; cover and refrigerate up to a day until ready to serve.)

4. Grease a 2-quart casserole or soufflé dish with the 1 teaspoon butter. Spoon the grits mixture into the prepared casserole and bake until a knife inserted in the center comes out clean, about 1 hour. Baked grits may be left in the turned-off oven for 10 minutes before serving.

Serves 8.

HOPPIN' JOHN

In the Deep South, black-eyed peas eaten on New Year's Day are supposed to bring good luck. Some insist the peas bestow luck only if they're prepared in Hoppin' John, which calls for dried black-eyed peas, as the flavor derives from the cooking liquid.

> 1½ cups dried black-eyed peas
>   (about ½ lb)
> 6 strips bacon, diced
> 1 medium onion, chopped
> ¾ cup long-grain white rice
> 2 tablespoons butter (optional)
>   Salt and pepper
>   Dash of Louisiana-style
>   hot sauce
> ½ cup minced green onions,
>   including crisp tops
> 3 tablespoons minced parsley

1. Rinse peas and pick them over. Cover with 3 cups of cold water, add 1 teaspoon of salt, and let stand overnight. (For a quicker soak, to serve peas the same day, place peas in a large pot and pour on 4 cups of boiling water. Heat to boiling again, and cook for 2 minutes. Turn off heat, cover, and let stand for 1 hour).

2. Drain peas, discarding water, and place in a large pot. In a separate pan, sauté bacon until crisp; add it to peas, reserving the rendered drippings. Add onion, ½ teaspoon salt, and 2 cups water. Bring just to a boil, lower heat, and simmer until peas are tender, about 30 minutes (longer in high-altitude and hard-water areas). A small amount of cooking liquid should remain; if liquid is absorbed too quickly during cooking, add fresh water by ¼ cups.

3. Cover rice with cold water. Bring to a boil, stir once, cover, and lower heat to the barest simmer. Simmer rice for 20 minutes.

4. When peas are tender, add cooked rice to pot. Stir in 2 tablespoons reserved bacon fat (or butter, if preferred), salt, pepper, and hot sauce to taste. Cover and simmer about 15 minutes longer so flavors mingle and rice absorbs some of the remaining cooking liquid. To serve, garnish with green onions and parsley.

Serves 6 to 7.

The sensual texture and exotic flavor of well-cooked okra are set off perfectly by tart, fresh tomatoes in this stew. Add rice and plump, tender shrimp and a homey side dish is transformed into an elegant main course: Shrimp Okra Pilau (recipe on page 36)—the mid-South's delicate version of Spanish paella or Louisiana jambalaya.

Served fresh from the oven with butter or warmed honey, this delightful, crumbly corn bread takes only minutes to mix. A treat at any meal, it tastes best when baked in an old-fashioned, cast-iron skillet, which produces a lovely, perfectly browned bottom crust.

OKRA AND TOMATO STEW

Okra is related to both hibiscus and cotton; the sticky fuzz (removed long before the okra reaches the grocery store) makes it as nasty to pick as cotton is. A native of Africa, it was popularized throughout the South during the era of slavery. (The Okra Pilau variation given below, native to the Georgia Sea Islands and the coastal lowlands, closely resembles a West African dish.) Okra is one vegetable that must be excluded from the current tendency to cook vegetables as briefly as possible. During cooking okra goes from crisp to slimy and finally to tender-crisp; it must be cooked long enough to recover from the slimy phase.

- 3 strips bacon
- 1 medium onion, finely chopped
- 1 small green bell pepper, finely chopped
- 1 pound fresh okra, trimmed and sliced into rounds, or 1 package (12 oz) sliced frozen okra
- 1 teaspoon flour
- 1 pound fresh tomatoes, peeled and coarsely chopped, or 1 can (14 oz) tomatoes, coarsely chopped
- 1 tablespoon light brown sugar
  Salt and black pepper, to taste

1. Cook bacon in a large skillet until crisp. Drain on paper towels, crumble, and reserve.

2. In bacon fat remaining in the skillet (about 3 tablespoons), sauté onion and green pepper over high heat, stirring until wilted (about 5 minutes). Add okra and cook over low heat for 10 minutes, stirring frequently.

3. Sprinkle flour over skillet and cook, stirring, for 1 minute, until flour loses its raw aroma. Add tomatoes, sugar, and salt and black pepper, to taste. Stir in bacon. Continue to cook over low heat until okra is tender and mixture is slightly thickened, about 10 minutes longer.

Serves 4 to 6.

Lowlands Okra Pilau Complete steps 1 and 2. Meanwhile, place 1 cup long-grain rice in 1½-quart saucepan with cover and add 2 cups cold water. Bring to a boil, stir once, cover, and cook over the lowest heat for exactly 12 minutes. Drain rice and add it to okra along with tomatoes, salt, pepper, and bacon (flour and sugar are omitted). Cover skillet and continue to cook over low heat until rice is tender, about 15 minutes longer.

Serves 6 to 8.

Shrimp Okra Pilau For a main dish, prepare Lowlands Okra Pilau and add 1 pound shelled medium shrimp and a dash of cayenne during the last 7 minutes of cooking.

Serves 4.

BREADS

Breads play a starring role at the southern table. Quick drop biscuits and souffléed spoon bread are at home equally at breakfast and at dinner, and lazy afternoons call for puffy tea cakes. And the chapter wouldn't be complete without the bouncy hush puppies and toothsome corn bread that seem made-to-order accompaniments for skillet-cooked entrées.

SALLY LUNN, GEORGIA STYLE

The purported creator of this recipe, Sally Lunn, the baker of Bath, is only a myth. These tea cakes originated in France under the name *Sol et Lune* (Sun and Moon) and became popular first in Bath, then throughout England, and finally in colonial America, under a slightly different pronunciation. This Georgia version, which owes its delicate texture to cake flour, may be mixed in a food processor. The square cakes may be served at breakfast, or in place of dinner rolls, as well as for snacks.

> ½ cup shortening
> ½ cup sugar
> 2 eggs
> 1 cup milk
> 2 cups sifted cake flour
> (measured after sifting)
> 1 tablespoon baking powder
> ½ teaspoon salt
> Butter (optional)

1. Heat oven to 425° F. Grease and flour an 8-inch square baking pan.

2. Using a wooden spoon, electric mixer, or food processor, cream shortening. Beat in sugar.

3. In a medium bowl beat eggs well, then blend with milk. In a separate large bowl, combine flour, baking powder, and salt. Beat about a quarter of egg mixture into creamed shortening mixture, then beat in about a quarter of the flour mixture. Repeat until all ingredients are blended, regularly scraping the sides of the bowl. The batter is done when it is thick, smooth, and satiny.

4. Turn batter into prepared pan and bake until top is golden and puffed (20 to 30 minutes). Cut into 2-inch squares and serve hot, with butter if desired.

Makes 24 squares.

GEORGIA DROP BISCUITS

These are the basic southern biscuits, and they're astonishingly easy. They take about the same amount of time to prepare as biscuits from a mix and yield a genuine homemade flavor.

> 1 cup self-rising flour (see Note)
> ¼ cup cold shortening
> ½ cup whole milk
> Additional flour

1. Preheat oven to 500° F. Lightly grease a baking sheet.

2. Put flour in a large bowl. Cut in shortening, using a pastry blender or rubbing between your fingers, until you have a coarse but even meal.

3. Make a well in the center of flour mixture and pour in milk. With a wooden spoon stir to make a wet, sticky dough. Beat with the spoon until milk is thoroughly integrated and dough is elastic. (Dough can now be left to sit at room temperature, covered with plastic wrap, for up to an hour before baking.)

4. Place about 2 tablespoons flour in a large bowl. Use more to flour your hands. For each biscuit, scoop out a tablespoon of dough, roll lightly between your hands to the size and shape of an egg, dip on all sides in the bowl of flour, and place on baking sheet. Do not crowd.

5. Bake in top third of oven until biscuits are puffed and starting to brown (about 10 minutes). Serve hot.

Makes about 8 medium-to-large or 12 small biscuits.

Note You can substitute all-purpose flour; sift in ½ teaspoon salt and 1 heaping teaspoon double-acting baking powder, then proceed with step 2.

SOUTHERN CORN BREAD

White cornmeal or yellow? Butter or shortening? Whole milk or buttermilk? The answers vary with the area of the South, and all the alternatives are almost equally tasty. White and yellow cornmeal are similar in taste; butter lends corn bread a richer flavor, but shortening produces a lighter texture. Buttermilk, however, wins hands down, providing both a tangy flavor and a yeasty element to lighten the bread. (If it's absolutely necessary, use whole milk, but the result just won't be the same.) Corn bread is best served fresh from the oven and still hot, but any leftovers can be reheated in a 350° F oven until warm.

> Butter to grease pan
> 1 cup cornmeal
> 1 cup flour
> 3 tablespoons sugar
> 4 teaspoons baking powder
> ½ teaspoon salt
> ⅓ cup butter or shortening
> at room temperature
> 1 egg
> 1 cup buttermilk

1. Preheat oven to 400° F. Grease a 10-inch cast-iron skillet (or an 8- by 8-inch baking pan) and place in oven to heat.

2. In a large bowl stir together cornmeal, flour, sugar, baking powder, and salt. Use a pastry blender, two knives, or fingers to cut in butter to make a coarse but even meal.

3. In a medium bowl beat together egg and buttermilk and pour into cornmeal mixture. Stir strongly but briefly, scooping from the bottom, just until thoroughly blended.

4. Pour mixture into heated baking pan. Bake for about 25 minutes, until top is lightly browned and corn bread shrinks from the sides of the pan. Serve warm.

Makes 16 squares or 8 large wedges.

HUSH PUPPIES

Hush puppies were reputedly invented by southern fishermen to bribe the dogs at outdoor fish fries. They're still at their best when cooked in fish-frying oil, but these light, satisfying, quickly made nuggets are probably too good for man's best friend.

  Cooking oil (peanut or corn oil preferred)
2 cups white cornmeal
1 cup flour
1 tablespoon baking powder
1 teaspoon salt
1 teaspoon sugar
½ teaspoon freshly ground black pepper
  Pinch of cayenne pepper
3 eggs
¾ cup milk
3 tablespoons melted margarine or butter
1 small onion, minced (about ¾ c)
1 large clove garlic, pressed or minced fine

1. In a deep skillet or Dutch oven, heat 2 inches of oil to 365° F. (If frying fish at the same meal, use oil from cooking fish.) Preheat oven to 325° F.

2. In a large bowl stir together cornmeal, flour, baking powder, salt, sugar, black pepper, and cayenne. In a medium bowl beat eggs until large bubbles form. Stir milk, margarine, onion, and garlic into eggs. Stir egg mixture into cornmeal mixture to make a stiff, bouncy batter.

3. Working in batches, drop heaping teaspoons of batter into hot oil, until skillet is full; do not crowd. Regulate heat so oil remains between 350° F and 385° F. The hush puppies will sink to the bottom, then rise to the top, turning and bubbling. When they are golden brown (in 1 to 2 minutes), remove from oil with a slotted spoon and drain on paper towels. Keep warm in oven until all the batches are complete. Serve hot.

Makes 30 to 40 hush puppies.

VIRGINIA SPOON BREAD

Spoon bread is not really a bread; it's an easy cornmeal-based soufflé, puffed and airy. Serve it whenever you'd like a light and festive starch dish, or as the main course at brunch.

6 tablespoons unsalted butter, cut in 6 pieces
3 cups milk
2 tablespoons sugar
1 teaspoon salt
½ teaspoon freshly ground black pepper
1 cup white cornmeal
4 eggs, separated, at room temperature

1. Thoroughly grease a 2-quart casserole or soufflé dish, using some of the butter. Preheat oven to 350° F.

2. In a large, heavy saucepan (at least 3 quarts), combine milk, sugar, salt, and pepper. Slowly pour in cornmeal, beating strongly with a wooden spoon until mixture is smooth.

3. Over medium heat, stirring constantly, heat the mixture until it boils and thickens (about 5 minutes). Lower heat, add the remaining butter, and stir until butter melts (about 2 minutes). Remove from heat.

4. Beat egg yolks lightly and beat into the cornmeal mixture.

5. Beat egg whites until stiff but not dry. Gently fold into the cornmeal mixture. Pour batter into buttered casserole. Bake, uncovered, until spoon bread is browned on top and puffed (30 to 35 minutes).

Serves 4 to 6.

Variations Create a richer version by using half-and-half in place of the milk. For a sweeter version, add a tablespoon of honey along with the sugar. For a cheese-flavored casserole, replace ½ cup of the milk with 1 cup of grated Cheddar cheese. Add cheese along with the butter.

CHURCH SOCIAL

Fried Chicken

Cream Gravy

Church-Social Potato Salad

*Tossed Salad and
Cole Slaw of
Your Choice*

Pecan Pie

*Iced Tea, Iced Coffee,
Soft Drinks*

Churches play an important social role in southern communities, providing an extended family for the members as well as spiritual guidance, fellowship, and prayer. The institution of the church supper allows the congregation to get together informally and renew family ties while showing off their best recipes at a neighborly (and only mildly competitive) potluck. Whether the supper takes place in the church basement or a park by the river, the only absolute rule is: There will be fried chicken and there will be potato salad, usually at least five versions of each. And for dessert, there will certainly be several pies, and at least two of them will be pecan.

BASIC SOUTHERN-FRIED CHICKEN

1 *frying chicken (2½ to 3 lb), cut in serving pieces*
Salt and freshly ground black pepper, to taste
½ *teaspoon cayenne pepper, or to taste*
½ *cup (approximately) flour*
Lard or peanut oil, for frying (about 1½ c per skillet)

1. Wash chicken and pat it dry with paper towels. Sprinkle both sides of each piece with salt, pepper, and cayenne to taste. Rub seasonings into the meat and skin. Dredge chicken on both sides with flour, shaking off excess.

2. In a large (12- or 14-inch) skillet, heat lard over high heat. (When melted, lard should be about ½ inch deep.) When fat reaches 360° F it will start smoking a little and a haze will form on top. Using long tongs and standing well back to avoid being burned, add the chicken legs and thighs, skin side down. To keep the chicken from turning greasy, leave ample room between the pieces as they fry, and keep the oil bubbling hot. Lower heat to medium-high, so that fat bubbles constantly but does not roar. (Use a spatter-shield over the pan, if possible.) After 7 minutes, raise the heat again, turn the legs and thighs, and add breast pieces, wings, and back, skin side down. Continue to cook over high heat for 1 minute, then lower heat to medium-high again, and cook about 6 more minutes. Finally turn all the pieces and cook until done, about 7 minutes longer. (See tips on frying, page 75.)

3. Remove chicken from skillet and drain on paper towels. If necessary, keep warm in a 200° F oven until ready to serve.

4. Pour Cream Gravy into a gravy boat and serve with chicken.

Serves 4.

Buttermilk-Battered Fried Chicken With Honey-Pecan Glaze

This coating is thicker than the previous one, but still light and crisp. Mix 2 cups buttermilk, 1 teaspoon Tabasco sauce, and 2 cloves garlic, peeled and crushed. Soak chicken in this mixture for an hour at room temperature or overnight in the refrigerator. Drain chicken (do not wipe off), and dredge in self-rising flour (you'll need 1½ to 2 cups). Shake off excess flour, then place on waxed paper and allow to sit for 15 minutes. Heat ½ inch vegetable oil in a large heavy skillet (or in two skillets) and fry as directed in step 2. Drain on paper towels and serve hot with glaze or cold, unglazed. *For glaze:* Melt ¼ cup butter in a small pan. Stir in ¼ cup honey, ¼ cup halved pecans, and, if desired, a dash of Tabasco. Bring just to a boil, remove from heat, and pour over hot chicken.

Maryland Oven-Fried Chicken

Preheat oven to 400° F. Pour ½ cup oil into a baking pan large enough to hold all chicken pieces in a single layer. In a medium bowl mix 3 tablespoons flour, 3 tablespoons fine dry bread crumbs, ½ teaspoon salt, ¼ teaspoon black pepper, and ⅛ teaspoon cayenne. Roll chicken in the mixture to coat. Place coated chicken pieces in pan, skin side down. Bake 30 minutes, turn pieces, and bake an additional 25 minutes. Remove chicken pieces from the fat and keep warm while making Cream Gravy. *For Maryland-style cream gravy:* Pour 2 tablespoons of the cooking fat into a skillet, heat it over medium heat, add 2 tablespoons flour, and cook until flour starts to color. Slowly add 1 cup milk and seasonings to taste. Cook, stirring, over high heat until mixture starts to boil. Lower heat and cook, stirring, until mixture thickens.

CREAM GRAVY

2 *teaspoons flour*
1 *cup half-and-half*
Salt and ground black pepper
⅛ *teaspoon ground nutmeg*
Pinch cayenne pepper

After frying chicken pour nearly all the fat out of the skillet. Leave the browned bits on the bottom and just enough fat to film the pan (about 2 tablespoons). Stir in flour and cook, stirring, over low heat a few seconds, scraping up the browned bits, until flour begins to color. Pour in the half-and-half, raise heat to medium, and cook, stirring, until mixture begins to boil and thicken slightly. Season to taste with salt, black pepper, nutmeg, and cayenne.

Makes 1 scant cup.

CHURCH-SOCIAL POTATO SALAD

This soulful potato salad combines elements from traditional French, German, and Creole recipes.

4 *large potatoes, peeled and halved*
½ *cup chopped red onion*
¼ *cup sliced green onions*
1 *stalk celery, chopped*
4 *hard-cooked eggs, peeled and chopped*

Dressing

3 *tablespoons vinegar*
1¼ *cups salad oil*
2 *tablespoons Dijon mustard*
1 *teaspoon horseradish*
1 *teaspoon salt*
1 *teaspoon dried tarragon*
½ *teaspoon cayenne*
½ *teaspoon black pepper*

1. Boil potatoes until tender (20 minutes), cool, and chop into chunks.

2. Combine red onion, green onions, and celery. Add to potatoes and blend gently. Add Dressing, fold in hard-cooked eggs, mix gently, and chill.

Serves 4 to 6.

Dressing Combine all ingredients and beat until smooth. Set aside.

Southern potluck dinners bring out prized family recipes for crunchy fried chicken, tasty potato salad, and pecan pie. Recipes start on page 38.

PECAN PIE

Pecan pie is a long-standing favorite that is generally among the most popular desserts at church suppers and elsewhere. The filling in this Mid-South version is a little less sweet than the Deep South's renditions.

> 3 *eggs, lightly beaten*
> ¾ *cup dark brown sugar*
> ½ *cup white corn syrup*
> 1 *tablespoon cider vinegar*
> 1 *teaspoon vanilla extract*
> 2 *tablespoons unsalted butter, melted*
>   *Pinch of salt*
> 1 *cup pecans, coarsely chopped*
> 1 *unbaked 9-inch pie shell (use ½ recipe Flaky Pastry, page 63), chilled in refrigerator*
> 1 *cup (approximately) pecan halves*
> 1 *cup heavy cream (optional)*

1. Preheat oven to 425° F. In a medium bowl, stir together eggs, sugar, corn syrup, vinegar, vanilla, butter, and salt. When mixture is well blended, stir in chopped pecans.

2. Pour mixture into pie shell. Arrange enough pecan halves side by side on surface of filling to cover it in a sunburst design.

3. Place pie on lowest rack of oven. Immediately lower oven temperature to 350° F and bake pie until crust is lightly browned and filling sets (about 45 minutes). Place on a wire rack to cool before serving.

4. If whipped cream topping is desired, beat heavy cream with an electric beater until stiff peaks form when beater is lifted. (Do not sweeten the whipped cream.)

Serves 8.

DESSERTS

Here are sensuous pies, airy puddings, and a fudgy "tipsy" cake that's pure southern hospitality.

MISSISSIPPI MUD CAKE

This "tipsy" cake includes nuts and raisins to lend extra texture.

>   *Butter and flour to dust cake pan*
> ¾ *cup strong black coffee*
> ½ *cup butter, cut in 8 chunks*
> 3 *ounces unsweetened chocolate, chopped coarsely*
> 1 *egg*
> ⅓ *cup bourbon or Tennessee whiskey*
> 1½ *teaspoons vanilla extract, divided*
> 1 *cup cake flour*
> 1 *cup sugar*
> ½ *teaspoon baking soda*
>   *Pinch of salt*
> ¾ *cup chopped pecans*
> ½ *cup seedless raisins*
> 1 *cup whipping cream*

1. Preheat oven to 275° F. Grease and flour a 9- by 4-inch loaf pan.

2. In a 2½-quart saucepan over very low heat, mix coffee, butter, and chocolate, stirring constantly; do not boil. When butter and chocolate have melted, remove from heat and let cool until tepid (about 10 minutes).

3. Beat egg lightly and stir in bourbon and 1 teaspoon vanilla. Stir into chocolate mixture until blended.

4. In a medium bowl, sift together flour, sugar, baking soda, and salt. With a wooden spoon or electric mixer, rapidly beat into chocolate mixture until smooth. Stir in pecans and raisins and pour into prepared loaf pan. Bake until firm but not completely dry, 45 to 55 minutes. Let cake cool for about 20 minutes, then turn out of pan.

5. In a medium bowl, whip cream with ½ teaspoon vanilla to stiff peaks. Cut cake in thin slices (it's very rich) and spoon some whipped cream over each slice.

Serves 8 to 12.

Note Cake recipe may be doubled for a large crowd. Turn batter into a greased, floured 9-inch tube pan. Bake about 1½ hours.

OZARK PUDDING

This light and amazingly easy pudding from Arkansas was once called Huguenot Torte—and, indeed, the ingredients hint at an origin in the French province of Normandy. Use any firm, tart, and juicy apple sold in your area.

>   *Unsalted butter for greasing pan*
> 2 *eggs*
> ½ *cup sugar*
> 1 *teaspoon vanilla extract*
> 3 *tablespoons flour*
> 2 *teaspoons baking powder*
> ⅛ *teaspoon salt*
> ½ *cup coarsely chopped pecans or walnuts*
> 2 *large tart apples, peeled, cored, and diced*
>   *About ⅛ teaspoon ground cinnamon*
> 1 *cup whipping cream*
>   *Additional vanilla extract*

1. Grease a 9-inch pie pan with butter. Preheat oven to 350° F.

2. Place eggs and sugar in a large mixing bowl and beat with an electric mixer until pale and thickened to the consistency of a light mayonnaise. Stir in vanilla. Stir in flour, baking powder, and salt. Fold in nuts and apples.

3. Pour apple mixture into buttered pie pan, and dust the top lightly with cinnamon. Bake until top is browned and puffy, about 30 minutes. Remove from oven.

4. Beat cream with a few drops of vanilla until stiff peaks form. Serve pudding warm or at room temperature with whipped cream.

Serves 4 to 6.

It takes less than half an hour to whip up Florida's legendary Key-Lime Pie with this sixty-year-old quick version of the traditional recipe. The tender, uncooked custard—its citrus freshness intensified by a touch of grated lime rind—is topped with an airy meringue.

LEMON CHESS PIE

If unexpected guests drop in, this sensuous, sweet-tart dessert can be whipped up from staples.

> 1 9-inch unbaked pie shell (use ½ recipe Flaky Pastry, page 63)
>
> 6 tablespoons butter (at room temperature for mixing by hand; may be chilled if using a food processor)
>
> 1 cup sugar
>
> 3 eggs
>   Grated rind (about 2 tablespoons) and juice (about ¼ cup) of 1 large, ripe lemon
>
> 2 teaspoons cornmeal
>   Pinch of salt

1. Preheat oven to 400° F. Fill pie shell with raw rice, beans, or pie weights and bake for 10 minutes (it will be partially done). Empty pie shell and set aside; turn oven down to 350° F.

2. Cream butter and sugar together until fluffy. Beat in eggs one at a time, beating after each addition until batter is smooth. Mix together lemon rind, lemon juice, cornmeal, and salt; beat into butter mixture until smooth. Pour batter into pie shell and bake until top is browned and slightly puffed and filling is firm but not dry, 35 to 40 minutes. Serve warm, at room temperature, or chilled.

Serves 6 to 8.

KEY-LIME PIE

This traditional Key West, Florida, recipe for a meringue-topped pie takes less than 30 minutes to prepare.

> ½ cup (scant) fresh lime juice (from about 6 Key limes or 3 large, ripe regular limes)
>
> 2 to 3 teaspoons grated lime rind, green part only
>
> 1 can (14 oz) sweetened condensed milk
>
> 4 eggs, separated
>
> 1 prepared graham-cracker pie crust (or baked pastry crust)
>
> 5 tablespoons sugar (or to taste)

1. Preheat oven to 400° F. Stir together lime juice, lime rind, and condensed milk until mixture thickens to the consistency of heavy pastry cream. (The acid of the lime juice thickens the milk.) Beat egg yolks until fluffy, thick, and lemon colored, and stir into milk mixture to make a light custard. Turn custard into the pie crust.

2. With an electric mixer (using clean, dry blades), beat egg whites until soft, droopy peaks form. Beat in sugar one tablespoonful at a time. (If a very sweet meringue is desired, use additional sugar.) Continue beating until meringue is shiny and forms stiff peaks when beaters are lifted.

3. Mound meringue over the top of pie. Place pie in oven and bake at 400° F, just until meringue is browned but still tender (about 10 minutes). Remove from oven, let cool, and chill before serving.

Serves 8.

GEORGIA PEACH COBBLER

A cobbler is a pie with a puffy "shortcake" biscuit crust—which can either go under or over the fruit. Use any soft, juicy, fresh fruit (blackberries, blueberries, nectarines, cherries) instead of or mixed with peaches. In winter make a cobbler with thawed frozen fruits packed without syrup. Include in the filling whatever juices the fruits render when they're sliced.

    Butter to grease pan
 4 cups peeled, pitted, and sliced
    peaches
 2 tablespoons flour
 ½ teaspoon cinnamon
 ½ to scant 1 cup sugar (to taste)
    Sugar and cinnamon (for
    top-crust version)
 1 pint ice cream or 1 cup
    whipped cream (optional)

Biscuit Crust

 1 cup flour
 ¼ teaspoon salt
 1 tablespoon sugar
 ½ rounded tablespoon baking
    powder
 3 tablespoons butter
 6 tablespoons (⅜ cup) half-and-
    half or rich milk
    Additional flour, for kneading

1. Preheat oven to 425° F. Grease thoroughly a baking pan (a 9-inch deep-dish pie pan, an 8- by 8-inch cake pan, or a 10-inch cast-iron skillet).

2. In a large mixing bowl, gently toss together peaches, any juice from peaches, flour, cinnamon, and sugar (adjust the amount of sugar to the sweetness of the fruit).

3. *To make cobbler with bottom crust:* Press Biscuit Crust onto bottom of prepared baking pan; trim off excess. Cover with fruit and bake until fruits are tender (about 35 minutes). *To make cobbler with top crust:* Turn fruit mixture into baking dish. Cut dough with a biscuit cutter or a cookie cutter into whatever shapes amuse you. Top the fruit mixture with the biscuits; sprinkle biscuits lightly with sugar and cinnamon. Bake until biscuits are browned (about 35 minutes).

4. Let cobbler cool for about 10 minutes, then serve warm or at room temperature, alone or with ice cream or whipped cream.

Serves 4.

Biscuit Crust In a medium bowl sift together flour, salt, sugar, and baking powder. With fingers or pastry blender, cut butter into flour mixture to make a coarse meal. Pour in half-and-half and stir quickly with a fork until mixture forms a dough. Turn dough onto a lightly floured work surface and knead briefly (about half a minute). Cover dough with a sheet of waxed paper and roll it out to a sheet ¼ inch thick.

LANE CAKE

This is pure "plantation cookery," Hollywood style. When Melanie (or Rhett) came to dinner, Scarlett O'Hara probably demanded that her cook turn out this bourbon-laden angel-food layer cake. The oldest recipes created a batter like bubble gum. In this modern version (suggested by Virginia-born ecologist Martha Ture), there is much less flour, and the batter mixes easily—ideally, in a food processor.

 1 cup seedless golden raisins
    or currants
 ⅔ cup bourbon
    Butter to grease pans
 2 cups cake flour
 2 teaspoons baking powder
 ¼ teaspoon salt
 2 teaspoons vanilla extract
 1 cup milk
 1 cup butter
 3 cups sugar
 8 eggs, separated
 ½ cup butter, cut in 8 chunks
 1 cup chopped pecans
    White icing of choice
    (optional)
    Shredded coconut (optional)

1. Preheat oven to 350° F. Place raisins in bourbon and let steep while you work. (You will use these ingredients in the filling.) Grease two 9-inch layer-cake pans with butter. In a large bowl sift together flour, baking powder, and salt; resift two more times to aerate. Mix vanilla into milk. In food processor fitted with metal blade (or in large bowl of an electric mixer), cream the 1 cup of the butter. Add 2 cups sugar, and continue to cream until fluffy. Beat in some of the flour mixture, then some of the milk. Continue beating in flour mixture and milk alternately, ending with the flour mixture.

2. In another large bowl beat egg whites to stiff peaks. Gently fold batter into beaten whites. Spoon batter into prepared cake pans and bake until tops are lightly browned (about 35 minutes). Let cool on a wire rack before turning out of the pans.

3. *To make filling:* In the top half of a double boiler, beat egg yolks until smooth; stir in 1 cup sugar. Add the 8 pieces of butter to yolk mixture. Cook over gently boiling water, stirring constantly and strongly until very thick. Remove from heat, then add steeped raisins with bourbon and pecans.

4. When cake layers have cooled, place one on a serving plate and spread with half of the filling. Cover with second layer and top with remaining filling. Refrigerate until filling is chilled and very thick. Cake may be served as is, but for grand occasions frost with any white icing and garnish with shredded coconut.

Serves 8 to 12.

Crisply fried scrapple, a meaty cornmeal mush, brightens this breakfast of eggs, sautéed apples, and cinnamon buns. Recipes start on page 47.

The Heartland

Heartland cooking ranges from familiar home-style favorites such as Roast Chicken With Minnesota Wild-Rice Stuffing (see page 52), Plump Blueberry Muffins (see page 56), and Michigan Sour-Cherry Pie (see page 62) to the more exotic fare of Morel Soup (see page 49) and Upper Peninsula Pasties (see page 50). Menus from the Midwest emphasize joyous abundance. A Fourth of July Picnic in the Park (see page 58) offers Grilled Polish Sausage, Corn on the Cob, and Red Marble Cake; and a substantial Sunday Breakfast (see page 47) includes Sautéed Apples, Cream-Basted Fried Eggs, Fried Scrapple, and Sticky Cinnamon Buns.

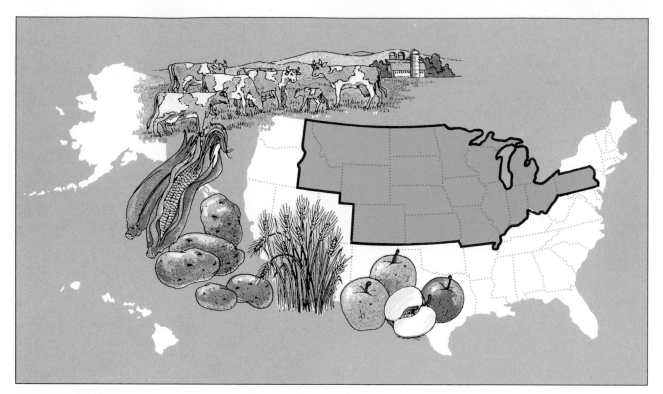

THE HEARTLAND

The classic dishes of America's vast Heartland, which stretches roughly from the Alleghenies to the Rockies, are as varied as the area is wide. The juxtaposition of a simply elegant porterhouse steak (see page 53) with a dazzling Hungarian goulash (see page 51) expresses the richness and diversity of heartland cooking.

The early settlers who pushed westward beyond the Ohio River into what was, in the late eighteenth century, the Northwest Territory, brought with them a liking for many New England foods.

As industry grew in the great urban centers of the Midwest, immigrants were drawn from all over Europe, bringing new foods and flavors to enliven the Heartland's spectrum of tastes. Midwestern fare today still owes much to all these origins, as the recipes in this chapter clearly show.

If you think of the foods on the table of the family in *The Little House on the Prairie,* you can picture the plain fare of the pioneers. It was based on grains; vegetables from summer gardens; a hog or steer, slaughtered when it could be spared; chicken; and orchard fruits. (John

"Johnny Appleseed" Chapman roamed the Midwest in the early 1800s, probably sowing the seeds of the Heartland's fondness for apple pie.) Game birds, animals, and fresh-water fish contributed to a festive dish on occasion.

Learning the lore of the edible wild was a skill the first settlers of the Heartland—and before them the trailblazers and trappers—could ill afford to overlook. Although seeking out such provender is more of a hobby than a necessity nowadays, the Midwest still boasts of many uncultivated delicacies: the tiny, tart wild persimmons of Indiana; the wild rice of Minnesota; and the chokecherries and thimbleberries, which make delicious preserves, and the sugar maples of Michigan.

Cultivated crops also shape the cooking of the Heartland. Wheat from the Great Plains, exported to the farthest corners of the world, shows up on heartland tables as home-baked breads and sweets, breakfast cereal, and a crusty loaf or basket of rolls with dinner. Sugar beets from Michigan, Nebraska, and Colorado sweeten them all. Feed grains fatten heartland livestock—beef, pork, and

chicken. Other cereal grains go into the beer that still makes Milwaukee—not to overlook St. Louis, Detroit, and Denver—famous.

Potatoes are grown throughout much of the upper Midwest, the better to be fried, baked, boiled, mashed, or dressed as potato salad (see page 57). They make up an essential part of any major meal the year around.

Dairying is important in the Great Lakes states. Butter lends much of the food of this region a luscious flavor and richness. Respected cheeses are produced in Ohio, Wisconsin, and Iowa. And a glass of cold milk is often the beverage of choice with lunch or supper.

It's no surprise that the Heartland, celebrated for a longstanding ethic of hard work in fields and factories, begins the day with a sturdy breakfast (see the menu on page 47). And it's no wonder that the Heartland, which gave us the hot dog at the 1904 St. Louis World's Fair, still likes grilled sausages for the Fourth of July (see page 58).

This region enjoys rib-sticking food—sturdy soups, hearty meat-based main dishes, and rich baked goods. You'll find an ample selection of these heartland dishes on the pages that follow.

SUNDAY BREAKFAST

Sautéed Apples
Cream-Basted Fried Eggs
Fried Scrapple
Sticky Cinnamon Buns
Milk and Coffee

A lazy Sunday breakfast is a meal to anticipate with pleasure. Scrapple—slices of cornmeal mush flavored with pork and savory herbs—is surprisingly light, and good with either tart sautéed apples or warm maple syrup. Accompany the scrapple with eggs in butter and cream and plump cinnamon buns. Both the scrapple and the rolls can be made ahead (refrigerate or freeze the scrapple; freeze the rolls, then reheat).

SAUTÉED APPLES

  2 tablespoons butter
     or margarine
  4 medium-sized tart cooking
     apples, peeled, cored, and
     sliced about ¼ inch thick
  1 tablespoon lemon juice
  ⅛ teaspoon ground nutmeg
  ⅓ cup sugar

1. Heat butter in a large frying pan over moderately high heat until butter foams. Mix in apples, lemon juice, and nutmeg. Cook, uncovered, stirring occasionally, until apples are almost tender (8 to 10 minutes).

2. Sprinkle with sugar and cook, stirring gently, until apples are tender (2 minutes longer). Serve warm.

Serves 4 to 6.

CREAM-BASTED FRIED EGGS

  2 tablespoons butter
     or margarine
  2 tablespoons whipping cream
  4 to 6 eggs
     Salt and white pepper, to taste

1. In a large, heavy frying pan over medium-low heat, melt butter. Swirl in cream. Break eggs into pan, being careful not to break yolks.

2. Cook, uncovered, occasionally spooning cream mixture over eggs, until whites are set and a pale, translucent film covers yolks (3 to 5 minutes). Serve at once, seasoned with salt and pepper.

Serves 4 to 6.

FRIED SCRAPPLE

  2 pounds boneless pork shoulder
  8 cups water
  1 teaspoon dried sage
  ½ teaspoon each salt and pepper
  ¼ teaspoon dried thyme
  ⅛ teaspoon ground nutmeg
  1½ cups yellow cornmeal
     Flour
     Butter or margarine
     Maple syrup (optional)

1. Trim off and discard excess fat from pork. Place in a deep 4½- to 5-quart pot and add 6 cups of the water, the sage, salt, pepper, thyme, and nutmeg. Bring to a boil over medium heat; cover, reduce heat, and simmer until pork is so tender it separates easily into shreds (about 2 hours). Lift meat from broth, reserving cooking liquid in pot. Chop pork finely; return to broth.

2. Place cornmeal in a large bowl. Using a whisk, gradually stir remaining 2 cups water into cornmeal. Stir cornmeal mixture into pork and broth. Return to medium heat and cook, stirring often with a long-handled wooden spoon, until mixture is very thick (about 30 minutes after it boils). Pour into 2 greased 4½- by 8½-inch loaf pans. Cover and refrigerate until firm (about 4 hours or until next day).

3. Cut scrapple into ½-inch slices. Dust lightly with flour on both sides. In a large frying pan over medium-high heat, melt butter, using enough to cover bottom generously. Add scrapple slices in a single layer (do not crowd pan) and cook, turning once, until crusty and golden brown (about 5 minutes total). Uncooked scrapple can be kept in refrigerator for up to 3 days. Serve hot, with Sautéed Apples or maple syrup, if desired.

Serves 10 to 12.

STICKY CINNAMON BUNS

- ½ cup warm (105° to 115° F) water
- 2 packages active dry yeast
- ¾ cup granulated sugar
- ½ cup warm (105° to 115° F) milk
- 1 teaspoon salt
- ½ cup butter or margarine, softened
- 5 to 5½ cups flour
- 2 eggs
- ½ cup firmly packed brown sugar
- 2 teaspoons cinnamon
- ¼ cup butter or margarine, melted
- 1 cup chopped walnuts
- ½ cup raisins
- 1 cup dark corn syrup

1. Put the water in large bowl of electric mixer; sprinkle yeast over water. Add 1 tablespoon of the granulated sugar. Let stand until yeast is soft (about 5 minutes).

2. Add remaining granulated sugar, the milk, salt, and the softened butter.

3. Add 3 cups of the flour. Mix to blend, then beat at medium speed until smooth and elastic (about 5 minutes). Beat in eggs, one at a time, beating until smooth after each addition. Stir in about 2 cups more flour to make a soft dough.

4. Turn dough out onto a board or pastry cloth coated with some of the remaining ½ cup flour. Knead until dough is smooth and satiny and small bubbles form just under surface (12 to 15 minutes), adding just enough flour to prevent dough from being sticky.

5. Place dough in a greased bowl and turn to coat with grease. Cover with plastic wrap and a towel; let rise in a warm place until doubled in bulk (1¼ to 1½ hours).

6. While dough rises, mix brown sugar and cinnamon in a small bowl.

7. Punch dough down. Cover with inverted bowl and let rest for 10 minutes. Roll dough out on a floured surface into an 18-inch square. Brush with the melted butter. Sprinkle with brown sugar mixture. Distribute walnuts and raisins evenly over the brown sugar mixture. Drizzle with about ¼ cup of the corn syrup. Pour remaining corn syrup into a greased 9- by 13-inch baking pan.

8. Starting from one edge, roll dough jelly-roll fashion; moisten long edge and pinch to seal. Cut into 12 equal slices. Place slices in prepared baking pan. Cover lightly with waxed paper. Let rise until doubled in bulk (about 1 hour). Preheat oven to 350° F.

9. Bake until well browned (30 to 35 minutes). Let rolls stand in pan on a rack for 1 minute; then invert carefully onto a serving tray. Let stand with pan in place for 30 seconds, then remove pan. Serve warm.

Makes 1 dozen rolls.

SUBSTANTIAL SOUPS

Sturdy, rib-sticking soups are a cornerstone of heartland cooking—welcoming warm-ups for winter lunches and suppers. And when a first course is called for to begin a more formal meal, soup of a somewhat less filling sort is often the answer.

WINTER-VEGETABLE BEEF SOUP

An abundance of nourishing winter vegetables backed up by plenty of beef makes this colorful soup a good choice for an informal main dish. Accompany it with crisp crackers, then serve warm gingerbread (see page 16) for dessert.

- 2 tablespoons butter or margarine
- 3 pounds beef shanks, sliced about 1 inch thick
- 1 thick slice (about 1½ lbs) beef knucklebone
- 2 medium onions, slivered
- 2 stalks celery, thinly sliced
- 3 cloves garlic, slivered
- 1 bay leaf
- 2 teaspoons salt
- ¼ teaspoon each *pepper* and *ground allspice*
- ¾ teaspoon *dried thyme*
- 1 large can (28 oz) tomatoes, coarsely chopped (reserve liquid)
- 3 large carrots, diced
- 1 large potato (about ¾ lb), diced
- 2 medium turnips (about ½ lb total), peeled and diced
- 8 cups water
- ½ cup frozen or fresh shelled peas
- 2 cups shredded chard leaves or cabbage

1. In an 8- to 10-quart kettle over medium-high heat, melt butter. Add beef shanks, knucklebone, brown well, and remove. Add onions, celery, garlic, and cook, stirring occasionally, until vegetables are limp (8 to 10 minutes).

2. Stir in bay leaf, salt, pepper, allspice, and thyme. Return all shanks and bone to the pan. Add tomatoes and their liquid, carrots, potato, turnips, and the water. Bring to a boil, cover, reduce heat, and simmer until soup is full flavored and beef is very tender (about 4 hours).

3. Remove and discard bay leaf. Remove beef shanks with slotted spoon. When cool, remove meat from bones and return to soup in generous chunks; discard fat and bones. If possible, cover and refrigerate soup for several hours or overnight.

4. To serve, skim and discard surface fat from soup. Boil soup over medium heat. Stir in peas and chard and boil gently, uncovered, until the last two vegetables are bright green and heated through (2 to 3 minutes). Add salt if needed. Serve at once.

Makes about 16 cups, 8 servings.

IDAHO WHITE-BEAN SOUP

After you've served baked ham for dinner, you'll have one of the key ingredients of this flavorsome bean soup—a meaty ham bone.

- *1 pound (about 2½ cups) dried Great Northern (large white) beans, rinsed and drained*
  Salt
- *1 meaty ham bone or 2 smoked ham hocks (about 1½ lbs total)*
- *1 large onion, finely chopped*
- *2 cloves garlic, minced or pressed*
- *1 bay leaf*
- *½ teaspoon dried thyme*
- *2 stalks celery with leaves, finely chopped*
- *2 medium carrots, shredded*
- *¼ teaspoon freshly ground pepper*

1. Place beans in a large bowl; add 2 teaspoons salt and 6 cups water. Cover and let stand for at least 8 hours or until next day; drain, discarding soaking liquid. (Or, to shorten preparation time, place beans in a 3- to 4-quart pan with 8 cups water, using *no salt;* bring to a boil, then boil briskly, uncovered, for 2 minutes. Remove from heat, cover, and let stand for 1 hour. Drain, discarding soaking liquid.)

2. In a 5- to 6-quart kettle, combine drained beans, 8 cups water, ham bone, onion, garlic, bay leaf, thyme, celery, and carrots. Bring to a boil over medium heat. Cover, reduce heat, and boil gently until beans are very tender and ham separates easily from bone (3½ to 4 hours).

3. Remove and discard bay leaf. Remove ham bone and set aside. Scoop out about 2 cups of beans with a little of the liquid, purée in a blender or food processor, and return to soup. When ham is cool enough to handle, remove meat from bone and return it to soup; discard bone and skin. Stir in pepper. Taste and add salt if needed.

4. Reheat soup, if necessary, and serve steaming hot.

Makes about 11 cups, 6 servings.

MOREL SOUP

Distinctive in flavor, texture, and appearance, wild mushrooms known as morels are one of the gloriously good-eating phenomena of spring found in the Midwest. Dedicated mushroom hunters seek them out each year in order to concoct this silken first-course soup. So that you can make the soup in any season, this recipe calls for dried morels. If you don't have the luck to discover your own wild morels to dry, you can obtain these rare and elegant mushrooms by mail from these sources.

Fresh & Wild
Box 917
Camas, WA 98607

American Spoon Foods
411 East Lake Street
Petoskey, MI 49770

- *1 cup (1 oz) dried morels*
- *¼ cup butter or margarine*
- *1 medium onion, finely chopped*
- *1 tablespoon flour*
- *½ teaspoon each salt and dry mustard*
  Pinch ground nutmeg
- *1 teaspoon catsup*
- *1½ cups chicken broth (not condensed)*
- *1 tablespoon lemon juice*
- *2 cups half-and-half*
- *2 tablespoons dry sherry*
  Chopped parsley, for garnish

1. Place morels in a medium bowl; cover with hot tap water. Let stand until soft (about 30 minutes). Drain, reserving ½ cup of the soaking liquid. Chop morels coarsely.

2. Melt butter in a 3-quart pan over medium heat. Add morels and onion; cook, stirring often, until onion is soft and beginning to brown.

3. Sprinkle with flour, salt, dry mustard, and nutmeg; add catsup. Remove from heat and gradually blend in reserved soaking liquid and chicken broth. Return to medium heat and bring to a boil; cover. Reduce heat; simmer until morels are tender (about 20 minutes).

4. Use a slotted spoon to remove about ¼ cup of the morels; set aside. Stir lemon juice into mixture in pan. Transfer morel mixture to a blender or food processor; whirl or process until smooth.

5. Return morel purée to cooking pan over medium heat. Gradually stir in half-and-half and reserved morels. Stir often until soup is steaming hot (do not boil). Taste and add salt if needed. Blend in sherry and serve at once, sprinkling each serving with parsley.

Makes about 5 cups, 4 servings.

HOMEMADE RELISHES

"Seven sweets and seven sours" accompany traditional meals in the Pennsylvania Dutch country. Two favorites are spicy apple butter and colorful corn relish. The first is wonderful on thick slices of homemade bread. Fruit butters are such a long-standing custom in the Heartland that an ample copper or cast-iron kettle for cooking apple butter is a family treasure, handed down from one generation to the next. Corn relish tastes good with country-style cooking such as fried chicken or pork products ranging from baked ham to sausages of all kinds.

TANGY APPLE BUTTER

    3 pounds tart cooking apples
      (about 6 large), peeled, cored,
      and quartered
    1 cup apple cider or water
    2 tablespoons lemon juice
 1½ teaspoons cinnamon
    ½ teaspoon ground allspice
    ¼ teaspoon each ground cloves,
      nutmeg, and ginger
    2 cups firmly packed brown
      sugar

1. Place apples in a large, deep, heavy saucepan with cider and lemon juice. Cover and bring to a gentle boil over medium heat. Cook until apples are tender when pierced (12 to 15 minutes).

2. Transfer mixture, half at a time, if necessary, to a food processor or blender and process or whirl until smooth.

3. Return apple purée to cooking pan and add spices and brown sugar. Cook, uncovered, over low heat, stirring occasionally and adjusting heat so mixture barely boils, until apple butter is thick and reduced to about 4 cups. As mixture thickens, stir often. Allow about 45 minutes to cook.

4. Pour hot apple butter into hot sterilized canning jars. Wipe off rims with a damp paper towel. Place scalded self-sealing lids on top; screw on rings.

Makes about 4 cups or 4 half-pints.

SWEET-SOUR CORN RELISH

    6 large ears corn, husks
      and silk removed
    ½ cup finely chopped red
      bell pepper
    1 stalk celery, finely chopped
    1 medium onion, finely chopped
    ½ cup sugar
    1 cup apple cider vinegar
    ½ cup water
    1 teaspoon salt
    ¼ teaspoon each celery seeds
      and ground turmeric
    1 tablespoon mustard seeds

1. Bring salted water to a boil in a large kettle; add corn and bring again to a boil. Cook, uncovered, for 2 minutes. Remove ears and plunge into a large bowl of cold water to stop cooking. Drain and cut corn kernels from cobs (you should have about 4 cups).

2. In a 3½- to 4-quart kettle, combine remaining ingredients. Add corn. Bring to a boil over medium heat, stirring until sugar dissolves. Reduce heat to medium-low, then boil gently, stirring occasionally, for 15 minutes.

3. Ladle relish into hot, sterilized canning jars, filling to within ½ inch of rim. Wipe off rims with a damp paper towel. Place scalded self-sealing lids on top; screw on rings.

4. Place jars on a rack in a deep kettle half full of hot water, and add more water to cover jars by 1 inch. Bring to a boil and process for 15 minutes. Remove from water and cool thoroughly.

Makes about 5 cups or 5 half-pints.

<u>Note</u> You may omit the heat processing in step 4; store relish in refrigerator and use within 2 months.

MAIN DISHES

In an area as ethnically diverse as America's Heartland, it's tricky to generalize about food preferences. However, there is one premise that isn't easily contradicted: This part of the country is where you'll find serious meat eaters.

Pork plays a big part in meal planning. And with the stockyards tradition of such centrally located cities as Chicago and Kansas City, beef is also an enduring favorite. Chicken on Sunday has long been a rural custom—roasted, pan-fried and served with a milk gravy, or tenderly simmered and bundled into a main-dish pie.

UPPER PENINSULA PASTIES

Pasties—individual meat-and-potato pies enclosed in a flaky pastry—first came to Michigan's Upper Peninsula with Cornish copper and iron-ore miners. Now they're a favorite with Scandinavians in the area as well, and the recipe has taken on some of the characteristics of Swedish and Finnish cooking. This version, from a cook of Swedish descent, goes together faster than other kinds of pasties (the *a* rhymes with that in the word *fast*) because you don't need to precook the filling. These pasties are plump and satisfying, a one-dish meal. Serve them plain or with brown gravy or catsup. Although some pasties are sturdy enough to eat sandwich style, these call for a plate and fork.

    1 pound ground beef, crumbled
    3 medium potatoes (about 1½
      lb), cut into ½-inch cubes
    1 cup finely chopped rutabaga
    ½ cup finely chopped carrots
    1 large onion, finely chopped
    1 teaspoon salt
    ¼ teaspoon pepper
    3 tablespoons butter or marga-
      rine, cut into small pieces

Pasty Pastry

2½ cups flour
1 tablespoon brown sugar
½ teaspoon salt
½ cup each lard and vegetable shortening
1 egg
1 teaspoon white vinegar

1. Have pastry ready in refrigerator. In a large bowl stir together ground beef, potatoes, rutabaga, carrots, onion, salt, and pepper for filling.

2. Preheat oven to 350° F. Divide pastry into 6 equal portions. On a well-floured board or pastry cloth, roll out each portion to a circle about 10 inches in diameter. Mound one sixth of the filling in center of each; dot with about ½ tablespoon of the butter.

3. Lift up edge of dough from two opposite sides, bringing together to overlap in center (it is unnecessary to crimp or seal edges). Repeat with other two opposite sides, making a somewhat square package. Use a fork to pierce pasty in several places.

4. Place pasties on a lightly greased baking sheet. Bake until lightly browned and vegetables in filling are tender when tested with a fork or skewer (about 1 hour). Serve hot.

Makes 6 pasties.

Pasty Pastry

1. In a large bowl mix flour, brown sugar, and salt. Using a pastry blender or two knives, cut in lard and shortening until mixture is crumbly and particles are the size of small dried peas.

2. Beat egg with vinegar in a measuring cup. Add enough cold water to make ½ cup. Add egg mixture to flour mixture, about 2 tablespoons at a time, adding liquid only until dough begins to cling together. With your hands press dough into a flattened ball. Enclose in plastic wrap and refrigerate while preparing filling.

PORK AND SAUERKRAUT GOULASH

In midwestern and Plains states, families with Hungarian roots enjoy this hearty stew, *Székely gulyás.* It can also be made using a combination of pork and veal. Serve it with egg noodles, rye bread, and dark beer.

2 tablespoons lard or vegetable shortening
2 pounds lean pork shoulder, cut in 1-inch cubes
2 large onions, finely chopped
1 clove garlic, minced or pressed
1 tablespoon sweet Hungarian paprika
1 teaspoon each caraway seeds and salt
¾ to 1 cup chicken broth (not condensed) or water
1 large can (27 oz) sauerkraut, well drained
1 to 2 cups sour cream
Chopped parsley, for garnish

1. Melt lard in a large, heavy frying pan or Dutch oven over medium-high heat. Add pork, about half at a time, and brown well on all sides; remove pork cubes as they brown and set aside. When all pork has been browned, reduce heat to moderate. Spoon off and discard excess fat, leaving about 2 tablespoons in pan. Add onions and cook, stirring often, until soft. Stir in garlic and cook for 1 minute longer.

2. Remove pan from heat and stir in paprika. Add browned pork and sprinkle with caraway seeds and salt. Return pan to heat and stir in ¼ cup of the broth. Cover, reduce heat, and simmer, stirring occasionally, until pork is tender (about 1 hour). While pork cooks, add more broth, ¼ cup at a time, as needed to keep mixture moist but not soupy.

3. Gently stir in sauerkraut. Cover again and continue to simmer for 15 minutes.

4. Blend in 1 cup of the sour cream, stirring over low heat just until sauce is heated through (do not boil). Sprinkle with parsley and serve with sour cream to taste.

Serves 6.

PAN-FRIED TROUT, ERNEST HEMINGWAY'S WAY

In a 1920 contribution to the *Toronto Star,* Ernest Hemingway—a native of Illinois, whose family summered in northern Michigan—described his method of cooking freshly caught trout while camping out. As straightforward and unembellished as Hemingway's prose, this cooking style can't be faulted. And it works just as well in a home kitchen. The response to trout cooked so impeccably shouldn't be a surprise. As Hemingway cautioned in the same dispatch, "The penalty for knowing how to cook is that the others will make you do all the cooking."

4 slices bacon
4 whole trout (about 8 oz each), cleaned
⅓ cup yellow cornmeal
Lemon wedges (optional)

1. Place bacon in a large, heavy frying pan over medium heat. Cook, turning occasionally, until bacon begins to brown.

2. While bacon cooks, dust trout with cornmeal to coat lightly on all sides.

3. Add trout to bacon drippings in pan; as you add each fish, place one of the bacon slices on top.

4. Cook trout until golden brown on all sides, turning once (about 10 minutes total) and replacing bacon on top of each fish. Serve trout hot, accompanied by bacon, and lemon (if desired).

Serves 4.

Juicy roast pork, glazed with cider, honey, ginger, and mustard, makes a handsome centerpiece for a harvest dinner when cooked with onions, apples, and sweet potatoes.

ROAST CHICKEN WITH MINNESOTA WILD-RICE STUFFING

Chippewa Indians in canoes harvest wild rice from the marshy lakes of northern Minnesota. The earthy flavor of wild rice—the seed of an aquatic grass only remotely related to cultivated rice—makes it a natural partner to wild game both furred and feathered. Seasoned with sage, mushrooms, and chicken livers, it's also a delicious complement to a plump roast chicken. The stuffing can be made ahead, then covered and refrigerated for up to one day.

    5- to 6-pound roasting chicken
    1 tablespoon butter or margarine
    2 tablespoons each *orange juice and dry sherry*
    1 tablespoon flour
    1 cup chicken broth (not condensed)

Wild-Rice Stuffing

    ½ cup wild rice
    1½ cups water
    ¼ teaspoon salt
      Liver from roasting chicken
    ¼ pound chicken livers
    3 tablespoons butter or margarine
    2 medium onions, finely chopped
    ¼ pound mushrooms, thinly sliced
    ¼ cup chopped parsley
    1 teaspoon chopped fresh sage leaves or ¼ teaspoon dried sage
    ⅛ teaspoon white pepper
    1 egg
    2 tablespoons dry sherry

1. Remove giblets from chicken, reserving liver for dressing. Rinse chicken and pat until dry. Preheat oven to 350° F.

2. Fill body cavity of chicken with Wild-Rice Stuffing. Use small skewers to fasten skin. Place chicken, breast up, on a rack in a shallow roasting pan. Tuck wing tips under. Insert a meat thermometer in thickest part of thigh. Skewer or tie drumsticks together. Melt butter in a small pan; stir in orange juice and sherry. Brush some of the mixture over chicken.

3. Roast, uncovered, brushing occasionally with orange juice mixture, until thermometer registers 180° F, chicken is well browned and leg moves freely when jiggled (2 to 2¼ hours). Remove chicken to a carving platter and cover loosely.

4. Discard all but 1 tablespoon of fat in roasting pan. Stir in flour and place over medium heat, stirring until bubbly. Gradually blend in broth and any remaining orange juice mixture. Cook, stirring constantly, until gravy thickens and boils. Strain to remove undissolved bits of pan drippings.

5. Remove stuffing, carve chicken, and serve with gravy spooned over.

Serves 6.

Wild-Rice Stuffing

1. Place wild rice in a strainer; rinse with cold water, then drain well.

2. Combine the water and salt in a 1½- to 2-quart saucepan. Bring to a boil over high heat. Stir in wild rice, cover, reduce heat, and boil gently until rice is tender and water is absorbed (30 to 35 minutes).

3. While rice cooks, chop all chicken livers coarsely. In a large frying pan over medium heat, melt butter. Add onions and mushrooms and cook, stirring, until onions are soft but not brown, and mushroom liquid is gone. Increase heat to medium-high and add chicken livers; cook, stirring often, until livers are lightly browned on all sides. Remove pan from heat.

4. To chicken liver mixture add cooked rice, parsley, sage, and white pepper. In a large bowl beat egg with sherry and blend well; stir in rice mixture.

Makes about 3½ cups.

BROILED PORTERHOUSE STEAK WITH SAVORY BUTTER

Fresh chives and parsley, snipped from a kitchen garden or pots indoors in a sunny window, flavor the butter that melts into a classic, thick steak. There's enough butter to use some of it to season baked potatoes or other vegetables as well.

⅓ cup butter or margarine, *softened*
1 teaspoon lemon juice
¼ teaspoon dry mustard
1 tablespoon chopped fresh *chives*
¼ cup finely chopped parsley
1½- inch-thick porterhouse *steak (1½ to 2 lbs)*

1. Beat butter in a medium bowl until fluffy; gradually beat in lemon juice until well combined, then blend in dry mustard. Mix in chives and parsley, distributing evenly. Shape butter mixture into a roll about 1 inch in diameter; enclose in plastic wrap and refrigerate until firm (about 1 hour).

2. Preheat broiler. Trim excess fat from edges of steak; slash remaining fat at about 1-inch intervals. Place steak on rack of broiler pan about 4 inches from heat.

3. Broil, turning once, for 6 to 8 minutes on each side for rare (increase time for medium or well-done). When you turn steak to broil second side, dot with about 1 tablespoon of the butter mixture.

4. Place broiled steak on a carving board. With a short pointed knife, cut around the T-shaped bone; remove bone. Cut the smaller loin portion of the steak across the grain into several slices. Then slice the remaining meat across the grain about ¼ inch thick. Serve slices from each portion on warm dinner plates. Accompany with slices of herb butter.

Serves 2 to 3.

CIDER-GLAZED PORK LOIN ROAST

The tart flavor of apples has an almost inevitable affinity with the sweet richness of pork. This handsome roast is glazed with spiced cider and honey and cooked with apples and onions. You can add to the feast by including peeled, quartered sweet potatoes to share the pan juices.

½ cup apple cider
¼ cup honey
½ teaspoon each *ground ginger and dry mustard*
2 medium onions
4½- to 5-pound loin pork roast
3 medium-sized tart apples
4 to 5 sweet potatoes, peeled *and quartered (optional)*

1. Pour cider into a small pan. Bring to a boil over high heat; continue boiling until reduced by half. Remove from heat and blend in honey, ginger, and mustard.

2. Preheat oven to 325° F. Peel onions and cut each into 6 equal wedges. Place roast, fat side up, in a shallow roasting pan; surround with onions. Insert a meat thermometer in center of roast. Brush roast generously with cider mixture, using about a third of it.

3. Roast pork until thermometer registers 150° F (1¾ to 2¼ hours, or about 25 minutes per pound). While pork roasts, peel and core apples; cut into quarters. After pork has cooked for 1 hour, add apples (and sweet potatoes, if used) around onions. Brush roast with about half of the remaining glaze. Brush on the rest of the glaze during last 15 to 30 minutes that the roast is in the oven.

4. Transfer roast to a carving board or serving platter; carve, cutting between rib bones. Arrange onions and apples (and sweet potatoes, if used) around meat to serve.

Serves 8 to 10.

BISCUIT-TOPPED CHICKEN POTPIE

Nearly every region of the central United States makes its own kind of chicken pie. In Pennsylvania Dutch country, chicken and generous squares of egg noodle dough simmer in a golden broth. Elsewhere boneless cooked chicken and vegetables nestle under a flaky pastry to make a hearty deep-dish pie. And in Kansas, the inspiration for this recipe, meaty chicken pieces are baked beneath buttery baking powder biscuits. A leafy salad with sliced tomatoes completes this family meal nicely. The filling can be prepared ahead and stored, covered, in the refrigerator for up to a day.

- 6 to 8 chicken thighs (about 2 lbs)
  Salt and white pepper
- 2 tablespoons butter or margarine
- ¼ pound medium mushrooms, quartered
- 1 bunch (about 20) baby carrots
- ¼ pound small white boiling onions
- 1 stalk celery, thinly sliced
- ½ cup dry sherry
- 1 cup water
- ½ cup frozen or fresh shelled peas
- 2 tablespoons cornstarch, smoothly mixed with ¼ cup cold water
- 1 recipe Buttery Baking Powder Biscuits (see page 56)

1. Lightly sprinkle chicken on all sides with salt and pepper. In a large frying pan over medium-high heat, melt butter. Add chicken and brown well on one side; turn chicken to brown second side and add mushrooms around chicken pieces.

2. Distribute carrots, onions, and celery evenly around chicken. Pour in sherry and water. Bring to a boil, cover, reduce heat, and simmer until chicken and carrots are just tender (30 to 40 minutes).

3. Using a slotted spoon, transfer chicken pieces and vegetables to a shallow 2½- to 3-quart casserole. Sprinkle with peas. Remove pan with cooking liquid from heat; using a whisk, blend in cornstarch mixture. Return to medium-high heat and bring to a boil, stirring constantly until thickened. Pour over chicken and vegetables.

4. Preheat oven to 425° F. Cut biscuit dough into 2- to 2½-inch rounds (or squares or diamonds of a similar size). Arrange biscuits, overlapping slightly, around edge of baking dish. (Bake any extra biscuits on an ungreased baking sheet for 15 to 20 minutes.)

5. Bake potpie until biscuits are well browned and chicken is thoroughly heated (25 to 30 minutes). Serve hot.

Serves 6 to 8.

CHICAGO-STYLE DEEP-DISH PIZZA

Chicago has its own style of pizza—a light, yeasty crust baked in a deep round pan. This version unites Italian sausage, cheese, mushrooms, and a fresh tomato sauce in a fairly traditional combination; feel free to substitute your own favorite pizza toppings, from anchovies to zucchini. Note that this recipe calls for preparing the pizza dough in a food processor. Pizza dough can also be made by hand, of course (see the California Culinary Academy book *Breads* for the recipe), but it takes much more time. Using a food processor to speed up the job makes homemade pizza really practical.

- ¾ pound Italian sausages
- 4 cups (1 lb) shredded whole-milk mozzarella cheese
- ½ pound mushrooms, thinly sliced
- ⅓ cup grated Parmesan cheese

Fresh Tomato Sauce

- 3 medium tomatoes (about 1 lb)
- 2 tablespoons olive oil
- 2 cloves garlic, minced or pressed
- ½ teaspoon each dried oregano and basil
- ¼ teaspoon salt

Food-Processor Pizza Dough

- 2½ to 2⅔ cups bread flour
- 1 package fast-rising active dry yeast
- ½ teaspoon salt
- 1 cup hot (115° to 125° F) water
- 1 teaspoon honey
- 2 teaspoons olive oil

1. Have Fresh Tomato Sauce and Pizza Dough ready. Remove casings from sausages; crumble meat into a large frying pan. Cook, stirring often, over medium heat until lightly browned. Spoon off and discard drippings. Set sausage aside.

2. Preheat oven to 450° F. Grease three 9-inch round pans (about 1½ inches deep). Divide dough into 3 equal portions; roll each portion out on a floured surface to about a 9-inch circle. Use your hands to pat and stretch dough to fit into each pan, pressing it against sides of pan to reach top edge.

3. Sprinkle ⅔ cup of the mozzarella over bottom of each portion of dough. Cover each with an even layer of mushrooms, then with cooked sausage. Spread a third of the Fresh Tomato Sauce over sausage in each pan. Cover with remaining mozzarella, dividing it evenly; sprinkle a third of the Parmesan over each pizza.

4. Bake on lowest rack of oven until crust browns well (20 to 25 minutes). Cut into wedges and serve at once.

Makes 3 medium pizzas, 6 servings.

Fresh Tomato Sauce

1. Pour boiling water over tomatoes to loosen skins. Peel, then chop fine.

2. Heat oil in a 2-quart saucepan over medium-high heat. Add tomatoes and garlic. Mix in oregano, basil, and salt. Bring to a boil, cover, reduce heat, and simmer for 15 minutes.

3. Uncover and cook over medium-high heat, stirring often, until sauce is thick and reduced to about 1 cup (about 15 minutes).

Food-Processor Pizza Dough

1. In work bowl of food processor, mix 2½ cups of the flour, yeast, and salt. Combine the hot water, honey, and olive oil in a measuring cup. With processor running, pour water mixture through feed tube in a steady stream, adjusting amount poured so flour can absorb it. Turn processor off when dough forms a ball. Dough should feel a little sticky. If it is too soft, add more flour, 1 tablespoon at a time, until dough has a firm consistency.

2. Knead by processing for an additional 45 seconds. Remove dough and shape into a ball.

3. Place dough in a greased bowl and turn to coat evenly with grease. Cover with plastic wrap and a kitchen towel and let rise in a warm place until dough is doubled in bulk (30 to 40 minutes). Punch dough down, cover with inverted bowl, then let rest for about 10 minutes before rolling out to fit pans.

Deep pans blackened by repeated trips through wood-fired brick ovens give Chicago-style pizza its unique shape. Made with light, yeasty crust that's easy to prepare in your food processor, fresh tomato sauce, and traditional toppings, it's a practical treat that can be created just about anywhere.

2. In a medium bowl beat egg with milk, butter, and lemon rind. Add egg mixture to flour mixture, stirring just until dry ingredients are moistened. Stir in blueberries with last few strokes.

3. Fill prepared pans about three fourths full. Sprinkle tops lightly with sugar-cinnamon mixture.

4. Bake until well browned (about 30 minutes). Serve warm.

Makes 9 muffins.

BUTTERY BAKING POWDER BISCUITS

The secret of flaky biscuits is to cut in the butter, using a pastry blender or two knives, until the particles are uniformly the texture of coarse crumbs. As the biscuits bake the butter melts, forming many tender layers. Serve these rich biscuits oven warm.

> 2 cups flour
> 1 tablespoon baking powder
> ½ teaspoon salt
> ½ cup (¼ lb) cold butter or margarine
> ¾ cup half-and-half
> Additional melted butter (about 2 tablespoons), for brushing

1. Preheat oven to 425° F. In a large bowl thoroughly mix flour, baking powder, and salt. Cut the cold butter into flour mixture until coarse crumbs form.

2. Add half-and-half, all at once, mixing gently just until a soft dough forms. Gather dough together with your hands and transfer it to a floured board or pastry cloth. Knead gently just enough to form dough into a uniform ball; turn to coat lightly with flour.

3. Roll or pat dough out to about ½-inch thickness. Using a 2½-inch round cutter, cut dough into biscuits. Place about 1 inch apart on an ungreased baking sheet. Brush tops lightly with the melted butter.

4. Bake until biscuits are golden brown (15 to 20 minutes). Serve hot.

Makes 1 dozen biscuits.

QUICK BREADS

A deft hand with golden muffins and a light touch with flaky, tender biscuits are much admired in the Heartland. These mouth-watering quick breads (pictured above) are equally appealing at breakfast, lunch, dinner or between meals, when a quick pick-me-up is needed.

Muffins, warm from the oven, can get brisk mornings off to a pleasant start, particularly when they contain such surprises as juicy blueberries—picked during the sun-filled days of summer, then frozen. Baking powder biscuits are a traditional accompaniment to fried chicken, but they're also welcome at breakfast if served with a pitcher of warm honey. And (as described on page 54), they also make an excellent topping for a supper casserole.

PLUMP BLUEBERRY MUFFINS

A gentle touch assures you of light, tender muffins—mix the batter just enough to moisten the dry ingredients. Stir in the berries with the last few strokes.

> 2 cups flour
> ⅓ cup sugar
> 1 tablespoon baking powder
> ½ teaspoon salt
> ¼ teaspoon ground nutmeg
> 1 egg
> 1 cup milk
> 3 tablespoons butter or margarine (melted and cooled) or salad oil
> ½ teaspoon grated lemon rind
> 1 cup blueberries
> 2 tablespoons sugar mixed with ⅛ teaspoon cinnamon

1. Grease 2¾-inch muffin pan. Preheat oven to 400° F. In a large bowl stir together flour, the ⅓ cup sugar, baking powder, salt, and nutmeg.

SIDE DISHES AND SALADS

Until recently the season dictated what produce appeared on the dinner tables of the Heartland. The abundance of summer, with legendary sweet corn on the cob and vines heavy with tomatoes, contrasted sharply with the monotony of winter vegetables—carrots, potatoes, onions, rutabagas, and squash. To bring variety to winter meals, housewives spent many a long summer day engaged in home canning (and, later, freezing), "putting up" vegetables and stirring bubbling kettles of tomato sauce.

Today supermarkets in much of the central area rival those of both coasts for variety throughout the year. But potatoes in some fashion are still most welcome at dinner every evening.

SWEDISH MASHED POTATOES AND RUTABAGA

Combining two dependable winter vegetables makes a golden purée with a savory flavor. In the Upper Peninsula of Michigan, this dish is known by the Swedish name, *rotmus*.

- 6 cups salted water
- 1 medium rutabaga (about 1 lb), peeled and diced
- 3 medium-sized boiling potatoes (about 1½ lb total), peeled and quartered
- 2 tablespoons butter or margarine
- ½ teaspoon salt
- ⅛ teaspoon white pepper

1. Bring water to a boil in a 3- to 4-quart pan; add rutabaga and bring again to a boil. Boil uncovered for 15 minutes. Add potatoes and continue to boil until potatoes and rutabaga are very tender (about 20 minutes). Drain well.

2. Add butter, salt, and pepper to cooked vegetables. Beat with an electric mixer or mash with a potato masher until fluffy. Serve hot.

Serves 4 to 6.

TWICE-BAKED POTATOES WITH WISCONSIN CHEDDAR CHEESE

For special dinners, potatoes put on company manners. These can be prepared ahead, then baked to serve with a sumptuous beef roast.

- 3 large baking potatoes (1½ to 2 lb total)
- 3 tablespoons butter or margarine
- ¼ teaspoon salt
- ⅛ teaspoon white pepper
- 1 egg yolk, beaten with 3 tablespoons milk
- 2 tablespoons chopped fresh chives
- 1½ cups (6 oz) shredded sharp Cheddar cheese (Wisconsin, if possible)

1. Preheat oven to 400° F. Scrub potatoes and pierce each in several places with a fork. Rub all over with butter, using about 1 tablespoon. Bake potatoes until they are tender in the center when tested with a fork (about 45 minutes).

2. Remove potatoes from oven and cut each in half lengthwise. Reduce oven temperature to 350° F. When potatoes are cool enough to handle, scoop out centers, leaving a shell about ¼ inch thick. Place shells in a shallow baking pan.

3. In a medium bowl combine hot scooped-out potato, the remaining butter, the salt, and pepper; add egg yolk mixture. Using an electric mixer, beat until fluffy and well combined. Stir in chives and 1 cup of the cheese.

4. Mound potato mixture into hollowed-out shells, dividing it evenly. Sprinkle with remaining cheese. (Potatoes can be prepared ahead to this point. Cover and refrigerate for up to a day; let stand at room temperature for about 30 minutes before baking.)

5. Bake until potatoes are heated through (15 to 20 minutes).

Serves 6.

WILTED GREEN SALAD WITH SWEET-SOUR DRESSING

Bacon and bacon drippings flavor this salad, a legacy of the German immigrants distributed throughout the Heartland.

- 1 tablespoon apple cider vinegar
- 2 tablespoons lemon juice
- 1 teaspoon each *sugar and dry mustard*
- ⅛ teaspoon pepper
- 8 cups lightly packed torn green leaf lettuce
- 4 slices bacon, cut crosswise into ½-inch strips
  Salad oil, if needed
- 6 green onions (including tops), thinly sliced
  Salt (optional)
- 1 hard-cooked egg, shredded

1. In a small bowl mix vinegar, lemon juice, sugar, dry mustard, and pepper, stirring until sugar dissolves; set mixture aside. Have lettuce ready in a large salad bowl.

2. In a 9-inch frying pan over medium heat, cook bacon until crisp and brown, stirring often; remove with a slotted spoon and set aside to drain on paper towels. Measure ¼ cup bacon drippings and discard excess (or add oil, if needed, to make ¼ cup). Return measured drippings to same frying pan and add green onions; cook, stirring, for about 30 seconds. Blend in vinegar mixture and bring to a boil. Remove from heat, taste, and add salt if needed.

3. Pour hot dressing over lettuce. Immediately mix lightly to coat lettuce with dressing. Sprinkle with reserved bacon and hard-cooked egg. Serve at once.

Serves 4.

AMANA COLONIES RADISH SALAD

One group of German immigrants, the Amana Society, founded seven villages in east-central Iowa, near Cedar Rapids, in the nineteenth century. For many years, the residents dined in communal kitchens. Their fare, of which this radish salad or *Rettigsalat* is typical, reflected both their German heritage and the abundance of the rich Iowa farmland.

> 3 bunches radishes
> 1 teaspoon salt
> ½ cup sour cream
> 1 tablespoon apple cider vinegar
> ⅛ teaspoon white pepper
> 2 tablespoons chopped fresh chives
> Butter lettuce leaves

1. Remove and discard radish leaves and roots; cut radishes into thin slices (about 3 cups). Mix radish slices lightly with salt. Place in a colander and let stand to drain for 30 to 45 minutes. Blot dry with paper towels.

2. In a medium bowl blend together sour cream, vinegar, white pepper, and chives. Add drained radishes and mix lightly to coat with dressing. Cover and refrigerate until ready to serve (up to 2 hours).

3. Serve salad in a bowl lined with butter lettuce leaves.

Serves 6.

FRIED GREEN TOMATOES

Early cold snaps in the upper midwestern and Plains states often catch unripened tomatoes on the vine. Green tomato preserves are one way to use these tart immature fruits; an even faster way is to pan-fry them to serve as a piquant vegetable.

> 4 medium-sized green tomatoes
> Salt and pepper
> About ⅓ cup flour
> Salad oil for frying
> 1 egg, lightly beaten

1. Slice tomatoes about ½ inch thick. Sprinkle lightly with salt and pepper. Dust slices with flour on all sides.

2. Pour oil into a large frying pan to a depth of about ¼ inch. Place over medium heat. While oil heats, dip tomato slices into egg to coat on all sides.

3. Fry tomatoes, about half at a time, turning once, until golden brown on both sides. Serve hot.

Serves 6.

STUFFED ACORN SQUASH

Here is a substantial side dish, baked squash halves filled with a moist, cheese-strewn sausage stuffing. It's good with roast chicken.

> 2 medium-sized acorn (Danish) squash (about 1 lb each)
> ½ pound bulk pork sausage
> 1 large onion, finely chopped
> 1 stalk celery, finely chopped
> 2 tablespoons chopped parsley
> 1 cup soft bread crumbs
> ½ cup shredded brick or Muenster cheese
> 1 egg, lightly beaten

1. Preheat oven to 350° F. Cut each squash in half; scoop out and discard seeds. Place squash halves, cut sides down, in a well-greased shallow baking dish just large enough to hold them in a single layer. Bake, uncovered, for 30 minutes.

2. While squash bakes, crumble sausage into a large frying pan. Add onion and celery; cook, stirring often, over medium heat until sausage browns and onions are soft. Remove from heat and mix in parsley, bread crumbs, half of the cheese, and the egg; mix lightly to combine thoroughly.

3. Remove squash from oven and turn each over. Mound a fourth of the sausage mixture into hollow of each squash half. Sprinkle with remaining cheese, dividing it evenly.

4. Return squash to oven and bake until tender when tested with a fork (20 to 30 minutes). Serve hot.

Serves 4.

menu

FOURTH OF JULY PICNIC IN THE PARK

Grilled Polish Sausage and Bratwurst

Mustard, Pickle Relish, Horseradish

Frankfurter Rolls

Corn on the Cob

German Potato Salad

Crispy Coleslaw

Red Marble Cake

Lemonade, Beer

Celebrate the star-spangled holiday with a menu filled with German-American flavors. This is a glorious-tasting Fourth, as it might be enjoyed at an Iowa potluck. The sausages are simmered in beer, which keeps them moist and juicy; then they're finished on the grill, nestled into warm rolls, and accompanied by piquant picnic salads. Dessert is an unusual marble cake or Marmorkuchen, mingling crimson- and cream-colored swirls. This version, so delicious with plump fresh strawberries, is from Iowa's Amana Colonies.

Farm-fresh corn on the cob and plump grilled sausages celebrate the glorious Fourth of July at this star-spangled heartland holiday picnic.

GRILLED POLISH SAUSAGE AND BRATWURST

- 4 bratwurst or bockwurst (about 1¼ lb)
- 4 individual-size, fully cooked Polish sausages or 1 large, fully cooked Polish sausage ring (about 1½ lb total) (see Note)
- 2 bottles or cans (12 oz each) beer
- 8 frankfurter rolls, split and warmed
- Mustard, pickle relish, and prepared horseradish

1. Pierce each sausage in several places with a fork. Pour beer into a large, deep frying pan or Dutch oven; bring to a boil over high heat. Add bratwurst, reduce heat to low, cover, and simmer gently (liquid should barely bubble or sausages will split) for 20 minutes. Add Polish sausages during last 5 minutes of simmering. Remove pan from heat and drain sausages well.

2. Place sausages on grill, 4 to 6 inches from heat, over low, glowing coals. Cook, turning often, until browned on all sides (8 to 10 minutes).

3. Serve whole sausages (or sliced Polish sausage ring) in split rolls. Add mustard, relish, and horseradish to taste.

Serves 8.

Note If Polish sausage is not precooked, add it to beer with bratwurst and simmer for 20 minutes.

GERMAN POTATO SALAD

- 4 large boiling potatoes (about 1½ lb)
- ½ pound sliced bacon, cut into ½- by 1-inch strips
- 1 large, mild-flavored onion, finely chopped
- ½ teaspoon salt
- ⅛ teaspoon white pepper
- 3 tablespoons apple cider vinegar
- Chopped parsley (optional)

1. Scrub potatoes with a stiff brush. Cook whole potatoes in a large pot in boiling salted water to cover, boiling gently just until tender when pierced with a fork (about 30 minutes). Drain, then slip off and discard skins as soon as potatoes are cool enough to touch.

2. While potatoes are cooking, cook bacon in a large frying pan over medium heat, stirring occasionally, until lightly browned.

3. Cut potatoes lengthwise into halves; slice into about ⅜-inch-thick pieces and place in a large bowl. Add onion and hot bacon (including drippings). To pan in which bacon cooked, add salt, pepper, and vinegar, stirring well; pour over potatoes. Mix lightly to combine all ingredients thoroughly.

4. Sprinkle salad with parsley, if desired. Serve at once, slightly warm, or cover and refrigerate until cold to blend flavors more completely (salad may be prepared up to a day in advance).

Serves 6.

CRISPY COLESLAW

- ½ cup each mayonnaise and sour cream
- ½ teaspoon salt
- 1 teaspoon sugar
- 2 teaspoons prepared mustard
- 1 tablespoon each prepared horseradish and apple cider vinegar
- 1 medium-sized green cabbage (1½ to 2 lb), thinly shredded
- 1 medium carrot, shredded
- 6 green onions (tops included), thinly sliced
- ¼ cup chopped parsley

1. In a medium bowl combine mayonnaise, sour cream, salt, sugar, mustard, horseradish, and vinegar; stir until well blended.

2. In a large bowl combine cabbage, carrot, green onions, and parsley. Pour dressing over vegetables; mix lightly to coat well. Cover and refrigerate to blend flavors for at least 2 hours (up to 8 hours).

Serves 6 to 8.

RED MARBLE CAKE

- 4 cups flour
- 1 tablespoon plus 2 teaspoons baking powder
- 1 cup (½ lb) butter or margarine, softened
- 1 cup granulated sugar
- 2 teaspoons vanilla
- 1 cup sour cream
- 5 eggs, separated
- 1 cup crystalline red decorating sugar
- Confectioners' sugar
- Strawberries

1. Generously grease a 10-inch bundt pan or other fluted tube pan (10- to 12-cup capacity); dust with flour. Preheat oven to 350° F.

2. Sift together flour and baking powder. To make the light-colored batter: Beat ½ cup of the butter with the white sugar; beat in 1 teaspoon of vanilla. Beat 2 cups of the flour mixture into butter mixture alternately with ½ cup of sour cream, beating smooth after each addition.

3. In a clean bowl beat egg whites until stiff but not dry. Stir a third of the egg whites into batter, then fold in remaining egg whites. Set aside.

4. To make the red batter: Beat remaining butter with red sugar; beat in remaining vanilla and egg yolks, one at a time. Add remaining flour mixture alternately with remaining sour cream, beating after each addition. (Both batters will be thick.)

5. Using a ¼-cup measure, scoop batter into prepared pan, alternating light-colored and red batters. Swirl a thin spatula through batter to marble.

6. Bake until a wooden pick inserted in thickest part comes out clean and cake pulls away from edges of pan (about 1 hour). Cool in pan on rack for 20 minutes. Invert cake onto rack and cool completely.

7. Sift confectioners' sugar over cooled cake, and serve with strawberries.

Serves 10 to 12.

DESSERTS

Baking is such an esteemed skill in the Heartland that it's hard to grow up in this far-flung area without a well-developed sweet tooth. Where heartland cooks really excel is in the creation of flaky-crust fruit pies. However, cake-baking is not neglected. And hardly a Midwesterner exists who doesn't boast of a grandmother whose cookie jar was legendary.

AUNT LOU'S BURNED-SUGAR CAKE

Caramelized sugar flavors both cake and frosting to make a handsome three-layer cake with a beautiful golden-amber color.

  2½ cups sifted flour
  1½ teaspoons baking powder
  ½ teaspoon baking soda
  ¼ teaspoon salt
  ½ cup (¼ lb) butter or margarine, softened
  1½ cups sugar
  1½ teaspoons vanilla
  2 eggs (at room temperature)
  ¾ cup water
    Chopped toasted pecans or walnuts

Burned-Sugar Syrup

  1 cup sugar
  ½ cup hot water

Burned-Sugar Frosting

  ¾ cup butter or margarine, softened
  1 egg
  3½ cups confectioner's sugar

1. Prepare Burned-Sugar Syrup and cool. Lightly grease three 8-inch-round layer-cake pans; line with rounds of waxed paper or baking parchment, then grease paper. Dust lightly with flour. Preheat oven to 350° F.

2. Sift together flour, baking powder, baking soda, and salt.

3. In large bowl of electric mixer, cream butter and sugar, beating until well combined. Beat in vanilla, then add eggs, one at a time, beating after

each addition until fluffy. Blend in ¼ cup Burned-Sugar Syrup; reserve remaining syrup for frosting. Add a third of the flour mixture; beat until fluffy. Blend in half of the water, then add another third of the flour mixture; beat until fluffy. Blend in remaining water, then add remaining flour mixture; beat until smooth.

4. Divide batter evenly into prepared pans. Bake until a wooden pick inserted near center of each layer comes out clean and cake springs back when touched lightly (20 to 25 minutes). Cool layers in pans for about 10 minutes, then turn out onto wire racks to complete cooling.

5. Place one cake layer on serving plate. Spread with Burned-Sugar Frosting to cover generously. Add a second layer and spread it with frosting. Cover with remaining cake layer. Spread sides and top with remaining frosting. Decorate with pecans.

Serves 8 to 10.

Burned-Sugar Syrup

1. Heat sugar in a large, heavy frying pan on medium heat until melted and a rich amber color (stir occasionally after sugar begins to melt).

2. Wearing an oven mitt to protect your hand from hot syrup, very gradually add the hot water, stirring constantly. Continue cooking after all the water is added, until caramelized sugar dissolves and syrup boils and reduces to about ¾ cup (2 to 3 minutes). Cool to room temperature before using in cake.

Burned-Sugar Frosting

1. Begin beating butter in large bowl of electric mixer. Add egg and beat until fluffy. Gradually beat in ½ cup Burned-Sugar Syrup.

2. Gradually blend in confectioners' sugar, beating until frosting is smoothly combined and of a good spreading consistency.

IPPERWASH BEACH SAND TARTS

These irresistible tarts—somewhere between an individual pie and a generous cookie—are a favorite at a Wisconsin summer vacation colony. For convenience, the pastry is made in a food processor. To prepare by hand, follow the instructions for Flaky Pastry on page 63.

  2 eggs
  1 teaspoon cinnamon
  ¾ cup sugar
  1 tablespoon flour
  ½ cup (¼ lb) butter or margarine, melted and cooled
  1 cup dried currants

Tart Pastry

  1⅓ cups flour
  ¼ teaspoon salt
  ½ cup (¼ lb) cold butter or margarine, diced
  2 to 3 tablespoons cold water

1. On a lightly floured board or pastry cloth, roll pastry out about ⅛ inch thick; cut with a 3½- to 4-inch round cutter. Press each round of pastry smoothly into a lightly greased 2½-inch muffin or tart pan.

2. Preheat oven to 350° F. In a large bowl beat eggs, cinnamon, and sugar until well combined, then blend in flour. Gradually beat in butter; stir in currants.

3. Divide currant filling into tart shells, filling them about three fourths full. Bake until filling is set and pastry is golden brown (25 to 30 minutes).

4. Cool tarts slightly in pans on a wire rack, then use a thin spatula to ease them out to complete cooling.

Makes eighteen 2½-inch tarts.

Tart Pastry

1. Combine flour and salt in food processor work bowl. Add butter; process, using short on-off bursts, until coarse crumbs form.

2. Add water through feed tube, 1 tablespoon at a time, processing just until mixture barely clings together. Use your hands to press pastry together into a smooth ball.

SOUR-CREAM SUGAR COOKIES

Sugar sprinkled and tasting faintly of nutmeg, these crisp and tender cookies are the sort that every heartland child from Pennsylvania to Idaho associates with the word *homemade.* Note that the dough needs to chill at least 2 hours.

   ½ cup (¼ lb) butter or
      margarine, softened
 1¼ cups sugar
   1 egg
   1 teaspoon vanilla
   ½ teaspoon baking soda
   ½ cup sour cream
   3 cups flour
 1½ teaspoons baking powder
   ¼ teaspoon each *salt and*
      ground nutmeg
      Chocolate sprinkles and addi-
      tional sugar, for decoration

1. In a large bowl beat butter until fluffy. Gradually add sugar, beating until light. Add egg and vanilla; beat again until fluffy. In a small bowl stir baking soda into sour cream. Blend into butter mixture.

2. In a medium bowl stir together 2 cups of the flour, the baking powder, salt, and nutmeg. Gradually blend flour mixture into butter mixture. Add the remaining flour, mixing in about ¼ cup at a time, until well combined.

3. Divide dough into 2 equal portions; enclose in plastic wrap and refrigerate until firm (about 2 hours or until next day).

4. Preheat oven to 375° F. Lightly grease baking sheets. Roll cookie dough out on a lightly floured board or pastry cloth until it is about ⅛ inch thick. Cut in 3-inch rounds or fancy shapes.

5. Place cookies on baking sheets about ½ inch apart. Sprinkle lightly with chocolate or sugar.

6. Bake until golden brown (8 to 10 minutes). Transfer to wire racks to cool.

Makes about 4 dozen 3½-inch cookies.

MICHIGAN SOUR-CHERRY PIE

The surrounding Great Lakes moderate the climate of Michigan's shoreline, and orchards abound there. Tart red cherries from such areas, although too sour to enjoy in the raw, are perfect for pies like this classic.

    Flaky Pastry (see page 63)
   6 cups pitted red sour cherries
     or *1 package (20 oz) frozen,*
     unsweetened pitted red sour
     cherries, thawed, or 2 cans
     (1 lb each) pitted red sour
     cherries
 1¼ cups sugar
   ⅓ cup flour
   ⅛ teaspoon ground nutmeg
     Pinch salt
   ¼ teaspoon almond extract
   2 tablespoons butter or
      margarine

1. Have pastry ready. If using frozen cherries, use cherries and their juice. If using canned cherries, drain; reserve ¼ cup of the juice for pie and discard the remainder. If using fresh cherries, reserve any juices yielded.

2. In a large bowl mix sugar, flour, nutmeg, and salt. Add cherries and their juice as specified in step 1. Sprinkle with almond extract. Mix lightly to coat cherries with sugar mixture.

3. Preheat oven to 400° F. Roll out half of the pastry on a lightly floured board or pastry cloth to a circle about 12 inches in diameter. Ease pastry into a 9-inch pie pan. Fill with cherry mixture. Dot with butter.

4. Roll out remaining pastry to a 9- by 12-inch rectangle; cut into 1-inch-wide, 9-inch-long strips. Weave strips over cherries into lattice; trim and flute edge.

5. Bake until filling bubbles up between lattice strips and pastry is golden brown (40 to 45 minutes). Cool on a wire rack, then serve warm or at room temperature.

Serves 6 to 8.

NORWEGIAN CHOCOLATE CAKE

This moist, densely chocolate cake makes a lovely birthday cake for a chocolate fancier.

   2 cups sifted flour
   2 teaspoons baking soda
   ½ cup (¼ lb) butter or
      margarine, softened
   2 cups firmly packed light
      brown sugar
   1 teaspoon vanilla extract
   2 eggs (at room temperature)
   2 ounces (2 squares) unsweet-
      ened chocolate, melted and
      cooled
   ½ cup each buttermilk and
      boiling water
   ½ cup whipping cream
   2 teaspoons confectioners' sugar
      Toasted sliced almonds

Fudge Frosting

   2 ounces (2 squares) unsweet-
      ened chocolate
   ¼ cup butter or margarine
   2 cups confectioners' sugar
   1 egg yolk
   1 teaspoon vanilla
   2 tablespoons whipping cream

1. Lightly grease two 8-inch round layer-cake pans; line with rounds of waxed paper or baking parchment, then grease paper. Dust with flour. Preheat oven to 350° F.

2. Sift flour with baking soda.

3. In large bowl of electric mixer, cream butter and brown sugar, beating until well combined. Beat in vanilla, then add eggs, one at a time, beating until fluffy after each addition. Blend in chocolate. Add a third of the flour mixture; beat until fluffy. Blend in buttermilk, then add another third of the flour mixture; beat until fluffy. Blend in boiling water, then add remainder of flour mixture; beat until smooth.

4. Divide batter evenly into prepared pans. Bake until a wooden pick inserted near center of each layer comes out clean and cake springs back when touched lightly (30 to 35 minutes). Cool layers in pans for about 10 minutes, then turn out onto wire racks to complete cooling.

5. Place one cake layer on serving plate and frost. Cover with second layer and frost sides. With electric mixer, beat cream and confectioners' sugar until stiff. Top cake with whipped cream and almonds. Refrigerate until served (up to a day).

Serves 8 to 10.

Fudge Frosting In a large heavy saucepan over low heat, melt chocolate with butter. Remove from heat; gradually beat in 1 cup confectioners' sugar. Blend in egg yolk and vanilla. Add remaining confectioners' sugar, then cream, 1 tablespoon at a time, beating until fluffy and spreadable.

MOM'S GREEN-APPLE PIE

In true melting-pot fashion, heartland apple pie (pictured at right) incorporates the best features of all its European ancestors.

    Flaky Pastry (at right)
¾ *cup sugar*
¼ *cup flour*
½ *teaspoon cinnamon*
⅛ *teaspoon ground nutmeg*
1 *teaspoon grated lemon rind*
5 *large green apples, peeled, cored, and thinly sliced (8 to 10 c)*
1 *tablespoon butter or margarine*
2 *tablespoons milk*

1. Have pastry ready. In a large bowl mix sugar, flour, cinnamon, nutmeg, and lemon rind. Add apple slices and coat lightly with sugar mixture.

2. Preheat oven to 375° F. Roll out half of the pastry on a lightly floured board or pastry cloth to a 12-inch circle. Ease pastry into a 9-inch pie pan. Fill with apple mixture. Dot with butter.

3. Roll out remaining pastry. Place over apples. Trim and flute edge. Pierce pastry in several places. Brush with milk; sprinkle with 1 to 2 tablespoons more sugar.

4. Bake until pastry is golden brown and apples are tender (1 hour to 1 hour and 10 minutes). Cool on a wire rack, then serve.

Serves 6 to 8.

Basics

FLAKY PIE CRUST

The moms whose apple pies are the most fondly recalled in the Heartland are the moms who made the best pastry—thin, flaky, almost ethereal on the tongue. An expert hand with pastry comes with practice. It's worth acquiring if you want to bake fruit pies as appealing as Mom's Green-Apple Pie, shown above (recipe at left).

Shortening in small particles forms layers as pastry is rolled out, making a pie crust flaky. The kind and amount of shortening determine the tenderness of the pastry. Lard has the greatest shortening ability, next comes vegetable shortening, and, last, butter. This pastry combines lard for tenderness and butter for flavor. Preparing pastry in a food processor (see Note) saves time and work; the results are so delectable that even your mom might be surprised. If you only need one crust, make the full recipe and freeze half, rather than try to make a half-recipe. Frozen pastry will keep in the freezer for up to 2 months.

FLAKY PASTRY

2 *cups flour*
¼ *teaspoon salt*
⅓ *cup each cold lard or vegetable shortening and cold butter or margarine*
3 *to 5 tablespoons cold water*

1. In a large bowl mix flour and salt. Using a pastry blender or 2 knives, cut in lard and butter until mixture is crumbly and particles are the size of small dried peas.

2. Mixing lightly with a fork, sprinkle on water, 1 tablespoon at a time, until dough begins to cling together. With your hands press dough into 2 flattened balls of equal size. Enclose in plastic wrap to prevent dough from drying out while preparing filling. To avoid stickiness, refrigerate for up to a day.

3. Roll out on a lightly floured surface, using short, firm strokes to achieve uniform thinness, according to recipe directions.

Makes two 9-inch pie crusts.

Note To prepare in food processor, combine flour and salt in work bowl. Add lard and butter. Process, using short on-off bursts, until coarse crumbs form. Add water through feed tube, 1 tablespoon at a time, processing until mixture barely clings together. Use your hands to press pastry together into 2 smooth balls.

*Seafood Gumbo, Jambalaya,
Raw Oysters, and Creole Slaw
are all Cajun classics that
can even be served directly from
the pots. Recipes start on page 82.*

Louisiana

The cuisine of Louisiana is as broad as it is rich and spicy. This chapter samples both Cajun and Creole cooking, and a wide range of shellfish recipes includes the two most popular Louisiana favorites—Jambalaya and Seafood Filé Gumbo (see page 83). Two classic and much-requested appetizers are presented: Oysters "Rockefeller" and Shrimp Rémoulade (see page 68). One festive menu gives all the recipes needed for a *Fais Dodo* dance-hall party (see page 82) with Raw Oysters, Jambalaya, and Seafood Gumbo. A second menu (see page 78) features a Boiled Seafood Dinner followed by Pralines.

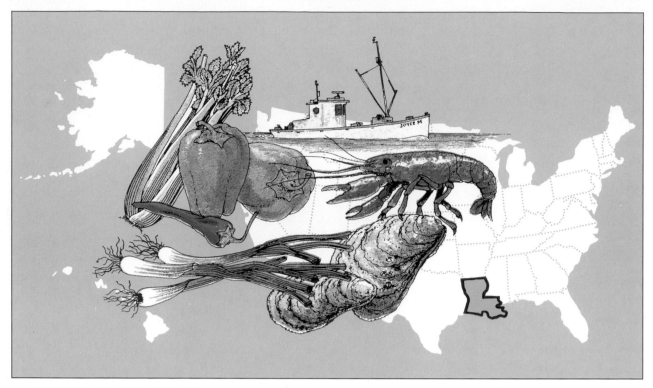

A REGION IN ONE STATE

In this book of regional American food, only one state warrants a chapter all to itself: Louisiana. There the cooking is so varied and distinctive that it is a cuisine unto itself, a synopsis of the ethnic influences that have mingled during the 300-year history of this part of the country. Within this fascinating cuisine, two major cooking styles—Cajun and Creole—dominate.

When the French arrived in the early eighteenth century, they came with a well-developed culinary history and style. Using local ingredients, they gradually developed a new cuisine. Other immigrating groups also contributed culinary traditions and flavors. Notable among them were the blacks from Africa; they not only brought a taste for spicy food, but also introduced seeds for new ingredients such as okra.

In addition, indigenous Indian tribes influenced the region's cooking, contributing such elements as filé powder, corn, herbs, and spices. And the culinary traditions of the Spanish, who ruled the colony for 40 years, melded further with the developing cooking style.

In the last 150 years, other European immigrants have come to Louisiana. Italians introduced the use of artichokes, eggplant, garlic, and aromatic herbs including basil, oregano, and rosemary. Germans added sausage and smoked meats, and the skills to prepare them. The result of a 300-year adaptation process is what we know today as Creole cooking, the style of Louisiana cities that is often synonymous with New Orleans.

Cajun cooking came to Louisiana around 1760, when the French Acadians began leaving Nova Scotia in search of a new home. They were farmers and fishermen who came to be known as Cajuns in the Louisiana countryside where they settled and developed a provincial, peasant style of cooking. It was, and is, a cuisine of the country. Compared with Creole cooking, the food of the Cajuns is less refined and more hearty. It uses local ingredients that come from the bayou, the sea, or the farm.

Much overlap exists between Cajun and Creole cooking. When Cajuns arrived, they adapted the already well-developed regional cooking style. Dishes such as gumbo and jambalaya are common to both groups. Although in today's Louisiana homes there are differences, as with any family-style

cooking, between Creole and Cajun dishes, in restaurants the distinction scarcely exists. It is simplest to refer to Cajun and Creole cuisines together as Louisiana cooking.

Specific ingredients and combinations of ingredients give Louisiana cooking its distinct flavor and character. The hallmarks include a heavy use of spices and the smoky flavors produced by brown roux (see page 77). Another characteristic is the mixture of onions, celery, and bell peppers—often called the Creole trilogy or Creole *mirepoix.*

Seafood and fish also play an important part in Louisiana cooking. Oysters, blue crabs, crayfish, shrimp, redfish, speckled trout, and pompano are fresh and plentiful. Often seafood such as shrimp and oysters is combined with smoked meats such as *andouille* and *tasso* in gumbos and other dishes with rich and wonderful flavors.

Louisiana cooking can best be summed up by an old French Creole word, *lagniappe,* which means "something extra." This one word captures the extremely generous spirit of both the people of Louisiana and their cuisine.

Basics

GLOSSARY

Andouille This heavily smoked, coursely ground, spicy Cajun sausage is used in many Louisiana dishes. Linguisa, Polish sausage, or chorizo may be substituted, but they will not offer the same flavor. Available in some areas in specialty delis and butcher shops; see below for mail-order sources.

Blue Crabs Native to the Gulf Coast and Chesapeake Bay, these are sweet and succulent and are available live, boiled, as softshells, or as crabmeat. If blue crab is not available in your area, use any fresh variety; do not use frozen.

Cayenne Pepper This hot, ground spice is responsible for the characteristic heat and tang in Louisiana cooking.

Chaurice Also called hot sausage, this is a spicy pork sausage available smoked or raw. It is usually flavored with parsley and onion. If unavailable, substitute any other fresh hot sausage such as Italian. See below for mail-order sources.

Crab, Crayfish, or Shrimp Boil This mixture of herbs, spices, and lots of cayenne pepper is used to flavor cooking water for crabs, shrimp, or crayfish. In some parts of the country, it is available packaged in net bags or as a concentrated liquid extract. You can also make your own; follow the instructions in step 2 of Boiled Seafood Dinner, page 78.

Crayfish This fresh-water crustacean is usually purchased live or as frozen tail meat. In Louisiana it is pronounced and usually spelled *crawfish*. If you cook it yourself, make sure you save the orange material in the head and tail meat to add flavor to crayfish dishes. If crayfish are unavailable, substitute shrimp, but the flavor will be different.

Étouffée The word means *smothered* and describes a dish braised with chopped vegetables and liquid.

Filé Powder Also called gumbo filé, this herb is often used to flavor and slightly thicken gumbo. It is made from ground sassafras leaves, and there is no substitute for it. It is available in many supermarkets and gourmet shops; for mail-order sources, see below.

Gumbo This is either a hearty soup or a stew, usually made with a dark roux (see page 77) and further thickened with okra or filé powder.

Jambalaya This rice dish contains sausages, smoked meats, seafood, chicken, and other meats. It is usually spicy and often contains tomatoes.

Louisiana-Style Hot Sauce A bottled mixture of fermented red peppers, salt, and vinegar is commonly used to add spice and flavor to dishes throughout the South and Southwest. The best-known brand is Tabasco, but others work equally well in these recipes.

Mirliton A pale green squash, mirliton (pronounced *MEL-i-ton*) is known in Mexican and Latin American cooking as *chayote* (see page 87); it is also sometimes referred to as *vegetable pear*. If you cannot find mirliton, try large patty-pan squash.

Okra This vegetable originates in Africa and is common throughout the South (see page 36). It is often used in gumbo or stewed to be served as a side dish.

Oysters These are always used fresh in Louisiana, where only local varieties are available. Do not use canned—instead, either shuck them yourself or try fresh-shucked bottled oysters.

Pepper Black and white pepper are used in Louisiana cooking. Both should be ground fresh before being used. White pepper is milder than black, but does not have the same range of flavor.

Redfish A member of the Drum family, redfish has fairly firm, white flesh with a delicate flavor. If it is not available, substitute sea bass, striped bass, halibut, rockfish, or some varieties of shark.

Roux In Louisiana cooking roux is a blend of flour and oil that is usually cooked to a rich brown color. It gives both flavor and body to gumbos, sauces, and étouffées. See page 77 for instructions on preparing a roux.

Shrimp In Louisiana they are usually sold fresh with the head on. If you can't find fresh shrimp, buy them frozen, uncooked, and in the shell.

Tasso This Cajun "seasoning meat" is usually made from lean pork shoulder cut into chunks. Richly seasoned with cayenne and heavily smoked, it gives a tangy, smoky flavor. Smoked ham is a substitute, but it does not have the same smokiness or intensity. Tasso is rarely available outside Louisiana; see below for mail-order sources.

Yellow Corn Flour A fine flour made from corn, this is not the same as yellow cornmeal. It is marketed commercially under several names, of which Fish-Fri is the most common. If you cannot obtain it, substitute an equal quantity of all-purpose flour; however, the flavor will not be the same. It is often found in health-food stores, groceries in black neighborhoods, and specialty shops; see below for mail-order sources.

Mail-Order Sources Aidells Sausage Company, 618 Coventry Road, Kensington, CA 94707; 415-420-1737 *(andouille, chaurice, tasso, chorizo)*. Oak Grove Smoke House, Route 6, Box 133, Baton Rouge, LA 70815; 504-673-6857 *(andouille, tasso)*. Louisiana Catalog, Route 3, Box 614, Cut Off, LA 70345; 504-632-4100 *(crab boil, Louisiana-style hot sauce, yellow corn flour, pecans, pecan rice, red beans, filé powder, and many other Louisiana products)*.

APPETIZERS AND SOUPS

Louisiana appetizers and soups make abundant use of the wonderful shrimp, crabs, oysters, and crayfish that come from bayou, lake, and gulf.

OYSTERS "ROCKEFELLER"

Of all the dishes to come out of New Orleans, Oysters "Rockefeller" has found its way onto more restaurant menus throughout the world than any other. Named after John D. Rockefeller because it is so rich, the dish is characterized by a sauce that is actually a compound butter. Although the original recipe, invented at Antoine's restaurant, remains a secret, many versions exist. The recipe given here is less rich than some and has a wonderful herb flavor. Any leftover butter can be stored, well wrapped, in the refrigerator for 2 to 3 days. It is excellent spread on crusty French bread toasted under the broiler. You can use a food processor fitted with metal blade to chop the spinach, lettuce, watercress, parsley, green onions, and celery.

    24 large eastern oysters with
        their shells
     1 cup loosely packed spinach
        leaves, well washed and dried,
        and chopped in 2-inch pieces
     6 large leaves romaine lettuce,
        well washed and dried, and
        chopped in 2-inch pieces
     1 bunch watercress, well washed
        and dried, and chopped in
        2-inch pieces
    ¼ cup coarsely chopped parsley,
        well washed and dried
    ¼ cup coarsely chopped green
        onion tops
     1 stalk celery, coarsely chopped
    ¾ cup unsalted butter, softened
     1 clove garlic, minced
    ½ cup dry homemade bread
        crumbs
    ½ teaspoon dried basil
    ½ teaspoon ground fennel seed
     1 teaspoon hot pepper sauce
    ¼ cup anise-flavored liqueur
        Salt and pepper, to taste
     1 pound rock salt
    ¼ cup Parmesan cheese
        (optional)

1. Shuck oysters and wash sand and grit from larger bottom shell.

2. In a food processor fitted with a metal blade, finely chop spinach, lettuce, watercress, parsley, green onions, and celery. Remove vegetables to a mixing bowl. Put the butter in processor bowl; cream with garlic, bread crumbs, basil, fennel seed, and hot pepper sauce. Add finely chopped greens and liqueur. Process until no lumps of butter remain. Taste and correct seasoning with salt and pepper, if needed.

3. Place an oven rack at the top of the oven; preheat to 500 °F. Place oyster shells on a ½- to 1-inch layer of rock salt in an ovenproof pan or platter. Drop an oyster into each shell and cover with 1 to 2 tablespoons of butter mixture. If desired, sprinkle with Parmesan cheese. Bake until sauce begins to bubble and oysters are plump and firm, about 10 minutes. Place oysters under broiler until top of butter mixture becomes lightly browned (30 seconds to 1 minute).

Serves 4.

OYSTER AND ARTICHOKE SOUP

This elegant soup is somewhat expensive, but don't compromise the flavor by using frozen or canned artichokes or oysters. Quite rich, it is best served as an appetizer in small servings.

     6 medium artichokes, stems
        trimmed
     4 cups chicken stock
    ½ cup unsalted butter
     2 leeks, split and sliced
     2 stalks celery, coarsely chopped
     4 shallots, chopped
     2 cloves garlic, minced
     1 cup cooked rice
    ¼ teaspoon thyme
    ¼ teaspoon basil
    ¼ teaspoon cayenne pepper
     2 cups raw oysters in their
        own juice
     1 cup cream
        Lemon slices, for garnish

1. Place artichokes and stock in a 2- to 3-gallon pot over medium heat and cook until artichokes are tender, about 45 minutes. Remove artichokes and let cool; reserve the cooking liquid. Remove leaves (if desired, scrape the soft pulp off and add it to the soup with the chopped hearts; or save the leaves to serve cold with a vinaigrette). Cut out the fibrous chokes; coarsely chop the hearts.

2. In a 12-inch frying pan over medium heat, melt butter. Add leeks, celery, shallots, and garlic and cook until they are soft, about 20 minutes. Add artichoke-cooking liquid, bring to a boil, reduce to a simmer, and cook 20 minutes. Add rice, thyme, basil, and cayenne.

3. In a small saucepan over medium heat, cook oysters in their own juice until plump (2 to 3 minutes). Add half the oysters and half the chopped artichoke hearts to the soup. In a food processor, blender, or food mill, purée the soup in batches. Add cream and strain soup through a sieve; gently warm soup. To serve, place one oyster and 1 tablespoon of remaining chopped artichoke heart in each soup bowl. Ladle in the soup and garnish with lemon slices.

Serves 8.

SHRIMP RÉMOULADE

In French cooking *rémoulade* is a flavored mayonnaise to which mustard, parsley, celery, capers, gherkins, fresh tarragon, chervil, and anchovies are added. This Louisiana version is more spicy and mustardy. Rémoulade dressing is also excellent with hard-cooked eggs, cold poached fish, and cold roast beef. It can be made ahead and stored in the refrigerator for 3 to 4 days. You can use a food processor fitted with the metal blade to chop the celery, green onions, and parsley.

     4 quarts water
     2 tablespoons salt
     1 pound (15 to 20) large
        shrimp, unshelled
    ½ cup coarsely chopped pimiento
    ½ cup Creole or Dijon-style
        mustard
    ¼ cup prepared horseradish
     1 cup mayonnaise
     2 tablespoons olive oil

¼ cup tarragon vinegar
1½ cups coarsely chopped celery
 1 cup coarsely chopped green
   onion
 ½ cup chopped parsley
 2 tablespoons paprika
 ½ teaspoon cayenne pepper
   Salt and pepper, to taste
 ¼ head iceberg lettuce, shredded
   (optional)

1. Place the water and salt in a 4-quart pot and bring to a boil. Add shrimp and cook until shrimp are pink and firm, about 7 minutes. Drain shrimp in a colander and cool under cold running water. Peel shrimp and refrigerate until served.

2. *To prepare rémoulade dressing with a food processor:* In a food processor fitted with metal blade, process pimiento to a purée. Add mustard, horseradish, and mayonnaise. With processor running, gradually add olive oil and vinegar. Add celery, green onions, parsley, paprika, and cayenne. Pulse for 1 or 2 seconds three times. Add salt and pepper to taste. *To prepare rémoulade dressing by hand:* Chop pimiento, celery, green onions, and parsley finely. Whisk in mustard, horseradish, mayonnaise, olive oil, and vinegar. Add paprika and cayenne and blend well. Add salt and pepper to taste.

3. To serve, place 6 or 7 shrimp on a plate, with shredded lettuce if desired, and spoon generous amounts of the rémoulade over shrimp.

Serves 4 to 6.

The original recipe for Oysters "Rockefeller" from Antoine's Restaurant remains a secret, but this variation is tasty and easy to prepare. Use medium to large oysters, and do not overcook. The oysters should be plump and juicy. Rock salt not only keeps the oysters from tipping over but helps to retain heat so the platter can be served piping hot. Make sure to use an ovenproof platter.

CRAYFISH BISQUE

Steve Armbruster is a talented chef at Christian's, an excellent restaurant in New Orleans. This dish, he says, "is so elaborate it's rarely done even here in New Orleans. It's the first dish I ever worked on, helping my mother when I was about 5 years old." Elaborate it may be, but it is also a Louisiana classic worth all the time and effort it takes.

5 pounds live crayfish
1 bag crayfish boil
    (see page 67)
¼ cup salt
2 whole heads garlic
2 onions, split in half
    Juice of 2 lemons
1 cup peanut oil
1 cup flour
2 cups chopped onions
¾ cup chopped celery
1 cup chopped bell pepper
1 tablespoon chopped garlic
1 cup finely chopped green
    onions
2 tablespoons tomato paste
½ teaspoon dried thyme
¼ teaspoon cayenne pepper
2 bay leaves
1 teaspoon black pepper

Stuffed Crayfish Heads

1 cup finely chopped meat
    from peeled crayfish tails
    (see step 3)
½ cup finely chopped onion
½ cup finely chopped celery
¼ cup finely chopped green
    onions
2 tablespoons finely chopped
    parsley
2 teaspoons minced garlic
1 egg
¼ teaspoon dried thyme
2 tablespoons crayfish fat
    or melted butter
1 cup (approximately) fine
    dry bread crumbs
    Salt and pepper, to taste
2 dozen cleaned crayfish head
    shells (see step 3)
8 cups vegetable oil, for
    deep-frying
1 cup flour

1. Purge crayfish by soaking them in cold salted water. Drain and rinse; repeat until crayfish are clean, and water is no longer muddy.

2. In a large stockpot boil 2 gallons of water. Add crayfish boil, salt, the garlic heads, the halved onions, and lemon juice. Boil for 10 minutes, then add crayfish. Boil slowly over moderate heat for 10 minutes. Place a colander over a large pot or bowl and strain the crayfish. Discard vegetables and reserve 2 cups of the liquid.

3. Break crayfish at junction between thorax ("head") and tail. Remove all material in head sections, except orange crayfish fat, and discard; reserve shells and fat. Remove meat from tail sections; reserve shells. Finely chop enough tail meat to make 1 cup for use in Stuffed Crayfish Heads; leave the rest whole (or chop coarsely, if desired) for use in step 6. Set aside the shells from 2 dozen heads and any fat. Combine remaining shells with 4 cups cold water and the 2 cups reserved boil liquid. Bring to a boil and reduce to a simmer for at least 45 minutes (use this time to prepare Stuffed Crayfish Heads and roux).

4. In a 6- to 8-quart Dutch oven, combine oil and flour and prepare a brown roux the color of peanut butter according to the instructions on page 77. Add the chopped onions and celery; cook 10 minutes. Add bell pepper and cook over medium heat for 5 minutes. Add the chopped garlic and green onions, and continue cooking an additional minute.

5. Remove simmering stock from heat and strain. Add to Dutch oven along with tomato paste, thyme, cayenne, bay leaves, and black pepper. Bring to a boil and reduce to a simmer. Simmer for 30 minutes.

6. Add Stuffed Crayfish Heads to bisque along with reserved chopped tail meat; simmer 5 minutes. Adjust seasoning and serve bisque with lobster forks, if available.

Serves 8.

Stuffed Crayfish Heads Combine tail meat, onion, celery, green onion, parsley, garlic, and egg. Add thyme, crayfish fat, and bread crumbs to bind mixture. Add salt and pepper if needed. Stuff mixture into head shells. Heat oil in deep pot to 350° F. Roll stuffed heads in flour and deep-fry 8 at a time until golden brown (7 or 8 minutes). Drain on paper towels and set aside.

CRABMEAT RAVIGOTE

This rich appetizer is made in Louisiana with lump blue crabmeat, but other crabmeat, shrimp, or scallops also work well.

¼ cup unsalted butter
¼ cup flour
½ teaspoon salt
⅛ teaspoon cayenne pepper
1 teaspoon minced garlic
1½ cups half-and-half
¼ cup vermouth
1 cup thinly sliced green onion
1 tablespoon white tarragon
    vinegar
1 tablespoon lemon juice
1 tablespoon fresh tarragon
    (optional)
1 pound choice lump crabmeat
    Salt and pepper, to taste
    Hot pepper sauce (optional)
    Fine dry bread crumbs

1. In a heavy saucepan melt butter over low heat. Gradually stir in flour, salt, cayenne, and garlic and blend well. Continue to stir over heat 5 minutes. Slowly add half-and-half, stirring constantly. Cook over low heat, still stirring, until the mixture thickens, then blend in vermouth, green onions, vinegar, lemon juice, and tarragon (if used). Add crabmeat and cook over very low heat until heated through, about 2 to 3 minutes. Add salt and pepper; add hot pepper sauce if you prefer it spicier.

2. Preheat oven to 350° F. Remove pan from heat and pour crab mixture into individual gratin dishes or ramekins. Sprinkle lightly with bread crumbs. Bake in oven for 8 to 10 minutes and serve warm.

Serves 6 to 8 as an appetizer.

VEGETABLES AND SIDE DISHES

Vegetables, and especially salads, do not play as important a part in the cooking of Louisiana as that in other parts of the country. However, many side dishes emphasize vegetables. Some, such as Oyster and Eggplant Casserole (at right) and Stuffed Mirliton (page 72), are so hearty that they can also be served as main dishes.

CORN MAQUECHOUX

This Creole version of creamed corn is best served in summer when corn is sweetest, peppers are at their best, and fresh basil is abundant. It makes a nice accompaniment to fried or roast chicken.

- 3 tablespoons unsalted butter
- 1 cup finely chopped onions
- 2 shallots, finely chopped
- ½ cup chopped red bell pepper
- ½ cup chopped green bell pepper
- ½ cup chopped yellow bell pepper, optional (or substitute red bell pepper)
- 3 to 4 cups fresh or frozen sweet-corn kernels
- 2 tablespoons chopped parsley
- 4 tablespoons chopped green onion
- 1 cup whipping cream
- ¼ teaspoon dried thyme
- 1 tablespoon chopped fresh basil or ½ teaspoon dried basil
- ½ teaspoon cayenne pepper
  Salt and pepper, to taste
  Sugar (if needed)

Melt butter in heavy 3- to 4-quart saucepan over medium heat. Add onions and shallots and sauté until vegetables are soft but not browned. Add peppers and cook another 2 to 3 minutes. Add corn, parsley, green onions, cream, thyme, basil, and cayenne and cook at a simmer for 10 to 15 minutes. Adjust taste with salt and pepper, and, if necessary, sugar.

Serves 4 to 6.

OYSTER AND EGGPLANT CASSEROLE

This unusual combination of eggplant, oysters, and smoked meats makes an excellent side dish with roast fowl or broiled fish or chicken.

- 2 medium eggplants, cut into 1-inch cubes
- ½ cup olive oil
- ¼ cup unsalted butter
- ¼ pound andouille, chopped (see page 67)
- ¼ pound tasso, chopped (see page 67)
- 1 cup finely chopped onion
- ½ cup chopped red or green bell pepper
- 2 tablespoons minced garlic
- 1 pint oysters, coarsely chopped into ½-inch pieces
- ½ teaspoon each oregano, basil, and thyme
- ½ to 1 cup coarse dry bread crumbs
  Salt and pepper, to taste
  Hot pepper sauce, to taste
- ¼ cup grated Parmesan cheese
- 1 cup grated sharp Cheddar cheese

1. Preheat oven to 400 °F. Toss eggplant cubes in olive oil and spread in one layer on a baking sheet. Bake until soft (about 30 minutes) and set aside. Reduce heat to 350° F.

2. In 12-inch frying pan over medium heat, melt all but 1 tablespoon of the butter. Add *andouille, tasso,* and onion and cook until onion is translucent, about 10 minutes. Add bell pepper and garlic and cook 5 minutes. Add oysters to pan and cook 2 minutes.

3. Remove pan from heat and place contents in a 12- to 14-inch mixing bowl. Add oregano, basil, and thyme. Mix in reserved eggplant and bread crumbs to bind the mixture. It should still be moist. Add salt, pepper, and 6 to 8 drops hot pepper sauce.

4. Butter a 3- to 4-quart casserole or gratin dish with remaining butter. Spoon in eggplant-and-oyster mixture. Combine cheeses and sprinkle over the top. Bake until cheese begins to brown, about 15 to 20 minutes.

Serves 6 to 8.

LEEKS BRAISED WITH TASSO

This dish demonstrates a typical and flavorful use of the Cajun seasoning meat tasso, which imparts a smoky, spicy tang to the leeks.

- 3 medium-sized leeks
- 1 carrot, diced
- 2 shallots, finely chopped
- 2 cloves garlic, minced
- ¼ pound tasso, finely chopped (see page 67)
- 2 cups beef stock
- 2 tablespoons butter

Split leeks and wash thoroughly. Place in a heavy pan over medium heat with carrot, shallots, garlic, *tasso,* stock, and butter. Cover, reduce to a simmer, and cook until leeks are tender when pierced, 30 to 40 minutes. Remove to warm serving dish and reduce liquid until it turns syrupy. Pour over leeks and serve.

Serves 4 to 6.

CAJUN HOME-FRIED POTATOES

An easy way to spice up home-fried potatoes. Add more sausage and you have a simple main course.

- ¼ cup unsalted butter
- 3 pounds red potatoes, diced into ½-inch pieces
- 1 large onion, chopped into ¼-inch pieces
- ½ pound andouille (see page 67) or smoked ham, diced into ½-inch pieces
  Salt and pepper
- ¼ teaspoon cayenne pepper
- ¼ cup chopped green onion

1. In a 12-inch cast-iron frying pan over medium heat, melt butter. Add potatoes and onions and fry over medium-high heat, turning occasionally for even cooking, until potatoes are browned, about 15 minutes.

2. Add *andouille,* ¼ teaspoon salt, ½ teaspoon black pepper, cayenne, and continue frying for 6 minutes.

3. Taste for salt and pepper and correct if necessary, sprinkle with green onions, and serve.

Serves 6 to 8.

Mirliton, a delicate squash-flavored vegetable, is actually a member of the cucumber family. It provides the perfect container for a spicy stuffing of sausage and fresh seafood. Try to use andouille for its naturally smoky flavor and lean chunky meat. (See mail-order sources, page 67.) If you cannot find mirliton (also called chayote), use patty-pan squash or large cucumbers. Cucumbers require less cooking time, about 5 to 7 minutes.

STUFFED MIRLITON

The mild flavor of mirliton takes well to the spicy stuffing given here.

- 2 *mirlitons (chayotes), cut in half lengthwise*
- 4 *cups water*
- ¼ *cup unsalted butter*
- ½ *pound andouille, chopped (see page 67)*
- 1 *cup chopped onion*
- ½ *cup chopped celery*
- ½ *cup chopped green bell pepper*
- 1 *tablespoon minced garlic*
- ½ *pound raw shrimp, shelled, deveined, and chopped*
- ½ *cup chopped green onions*
- ½ *teaspoon basil*
- ¼ *teaspoon thyme*
- ½ *teaspoon cayenne pepper*
- 1 *teaspoon Worcestershire sauce*
- ¾ *to 1 cup dry bread crumbs Salt and pepper, to taste*

1. Place halved mirlitons in a pan large enough to hold them in a single layer, cover with the water, and bring to a boil. Boil over medium heat until flesh of squash is tender, about 30 minutes. Remove from pan and cool under cold water. Remove seeds and scoop out pulp, being careful not to break through skin of mirliton. Chop pulp; reserve pulp and shells.

2. Preheat oven to 350° F. In a 12-inch frying pan over medium heat, melt butter. Add *andouille* and cook until slightly browned, about 5 minutes. Add onion and celery and cook until vegetables are soft, about 10 minutes. Add green pepper and garlic and cook for another 2 minutes. Add chopped shrimp and cook until shrimp turns pink, about 1 or 2 minutes. Add green onion, basil, thyme, cayenne, Worcestershire, and chopped mirliton pulp. Add enough bread crumbs to just bind the stuffing. Taste for salt and pepper; correct if necessary. Fill mirliton shells with stuffing and bake for 30 minutes.

Serves 4.

MAIN DISHES

As with appetizers, Louisiana main dishes often feature fish and seafood. Many, such as Red Beans and Rice (page 74), Grillades (page 78), and Chicken Étouffée (at right), are sturdy, rib-sticking dishes.

BAKED FISH WITH CREOLE BUTTER IN FOIL PACKAGES

This is a simplified and lighter version of the classic fish *en papillote* (fish baked in an envelope of baking parchment). Aluminum foil works as well as parchment, but if you have the parchment you can certainly use it. Any mild-flavored fish fillet can be used for this recipe. However, be sure it is no thicker than ½ inch, or it will not cook properly. You can use any combination of seafood garnishes. Try one of these: ¼ pound lump crabmeat, 8 to 12 small raw oysters, 8 to 12 medium raw shrimp (peeled), or 8 to 12 large crayfish tails. Or you can leave the garnishes out of the dish altogether.

> 1½ to 2 pounds fish fillets (see Note) in ½-inch-thick pieces, about 2½ inches by 5½ inches
> Lemon juice
> Black pepper
> ½ red bell pepper, cut crosswise in very thin strips
> Garnishes (optional, see above)

Creole Butter

> 1 ounce tasso (see page 67)
> ½ red bell pepper, roasted and peeled (see page 96)
> 1 cup softened unsalted butter
> Black pepper, to taste
> 2 teaspoons lemon juice
> 1 tablespoon finely chopped green onion
> 1 teaspoon minced garlic
> ½ teaspoon Worcestershire sauce
> 1 teaspoon fresh thyme or ¼ teaspoon dried thyme
> Salt, to taste
> Tabasco, to taste (optional)

1. Preheat oven to 450° F. For each fish piece, spread a 12- by 10-inch sheet of aluminum foil on a flat surface. Lightly spread Creole Butter on half of the foil.

2. Sprinkle fish with lemon juice and black pepper. Place fish skin side down on buttered surface. Spread about 2 tablespoons of Creole Butter on each fish. Garnish with bell pepper and with whatever seafood garnish you have chosen. Fold other half of foil over fish and completely seal all edges. Place in a sheet pan or on a baking sheet; bake for 10 to 12 minutes. Place packets on serving plates. Cut into center of each with scissors or paring knife and peel foil back. Serve immediately.

Serves 4.

Creole Butter In a food processor fitted with a metal blade, mince *tasso*. Add red bell pepper and purée. Taste for black pepper. Stop machine, remove lid, and add butter, lemon juice, green onion, garlic, Worcestershire, and thyme. Briefly pulse several times until well mixed. Add salt if needed and Tabasco if desired. Set aside at room temperature while you prepare fish. *To prepare in a blender:* Follow food-processor method, but start with extremely soft butter. Any leftover Creole Butter can be refrigerated for one week or frozen.

Note Any of these fish will work: redfish, speckled trout, sea bass, halibut, red snapper, rock cod, or cod.

CHICKEN ÉTOUFFÉE

Not only does this hearty dish benefit from long, slow cooking, but it's equally good reheated the next day. So make plenty well ahead of time.

> Salt and pepper
> 1⅛ teaspoon paprika
> ⅝ teaspoon cayenne pepper
> ⅝ teaspoon thyme
> 1 chicken (3½ pounds), quartered, with last 2 joints of wing removed
> Melted butter (about ¼ cup)
> ½ cup peanut oil
> ½ cup flour
> Pinch of sage
> 1 cup finely chopped onion
> ½ cup finely chopped celery
> ¼ cup finely chopped green bell pepper
> ¼ cup finely chopped red bell pepper
> 3 cups rich chicken stock
> ¼ pound unsalted butter
> ¼ pound tasso, in ¼-inch dice (see page 67)
> 1 cup green onions, finely chopped
> 2 tablespoons minced garlic
> 2 tablespoons tomato paste

1. Preheat oven to 375° F. Mix together ¼ teaspoon black pepper, 1 teaspoon salt, the paprika, ½ teaspoon cayenne, and ½ teaspoon thyme. Brush chicken with melted butter and sprinkle generously with the spice mixture. Place chicken on a rack; place rack over a roasting pan and bake for 45 minutes. Remove from oven and set aside.

2. Meanwhile, using a 6- to 8-quart Dutch oven, follow directions on page 77 to prepare a deep red-brown roux, using peanut oil and flour. When roux is deep brown, add sage, ⅛ teaspoon each salt and pepper, and the remaining cayenne and thyme. Immediately remove from heat and add half the chopped onion, half the celery, and half the bell peppers. Return to heat and continue to cook, stirring occasionally, until the vegetables are soft. The roux will continue to darken. Add stock and continue to cook over low heat.

3. Meanwhile, in a 12-inch skillet over medium heat, melt ¼ pound butter. Add *tasso* and fry for 2 to 3 minutes. Add remaining onion, celery, and peppers. Cook for 10 minutes or until wilted. Add green onions and garlic and cook for 2 more minutes. Add this vegetable mixture to sauce along with tomato paste and cook for another 30 minutes or more. About 15 minutes before serving, add the chicken pieces. Adjust the seasoning, if necessary, and serve.

Serves 4.

The classic Monday night dinner of New Orleans, Red Beans and Rice, is embellished with Louisiana sausages and smoked meats. The hot sausage here, called chaurice, is flavored with fresh onions, parsley, and chiles and lightly smoked. Also pictured is tasso, a Cajun seasoning meat, which is more spicy and smoky than ham. If tasso is unavailable, you can use a smoked ham.

RED BEANS AND RICE

This is the traditional Monday night dinner of New Orleans. The tradition probably began because folks had spent all their money on the weekend and needed a cheap but substantial way to feed themselves. Although it is an inexpensive meal, it does not lack in flavor and appetite appeal; it makes an ideal dish for informally entertaining a large group. Note that the beans first have to soak overnight, and then when cooked should be refrigerated at least overnight.

    1 pound dry red beans
    4 quarts water
    2 meaty ham hocks
    8 cups beef or chicken stock
    4 bay leaves
    ½ teaspoon thyme
    1 teaspoon cayenne pepper
    1 teaspoon black pepper
    1 pound andouille (see page 67)
    ¼ pound tasso, chopped (optional; see page 67)
    2 cups chopped onion
    ½ cup chopped celery

    1 bell pepper, chopped
    1 bunch green onions, chopped
    1 tablespoon minced garlic
    2 pounds (8 individual) chaurice sausage or other fresh hot sausage (see page 67)
       Salt and black pepper, to taste
       Red wine vinegar, to taste
    4 cups cooked hot rice
       Hot pepper sauce, to taste

1. Wash beans and soak overnight in the water. The next day drain beans and wash well under cold running water. Place beans, ham hocks, and stock in a heavy 6- to 8-quart stockpot or Dutch oven. The beans should be covered by about 2 to 3 inches of liquid; add more liquid if necessary. Bring to a boil and skim any scum that collects on the surface. Reduce heat to a simmer and add bay leaves, thyme, cayenne, and black pepper. Simmer for 30 minutes while you prepare the vegetables.

2. Chop ¼ pound of the *andouille* into ¼-inch pieces. Place it in a 12-inch cast-iron frying pan (or other heavy frying pan) with *tasso* if you are using it. Fry for 5 minutes to render the fat and brown the meat. Add chopped onion and celery and cook until the vegetables are soft, about 10 minutes. Add bell pepper, green onions, and garlic. Cook an additional 5 minutes, then add to the simmering pot of red beans. Continue to cook beans until they are soft and some begin to break apart, about another hour. Allow the beans to cool; refrigerate, covered, overnight or for up to 4 days.

3. When ready to serve, bring beans to a simmer. Place chaurice whole in a covered heavy frying pan and fry over medium heat for about 15 minutes, checking sausages frequently and turning them as they brown. Meanwhile, slice remaining andouille into ¼-inch slices and add to beans. Cook in the beans for about 10 minutes. Taste the beans for salt and pepper and correct if necessary; add a little vinegar if you wish. To serve, place about ½ cup rice in center of each plate, spoon beans over rice, and accompany with 1 chaurice. Serve with hot pepper sauce.

Serves 8.

LOUISIANA SEAFOOD FRY

Traditionally Saturday night in New Orleans meant fried seafood. These days the custom may be dying out at home, but just about every neighborhood restaurant and po'boy shop still knows how to fry seafood perfectly. Here are a few tips so you can duplicate this perfection. Always start with good-quality fresh oil. Peanut oil is best, but corn, safflower, or ordinary salad oil will also work fine. Heat the oil to 375° F. As you cook, be sure to maintain the temperature between 360° and 375° F by frying in small batches and waiting a minute or so after frying each batch for the oil temperature to come back up to the desired level. (This is a lot simpler with the type of thermometer that can be clipped to the side of pan.) Watch the color of the seafood and remove it when it is a light golden brown. Pay more attention to this visual signal than to the cooking times given here, which can only be approximate.

- *1 pound fresh large shrimp (15 to 20), peeled and deveined, with tails left on*
- *2 dozen medium oysters, shucked*
- *6 dozen peeled crayfish tails (optional)*
- *4 cups oil for deep-frying*
- *1 cup milk*
- *1 egg, beaten*
- *1 cup all-purpose flour*
- *2 cups yellow corn flour (see page 67)*
- *1 tablespoon salt*
- *½ teaspoon cayenne pepper*
- *2 teaspoons paprika*
- *1 teaspoon dried basil*
- *2 teaspoons black pepper*

Creole Tartar Sauce

- *2 tablespoons (or more) fresh lemon juice*
- *1 tablespoon Creole mustard or other coarse mustard*
- *2 eggs*
- *1½ cups olive oil*
- *½ teaspoon cayenne pepper*
- *1 teaspoon salt (approximately)*
- *½ teaspoon black pepper*
- *½ cup finely chopped green onions*
- *¼ cup finely chopped parsley*
- *½ teaspoon soya sauce*
- *¼ teaspoon Worcestershire sauce*
- *¼ cup finely chopped dill pickles*
- *2 tablespoons finely chopped fresh dill (optional) Louisiana-style hot sauce (optional)*

1. Wash and dry shrimp. Drain oysters and crayfish tails (if used). In a deep pot, wok, or deep-fryer, heat oil over medium-high heat to 375° F.

2. Add milk to egg and mix well. Combine flours, salt, cayenne, paprika, basil, and pepper; mix well and place in a shallow bowl or pie pan.

3. Dip shrimp in egg mixture and coat well with seasoned flour mixture. Deep-fry 6 to 8 shrimp at a time for 2 to 3 minutes. Remove with a skimmer or slotted spoon and drain on paper towels. Repeat with crayfish tails, frying for 1 to 2 minutes.

4. Roll oysters directly in seasoned flour and fry 6 to 8 at a time for 1 to 2 minutes.

5. Either serve fried seafood direct from the pan or keep finished batches warm on a platter lined with paper towels in a 200° F oven. Serve with Creole Tartar Sauce.

Serves 4 to 6.

Creole Tartar Sauce

1. Into a food processor fitted with a metal blade, place 2 tablespoons lemon juice, mustard, and eggs. With the motor running, gradually add olive oil. When sauce begins to thicken, add remaining oil in a steady stream. Sauce will be thick and fluffy. *Or:* Use a blender, hand-held electric mixer, or wire whisk; substitute 1 egg and 1 egg yolk for the 2 eggs. Proceed with step 2, beating instead of processing.

2. Remove processor lid and add cayenne, salt, pepper, green onions, parsley, soya sauce, Worchestershire, dill pickles, and fresh dill (if desired). Replace the lid and pulse the processor 2 or 3 times for 1 second each time. Taste and add more lemon juice, salt, or hot sauce if needed. Sauce can be stored, covered, in refrigerator for about one week.

Makes 2 to 3 cups.

PORK CHOPS WITH OYSTER STUFFING

Oyster stuffing is an excellent complement to pork chops but also goes well with roast chicken, turkey, or pork roast. If you put the stuffing inside poultry, use a little less liquid to moisten it, since it will absorb liquid as the bird cooks. The recipe below makes enough for a 5- to 6-pound roasting chicken or a small turkey.

- ¼ teaspoon dried rosemary
- ¼ teaspoon dried thyme
- ¼ teaspoon dried sage
- ½ teaspoon black pepper
- ¼ teaspoon cayenne pepper
- ½ teaspoon salt
- 4 pork chops, ¾ inch to 1 inch thick
- 1 tablespoon salad oil

Stuffing

- 2 tablespoons unsalted butter
- ¼ pound andouille, finely chopped (see page 67)
- ¼ pound (about 1 link) chaurice (see page 67) or hot Italian sausage, casing removed
- ½ cup finely chopped onion
- ¼ cup finely chopped celery
- ¼ cup finely chopped green bell pepper
- ¼ cup finely chopped red bell pepper
- ½ cup finely chopped green onions
- 1 teaspoon minced garlic
- 8- to 10-ounce jar oysters
- ¼ teaspoon dried thyme
- ½ teaspoon dried sage
- ¼ teaspoon dried rosemary
- ½ teaspoon black pepper
- 3 cups coarse bread crumbs, homemade from dry French bread
- 1 cup (approximately) chicken stock
  Salt and Louisiana-style hot sauce, to taste

1. Prepare Stuffing. To prepare pork chops, mix rosemary, thyme, sage, black pepper, cayenne, and salt. Rub this mixture well into both sides of the chops.

2. In a 12-inch cast-iron or enameled frying pan, heat oil over high heat until it just begins to smoke. Add pork chops, reduce heat to medium-high, and brown for 5 to 7 minutes on each side.

3. Place chops over oyster stuffing and cover with foil. Bake 15 minutes. To serve, place a generous portion of stuffing on each plate and cover it with a pork chop.

Serves 4.

Stuffing

1. Preheat oven to 350° F. In a 12-inch heavy frying pan over medium-high heat, melt butter. Add *andouille* and *chaurice*. Cook for 5 minutes, making sure that chaurice is well broken up. Lower heat to medium and add onion and celery; cook until they begin to show color (10 minutes). Add bell peppers, green onions, and garlic; cook 5 minutes more.

2. Drain oysters, saving liquid. If they are large, coarsely chop into ¾-inch pieces; otherwise, leave them whole. Add oysters to sausage mixture and cook for another 2 minutes. Remove pan from heat and add thyme, sage, rosemary, black pepper, and bread crumbs; mix well. Add reserved oyster liquid and enough chicken stock to make stuffing moist but not soggy. Add salt and Tabasco; mix well. Lightly smooth the surface with a spatula. Bake uncovered for 20 minutes while you prepare pork chops.

CREOLE BAKED EGGS WITH ANDOUILLE, HAM, AND ASPARAGUS

This dish, inspired by the Spanish dish *Huevos a la Flamenca*, is good for breakfast, but it also makes an excellent lunch or light supper. The added plus is that the leftovers are good cold.

- ½ pound andouille, cut into ¼-inch rounds (see page 67)
- ¼ pound diced smoked ham
- 4 quarts salted water
- 12 spears asparagus
- 1 whole pimiento or red bell pepper, cut into strips
- 6 eggs

Tomato Sauce

- 2 tablespoons olive oil
- ¼ cup finely chopped onion
- 6 medium green onions—white part finely chopped, green tops thinly sliced for garnish
- 1 teaspoon minced garlic
- ½ cup diced green bell pepper
- ¼ pound andouille, finely chopped or ¼ pound smoked bacon
- ¼ cup dry sherry
- 6 plum tomatoes (fresh or canned), peeled and quartered
- ½ teaspoon cayenne pepper
  Salt and pepper, to taste

1. Place sliced *andouille* in a heavy 12-inch frying pan and fry over medium heat until browned, about 5 minutes on each side. Add ham and cook 2 minutes. Remove pan from heat and set aside. In a large saucepan bring the water to a boil. Add asparagus and blanch for 4 minutes. Cool under running cold water and set aside.

2. Preheat oven to 450 °F. Spread Tomato Sauce on the bottom of a 14- by 8-inch gratin or baking dish. Distribute fried sausage and ham over sauce; arrange asparagus spears and pimiento strips on top. One at a time, break eggs into the dish, distributing them evenly and taking care not to break the yolks. Garnish with the green onion tops and bake until the egg whites are set but the yolks are still soft, about 10 minutes.

Serves 6.

Tomato Sauce In a 2-quart saucepan heat olive oil over medium heat. Add onion, chopped green onions, and garlic and sauté until soft (about 10 minutes). Add green pepper and chopped andouille and cook for an additional 2 to 3 minutes. Add sherry, tomatoes, and cayenne. Cook for about 10 minutes. Season with salt and black pepper.

MAKING ROUX

Roux is an essential part of Louisiana cooking. In French cooking the word *roux* refers to a mixture of flour and butter. In Louisiana cooking the same word refers to a mixture of flour and oil. The Louisiana roux is cooked much longer than that of French cuisine; it can become a rich reddish brown or even black. The function of roux in French cooking is to thicken sauces. In Louisiana cooking roux not only adds body but functions as an important flavoring ingredient that gives soups, stews, and sauces a nutty, smoky taste and aroma.

Making roux takes between 45 minutes and 1 hour. Because the roux must be stirred continuously, make sure that you have at least one uninterrupted hour for this project. Stored in the refrigerator, roux will keep for 2 to 3 weeks, so it's smart to make a large quantity, cool it, and refrigerate whatever you don't need immediately in an airtight jar. When you want to use it, spoon out what you need, gradually heat it, and proceed with the recipe. During storage some oil will come to the surface. Either pour this off or mix it back in (allow roux to come to room temperature first). **Caution** While it is cooking roux becomes quite hot. If it hits your skin, it will burn you instantly. Use a high-sided, heavy frying pan and make sure it will never be more than one quarter full. Always stir with a long-handled spoon or spatula.

To make the roux you will need equal proportions of flour and oil. This chef prefers peanut oil and unbleached white flour, but any cooking oil (except olive) will do. The first time you make roux, start with 1 cup oil and 1 cup flour. When you're comfortable with the process, you can increase the quantities to as much as 5 cups of each. Make sure that your vegetables and seasoning mixtures are prepared ahead of time.

If the roux begins to darken more quickly than you can stir, remove from the heat and stir. Lower the heat, then cook until it reaches the desired color. If black specks appear, you have burnt the roux and must start over—burnt roux will ruin your dish. Pour it into a heatproof container to cool before discarding.

When the roux has reached the desired color, stop the cooking by removing the pan from the heat and stirring in the chopped vegetables called for in the recipe. (If you're preparing extra roux for later use, ladle out the excess before adding the vegetables.) Keep stirring until the mixture stops bubbling (it will darken slightly), then return it to low heat and cook 5 minutes more.

1. *In a 10-inch cast-iron skillet or other heavy frying pan, heat oil over medium heat for 5 minutes. Remove from heat and gradually stir in flour. (A wooden or metal spatula will get into the corners of the pan better than a wire whisk.) Return pan to medium heat and cook, stirring continuously and making sure to get into the corners. As you cook the roux, it will go through several stages of coloring. The first is tan (shown above); it takes about 20 minutes to reach this color. Tan roux is not used too often in Louisiana cooking although it is an effective base for lighter sauces. Cajun chefs would use a tan roux with red meats like beef, venison, or wild duck.*

2. *After 5 to 10 more minutes, the roux turns light brown (the color of peanut butter). Light-brown roux is used in dishes such as Creole duck, Seafood Filé Gumbo (see page 83), and Georgia Rabbit and Oyster Gumbo (see page 30).*

3. *After another 5 to 10 minutes, the roux will have turned brown. Brown roux is used in such dishes as Grillades (see page 78), Crayfish Bisque (see page 70), and some gumbos.*

4. *After another 5 to 10 minutes, the roux turns deep red brown. Deep red brown roux is used in Chicken Étouffée (see page 73).*

GRILLADES

This traditional Creole breakfast dish also makes a fine dinner entrée.

- 2 pounds bottom round of beef, sliced about ¼ inch thick
  Salt and black pepper
- 2 teaspoons cayenne pepper
- 4 tablespoons minced garlic
- 1¼ teaspoons each *sage and thyme*
- 3 cups flour
- 2 tablespoons each *butter and olive oil*
- ¼ cup salad oil
- ¼ pound tasso, finely chopped (see page 67)
- ½ pound chaurice, chopped (optional; see page 67)
- 1½ cups chopped onion
- ½ cup each *finely chopped celery, green bell pepper, and red bell pepper*
- 2 cups tomato purée
- 2 cups rich beef stock
- 2 tablespoons red wine vinegar (optional)
  Hot pepper sauce (optional)

1. If beef slices are larger than 2 inches by 3 inches, cut smaller. In a small bowl mix salt, pepper, cayenne, garlic, and 1 teaspoon each of the thyme and sage. Rub mixture into meat pieces. Pound slices with the flat side of a cleaver. Roll in flour, shaking off excess. Save ¼ cup of coating flour for the roux. In a 12-inch cast-iron frying pan, heat butter and olive oil over high heat. Add meat and fry 2 to 3 minutes per side. Remove to a plate.

2. Follow directions on page 77 to make a brown roux, using salad oil and the reserved ¼ cup flour. Add *tasso,* and *chaurice* if used, and fry over medium heat 2 to 3 minutes. Add onion, celery, and bell peppers and cook until soft, about 10 minutes. Add tomato purée, beef stock, and remaining sage and thyme. Bring to a boil, reduce to simmer, and add meat. Simmer, uncovered, until meat is tender, about 1½ hours. Add salt and pepper to taste; add vinegar and hot pepper sauce if you wish. Serve with grits or rice.

Serves 4 to 6.

Menu

BACKYARD SEAFOOD DINNER

*Boiled Seafood Dinner:
Crayfish, Crabs, Shrimp,
Red Potatoes, Onions, Corn*

French Bread

Pralines (see page 81)

Beer, Soft Drinks, Coffee

In Louisiana boiled seafood is eaten spicy, either hot or cold. This recipe calls for serving it hot because the flavors come through more. If you cannot find blue crabs or live crayfish in your part of the country, use just shrimp; about 6 pounds should be enough for 12 people. This meal is messy and is best served outside on tables spread with lots of newspaper. Be sure to provide plenty of napkins, and bags to collect the shells.

BOILED SEAFOOD DINNER

The liquid prepared in step 2 constitutes a homemade crab boil (see page 67). It can be reused 3 or 4 times. It should be refrigerated, and if you're not going to use it for over a week, it should be frozen.

- 5 pounds live crayfish
- 2 gallons water
- 2 cups salt
- 1 cup lemon juice
- ½ cup cayenne pepper
- ¼ cup whole black pepper
- 2 teaspoons whole allspice
- 1 tablespoon whole cloves
- 1 tablespoon dried thyme
- 12 bay leaves
- 2 teaspoons whole celery seed
- 2 tablespoons coriander
- 3 heads garlic
- 6 onions, halved
- 24 small red potatoes
- 12 blue crabs (see page 67)
- 3 pounds shrimp
- 12 ears corn, cut in half widthwise

1. Purge crayfish by soaking in cold salted water. Drain and rinse; repeat this process until the soaking water is no longer muddy. Set crayfish aside.

2. In a 4- to 5-gallon pot, bring the 2 gallons water and salt to a boil over high heat. Add lemon juice, cayenne, black pepper, allspice, cloves, thyme, bay leaves, celery seed, and coriander; continue boiling for 20 minutes.

3. Add garlic, onions, and potatoes; boil another 10 minutes. Add crabs and boil 5 minutes. Add crayfish and continue boiling for 5 minutes. Add shrimp and corn and boil until shrimp are pink and firm (about 5 to 7 minutes). Drain boiled food through a colander suspended over a large pot.

4. Serve seafood and vegetables in large, shallow bowls or platters.

Serves 12.

This spicy boiled dinner uses three seafoods found fresh in Louisiana: blue crabs, crayfish, and shrimp. Or, if you prefer, any of these can be used alone.

Bananas Foster, Pralines, and Bread Pudding, all southern dessert stars, are usually served with the strong chicory-flavored coffee popular in Louisiana.

DESSERTS

Except for a few famous desserts such as Bread Pudding, Pralines, and Bananas Foster (all on this page), desserts tend not to be the main focus of Louisiana meals. However, desserts eaten in other parts of the South, like Pecan Pie (see page 41), are popular in Louisiana and appropriate as the finale to any meal there.

PRALINES

Regina Charboneau grew up in a restaurant family in Natchez, Mississippi. From a young age she helped her father and learned how to make Cajun-Creole dishes. Since then she has had her own restaurants, first in Alaska and now in San Francisco. Considered San Francisco's master Cajun chef, she brings an original and individual approach to classic Creole and Cajun dishes such as this dessert. A mixture of caramelized sugar and nuts, pralines are usually crisp, but her recipe, which follows, produces a softer candy. The use of buttermilk gives her version of this Louisiana classic a nice tang. Traditionally these candies are eaten after a meal with strong black coffee.

- *2 cups buttermilk*
- *2 cups white sugar*
- *1 teaspoon baking soda*
- *½ cup unsalted butter*
- *1½ cups coarsely chopped pecans*

1. In a heavy 4- to 6-quart saucepan, combine buttermilk, sugar, baking soda, and butter. Cook over medium heat, stirring frequently with a wooden spoon and monitoring temperature with a candy thermometer. First the mixture will foam, then darken as it thickens. It is done when it reaches 236° to 238° F (soft ball stage).

2. Remove mixture from heat and stir in pecans with a wire whisk. Beat mixture until it cools to about 220° F. While it is still soft, spoon onto waxed paper in 1- to 2-tablespoon mounds. As the pralines cool, they will become firm and can be removed from the waxed paper.

Makes 2 to 3 dozen.

BREAD PUDDING WITH BOURBON SAUCE

Regina Charboneau's version of bread pudding is somewhat like a steamed spice cake. Unusual in that it is prepared in individual ramekins, it also features a sauce less rich and caloric than the usual, which would be made with butter.

- *½ loaf dry sliced bread, whole wheat or white, torn into pieces*
- *3 cups brown sugar*
- *2 cups half-and-half*
- *1 cup whipping cream*
- *4 eggs, beaten*
- *1½ cups chopped pecans*
- *1 cup raisins*
- *2 teaspoons cinnamon*
- *2 tablespoons butter*

Bourbon Sauce

- *3 cups brown sugar*
- *Juice of 2 fresh oranges*
- *1 cup bourbon*

1. Preheat oven to 350° F. In a large bowl mix all ingredients until batter is as smooth as possible. (Batter can be stored, covered, in refrigerator for 4 to 5 days.)

2. Butter six 3-inch ramekins or ovenproof coffee cups and fill three fourths full. Put them in a large baking pan and add water to come 2 inches up sides of ramekins. Bake 50 minutes. Let cool briefly, then turn out of ramekins onto serving plates. Pour Bourbon Sauce over pudding. Both pudding and sauce should be served hot; reheat if necessary.

Serves 6.

Bourbon Sauce In a medium saucepan mix brown sugar and orange juice. Slowly simmer for 15 minutes until a syrup forms, then add bourbon carefully (it may flame). Let cook for 3 to 4 more minutes; serve hot.

BANANAS FOSTER

This flaming dessert makes an impressive finale to a dinner for guests. It's simple but must be prepared at the last minute in small batches; do not attempt it for a large dinner party. Use an omelet pan with slanted sides or a sauté pan. Flaming desserts are easier to prepare over a gas burner (see the directions in step 2). If you are cooking on an electric burner, heat the rum in a small saucepan until it just begins to boil. Then pour it over the bananas and use a match to ignite it.

- *2 tablespoons unsalted butter*
- *2 tablespoons light or dark brown sugar*
- *Pinch cinnamon*
- *Pinch nutmeg, preferably freshly grated*
- *2 small firm bananas, cut in half lengthwise*
- *¼ cup Drambuie liqueur*
- *¼ cup dark rum*
- *2 scoops vanilla ice cream*

1. In a 10-inch omelet or sauté pan over medium heat, melt butter. Add sugar, cinnamon, and nutmeg; mix well. Add bananas and sauté until they begin to soften, about a minute on each side.

2. Pour in liqueur and rum. Turn up heat and tilt pan to ignite liquor. Shake pan slightly to prolong flames. When flames burn out, place 2 banana halves on each serving plate. Place a scoop of ice cream between the banana halves and spoon the sauce over all.

Serves 2.

BERRY GRATINÉ

Assistant Chef Steve Armbruster of Christian's Restaurant in New Orleans suggests this simple but elegant dessert. Any fresh berry will work well; Chef Armbruster suggests mulberries.

- 2 cups fresh berries (blueberries, huckleberries, mulberries, raspberries, blackberries, olallieberries, or strawberries)
- ¼ cup fruit liqueur
  Pinch ground cardamom
  Sugar, to taste
- 2 cups milk
- 6 egg yolks
- ⅔ cup sugar
- 1 teaspoon vanilla extract
- ½ cup flour
- 1 cup whipping cream

1. Place berries in a large bowl and add liqueur and cardamom. Add sugar if fruit is too sour. Let sit for at least 30 minutes.

2. *To make vanilla custard cream:* Bring milk to a boil; set aside. In a 10-inch mixing bowl whisk together egg yolks, the ⅔ cup sugar, and vanilla. The mixture should be pale yellow, and when lifted from the bowl with the whisk, it should fall back into the bowl like folded ribbons. It will take 3 to 4 minutes of whisking to achieve the proper consistency. Add half the milk to the egg mixture and mix well. Gradually pour the mixture into the remaining milk, mixing continuously. Slowly whisk in flour, continuing to mix well. Return custard to medium heat and gradually bring to a boil, stirring continuously. When custard appears to have stopped thickening, reduce heat and simmer for 1 to 2 minutes. Cover with plastic wrap and set aside to allow custard to cool.

3. In a medium bowl, beat whipping cream until it forms peaks. Fold into cooled custard.

4. Preheat broiler. Place ½ cup berries in each of 4 ovenproof ramekins. Cover with custard and brown under broiler.

Serves 4.

Menu

FAIS DODO

Raw Oysters With Cocktail Sauce

Creole Slaw

Chicken, Andouille, and Tasso Jambalaya

Seafood Filé Gumbo

Ice Cream

Beer and Iced Tea

Out in Cajun country good food and music are the vehicles for bringing people together. That is the spirit of a Fais Dodo, a dance party that may take place in the town dance hall, a church, or outdoors. The gathering may be as small as a single family or as large as the whole town, but the air of festivity is always the same. When the whole town turns out, gumbo simmers away in large soup pots while men prepare jambalaya in giant caldrons. Even cooked on this massive scale, the food turns out to be as flavorful as if it were prepared in small batches. In the background local Cajun bands play, and on the dance floor, folks dance the two-step.

RAW OYSTERS WITH COCKTAIL SAUCE

In the stand-up oyster bars that pepper New Orleans' French Quarter, the patrons mix their own cocktail sauce. The raw oyster is dipped in this sauce and eaten on a soda cracker.

- 4 dozen small to medium oysters in the shell, well chilled
- 1 cup catsup
- 2 tablespoons lemon juice
- ¼ cup prepared horseradish
  Louisiana-style hot sauce, to taste
  Soda crackers

1. Open oysters and set each out on the half shell.

2. Mix together catsup, lemon juice, horseradish, and hot sauce. Serve in a small bowl with crackers on the side.

Serves 8.

CREOLE SLAW

This cabbage salad contains no mayonnaise. The dressing is also good for lettuce or potato salads or as a marinade for blanched broccoli or green beans. It is best to dress the salad an hour before serving.

- 1 head cabbage, thinly shredded
- 1 large carrot, shredded
- 2 cups finely chopped red onion
- 1 cup thinly sliced green onions
- ¼ cup olive oil

Dressing

- 2 green onions, coarsely chopped
- 3 tablespoons coarsely chopped parsley
- 1 tablespoon chopped garlic
- 2 teaspoons Dijon mustard
- 1 teaspoon dried oregano
- ½ teaspoon dried thyme
- ¼ cup red wine vinegar
- 1 beef-bouillon cube
- ½ teaspoon Worcestershire sauce
- 6 to 8 drops hot pepper sauce
- ½ cup olive oil
  Salt and pepper, to taste

Put cabbage, carrot, red onion, and green onions in a 14-inch mixing or salad bowl. Add olive oil and mix well into the vegetables. Let sit at least 30 minutes or as much as 4 hours. Add Dressing to vegetables, mix well, and serve.

Serves 8.

Dressing Put green onions, parsley, and garlic in food processor fitted with a metal blade and chop fine. Add oregano, thyme, vinegar, bouillon cube, Worcestershire sauce, and hot pepper sauce. With processor running, gradually add olive oil in a continuous stream. Taste and add salt and pepper as desired.

CHICKEN, ANDOUILLE, AND TASSO JAMBALAYA

A one-pot meal that can be made with any combination of seafood, sausage, smoked meats, and chicken, jambalaya is wonderfully satisfying and easy to prepare for small or large groups. The recipe can be increased almost indefinitely. This type of jambalaya, which contains no tomato, is usually referred to as a brown jambalaya. The color comes from the browned onions and smoked meats.

    8 cups chicken stock
    1 chicken, about 3 pounds
    2 pounds andouille, sliced into ¼-inch rounds (see page 67)
    ½ pound tasso, cut into ½-inch dice (see page 67)
    4 cups chopped onion
    ½ cup chopped celery
    2 tablespoons soy sauce (see Note)
    1 cup chopped green onions
    1 tablespoon minced garlic
    1 cup finely chopped green pepper
    ½ teaspoon cayenne
    2 bay leaves
    ½ teaspoon thyme
    ½ teaspoon sage
    2 cups long grain or converted rice
      Salt and pepper, to taste

1. Put stock in a stockpot or Dutch oven and add chicken. Bring to a boil and reduce to a simmer; cook, uncovered, for 45 minutes. Remove chicken from stock; reserve stock and allow chicken to cool. When chicken is cool, remove meat and cut into ½-inch pieces.

2. In a Dutch oven over medium heat, gently fry andouille and tasso until lightly brown, about 10 minutes. With a slotted spoon, remove meat from pan and set aside.

3. Add onion and celery to the pan and fry over medium heat until they are deep brown, about 30 minutes. Add soy sauce and cook another minute. Add green onions, garlic, and green pepper and fry for 5 minutes. Add cayenne, bay leaves, thyme, and sage to the mixture.

4. Add 3 cups of the reserved stock to the pan. Bring to a boil and add rice. Reduce heat to a simmer. Cover and cook about 20 minutes. Stir in chicken and reserved meats; cook until all the liquid is absorbed and the rice is cooked but firm, about another 10 minutes. Taste for seasonings, and add salt and pepper if desired.

Serves 8.

<u>Note</u> Soy sauce is not a traditional ingredient, but it is effective in producing the desired brown color.

SEAFOOD FILÉ GUMBO

For the best gumbo, use a rich home-made stock, high-quality smoked *andouille*, and fresh seafood. Once all the seafood has been cooked, serve immediately so it does not get overcooked. The recipe can be multiplied to serve a crowd. If you do so, cook the seafood separately in small quantities of the gumbo base as you serve it. Once the filé powder is added, the gumbo should not boil because the filé can become stringy.

    1 cup peanut oil
    1 cup flour
    4 cups chopped yellow onion
    1 cup chopped celery
    2 cups chopped red bell pepper
    1½ cups chopped green bell pepper
    2 cups chopped green onions
    3 tablespoons minced garlic
    ½ cup parsley
    6 bay leaves
    1 teaspoon thyme
    ½ teaspoon each oregano and sage
    ½ teaspoon cayenne pepper
    1 teaspoon black pepper
    12 cups chicken, seafood, or fish stock
    ¼ cup tomato paste
    ¼ cup lemon juice
    1½ pounds andouille, sliced in ¼-inch rounds (see page 67)
    ¾ pound medium shrimp, peeled and deveined
    4 to 5 small blue crabs, broken in half (see page 67)
    24 oysters, shucked
      Salt and pepper, to taste
    2 to 3 tablespoons filé powder (see page 67)
    2 cups cooked rice

1. In a 4- to 6-quart Dutch oven combine oil and flour and prepare a light-brown roux the color of peanut butter according to the instructions on page 77. Remove roux from heat and add onions and celery. Return to medium heat and brown vegetables for 10 minutes, stirring frequently. Add bell peppers, green onions, garlic, and parsley; cook another 5 minutes. Add bay leaves, thyme, oregano, sage, cayenne, and black pepper. Cook another 5 minutes. Add stock, tomato paste, and lemon juice. Bring soup to a boil. Reduce to a simmer and cook for 1 hour. Refrigerate overnight or go on to step 2.

2. Add andouille and cook for 10 minutes. Add shrimp and crabs and simmer 5 minutes. Add oysters and cook no longer than 5 minutes. Taste for salt and pepper and adjust if necessary. Remove gumbo from heat and mix in filé powder. Place about 4 tablespoons of cooked rice in each bowl and pour gumbo over it.

Serves 8 to 10.

Saucy grilled pork ribs are not
lone stars at a Texas barbecue.
Piquant salads, buttered corn,
and beans deserve equal billing.
Recipes start on page 100.

The Southwest

The land along the Mexican border has a varied cuisine marked by a pervasive Hispanic influence. Nonetheless, signs of Cajun, Deep South, German, and Native American cookery also abound. Two menus are offered here: a tasty Texas Barbecue (see page 100) of succulent Barbecued Pork Ribs and a Noche Buena Feast (see page 90), a Christmas Eve turkey dinner. A selection of sauces (see page 95) includes three salsas and Guacamole. Two easy and unusual bread recipes (see page 98) are presented—Navaho Fry Bread and Sopaipillas—and an array of desserts includes a luxurious, nut-flavored Flan de Almendras (see page 103).

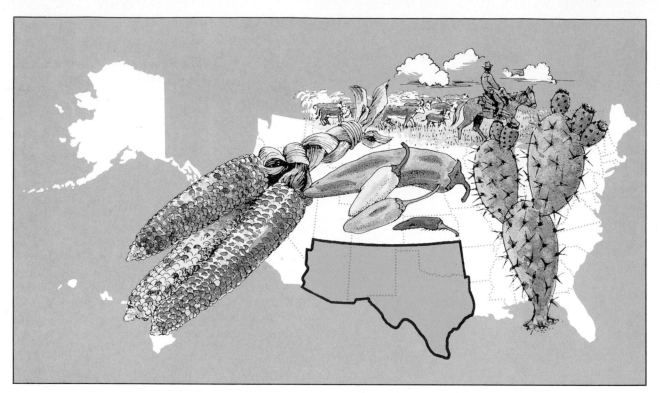

NORTH OF THE BORDER

The land that snakes along the Mexican border (extending some miles to the north and south) is neither Mexico nor America; it's really a third country, with its own special magic.

Up until 1848, Texas, New Mexico, and Arizona were all part of Mexico, and this geopolitical fact is delightfully evident at the dinner table. In addition to corn and flour tortillas, Southwesterners take for granted such exotic south-of-the-border ingredients as avocados, jalapeño chiles, and tomatillos.

Fresh limes and cilantro (coriander) are used as off-handedly as Yankees use lemon juice and parsley. And when a touch of cooking liquor is needed in a stew or dessert, it's likely to be tequila or triple sec—ingredients of a margarita, the Mexican cocktail.

Even chili powder, a crucial ingredient in Texas-style chili, is based on Mexican spices (we recommend using a brand made in Texas, such as Gebhardt's, which is nationally distributed).

Despite the pervasive Hispanic influence, southwestern cooking is anything but monolithic. Texas, for instance, is *so* big that it offers as many different cuisines as some medium-sized countries—from the Cajun influences near the eastern border to the German and Polish smokehouses of the San Antonio–Austin corridor, to the hearty chuck-wagon cookery of the central rangelands.

And in the southern half of the state, earthy Tex-Mex flavors invigorate incendiary delicacies with twice as much "heat" as their counterparts across the border. Farther west in New Mexico, hot and mild chiles are grown and used both fresh and dried in dishes such as Elotes (see page 101), Salsa Roja (see page 95), and Guajolote Relleno (see page 92).

New Mexico's famed blue cornmeal comes from an ancient genetic strain of Indian corn that was saved from extinction; local cooks reintroduced it in mauve corn bread and in the purple tortillas that are casually picked up at Santa Fe groceries.

Arizona, meanwhile, is the source of that fabled revision of the burrito, the giant-sized, ultraluscious chimichanga (see page 89), not to mention those airy, crisp-tender sopaipillas (see page 98), which are served as special treats at both breakfast and dinner.

Native Americans have added their flavors to the excitement of the desert cuisine. Navaho Fry Bread (see page 98), eaten as is or piled high with a spicy filling, is a popular snack from Yuma to Houston. Zuni Lamb, Chile, and Hominy Stew (see page 89) is the favored dish using lamb or mutton—staples of the arid reservation territories in this region. Walaxshi (see page 103), an Oklahoma dessert, originated with the Choctaws.

Throughout the Southwest no one is afraid to try the exotic produce that flourishes in the merciless heat, whether it's the delicate but odd-looking chayote (see Chayote in Cream-Cheese Sauce, page 98) or the spine-covered nopal cactus, which yields both a savory vegetable (see Nopalito Salad, page 94) and a startling red fruit (see Nieve de Tunas, page 94). It took adventurous people to settle the "wild" West, and southwestern cooking remains spectacularly adventurous.

MAIN DISHES

These southwestern main dishes include north-of-the-border variations on the rich cuisine of Mexico along with Native American recipes.

FAJITAS

Fajitas are the strips of marinated and grilled skirt steak that give this dish its name.

1½ pounds skirt steak, trimmed
¼ cup olive or peanut oil
Juice of 2 limes
1 tablespoon chopped cilantro
2 cloves garlic, crushed
1 teaspoon crushed red pepper or 1 jalapeño chile, seeded and diced fine
¼ teaspoon each *salt and black pepper*
⅛ teaspoon smoke flavoring
8 to 12 large (8½ in.) flour tortillas
Guacamole (see page 95) or 3 avocados, sliced and sprinkled with lime juice
Refried Beans or Frijoles (see page 97)
Salsa Cruda (see page 95)

1. To flatten and tenderize meat, pound steak with a meat mallet.

2. Mix oil, lime juice, cilantro, garlic, red pepper, black pepper, salt, and smoke flavoring (if desired). Pour over steak; marinate in refrigerator, turning occasionally, for 1 to 4 days.

3. Preheat oven to 350° F. *To cook fajitas outdoors:* Baste occasionally with marinade. (Fajitas are usually served well-done.) *To cook indoors:* Broil or pan-fry steak. Wrap flour tortillas (in twos or threes) in aluminum foil and heat in oven for 12 minutes.

4. Cut cooked steak across the grain in slices 1 inch long and 3 inches wide. Place slices on a warm platter. Place Guacamole, Refried Beans, Salsa Cruda, and warm tortillas in separate serving dishes. Diners may wrap the steak and garnishes in a tortilla or they may place them separately on their plates.

Serves 4 to 6.

Basics

TYPICAL INGREDIENTS OF SOUTHWESTERN COOKING

Chayote This pale green, Latin American squash has a delicate, slightly sweet flavor and a nutty-tasting edible pit. It can be found in well-stocked greengrocers and Latin markets.

Chiles, dried Powdered *chile pasilla* (semihot), *chile ancho* (mild), New Mexico chile (hot and mild), as well as whole dried chiles of all types can be found at Latin groceries or mail ordered from Casa Moneo, 210 West 14th Street, New York, NY 10011 (catalog $2).

Chorizo This coarsely ground and highly spiced, medium-sized pork sausage can be found in well-stocked delicatessens and supermarkets as well as in Latin groceries. (Also available by mail order; see page 67.)

Cilantro Also called *Chinese parsley*, this garnish is the leaves and stems of the coriander plant. It is always used fresh. Cilantro can be found in well-stocked supermarkets as well as Chinese, Southeast Asian, East Indian, and Latin groceries.

Cornmeal, blue This cornmeal is now widely available (coarsely ground for corn bread or finely ground for tortillas) at large supermarkets and gourmet shops. It may be mail ordered from G. B. Ratto's, 821 Washington Street, Oakland, CA 94607, 800-325-3483 (in California, 800-228-3515; small charge for catalog refundable with order) or from Dean and DeLuca, Mail-Order Dept., 110 Greene Street, Suite 304, New York, NY 10012, 800-221-7714.

Jicama A large root vegetable with a slightly sweet flavor and a crunchy texture, it's readily available almost the year around in Latin, Chinese, Filipino, and Southeast Asian markets.

Mole poblano paste This mixture of ground chocolate, spices, chiles, nuts, and toast is available bottled and canned. It can be found at Latin groceries and many large supermarkets or can be mail ordered from Casa Moneo (see Chiles) or Dean and DeLuca (see Cornmeal).

Nopalitos Young leaves of the nopal cactus, this delicacy can be found fresh, but it's safer to buy bottles of *nopalitos tiernos en rajas*, already despined, poached with jalapeños, and sliced. Bottles may be found in Latin groceries and many large supermarkets or can be mail ordered from Casa Moneo (see Chiles).

Pine nuts (*piñones*) These tiny, rich-tasting white nuts are available in large supermarkets, Italian and French specialty groceries, or by mail from G. B. Ratto's (see Cornmeal).

Prickly pears The oval fruits of the prickly-pear (nopal) cactus can be found in Latin groceries and gourmet greengrocers. Resembling vegetable hand grenades, they're the size of small avocados; their splotchy rinds—mingling dark red, purple, green, and yellow—are covered with little bumps where the spines were (mostly) burned off. Choose fruits with more red and purple than green (these are the ripest and will yield the most pulp), and use plastic bags to handle them at the market and rubber gloves in the kitchen.

Tomatillos These are small, green fruits related to the ground cherry (and not to the tomato). Canned, they may be found in Latin markets and well-stocked supermarkets, or they may be mail ordered from Casa Moneo (see Chiles) and Dean and DeLuca (see Cornmeal).

Arizona's legendary chimi-changa throws culinary caution to the winds; this wild-West specialty—a giant, crisply fried burrito with a rich, melted stuff-ing—is covered with three different toppings, which eventually find their way into the heap of salad in-variably sharing the plate.

CHEROKEE GREEN ONIONS AND EGGS

Oklahoma Cherokees use local wild onions for this dish, which was reput-edly a favorite of Will Rogers. Green onions provide a similar flavor, but the dish can be varied by substituting shallots, chives, garlic (or "Chinese") chives, young leeks—or any combi-nation thereof—for as much as half the green onions. Home gardeners who grow Egyptian onions will find this a delicious use for the bulblets and the greens. Serve Cherokee Green Onions and Eggs for breakfast or lunch, or even for a light supper.

> 3 tablespoons bacon fat
> 2 bunches green onions, whites and crisp green tops, trimmed and sliced in ¼-inch rounds
> Salt, to taste
> ¼ cup water
> 7 large eggs or 6 jumbo eggs
> Freshly ground black pepper (optional)

1. Heat bacon fat in a large, heavy skillet over medium heat. Add green onions and turn in fat to coat. Lower heat, cover, and simmer for about 5 minutes. Uncover, sprinkle lightly with salt, and add water. Cook over low heat for about 10 more minutes, stirring occasionally, until green on-ions are tender but not brown. If water is all absorbed, add more by tablespoons.

2. Break eggs into the skillet and stir with a fork until they are scrambled. Raise heat to medium. Continue to stir until eggs are cooked as desired. When they are nearly done, adjust seasoning.

Serves 3 to 4.

ZUNI LAMB, CHILE, AND HOMINY STEW

The mildly spicy lamb stew of the Zuni Indians is rich in flavor. Accompany with Navaho Fry Bread (see page 98), Sopaipillas (see page 98), deep-fried flour tortillas, or rice.

     ¼ cup flour
       Salt and black pepper
  2¼ pounds boneless lamb stew
       meat, trimmed and cut in
       1-inch cubes
     2 tablespoons peanut oil
     1 medium onion, chopped
    16 juniper berries
     1 can (13 oz) tomatillos
     4 semimild, thin-skinned green
       chiles or 2 bell peppers plus 1
       can (4 oz) diced green chiles
     1 can (14½ oz) whole hominy
     2 small dried red peppers or
       1 teaspoon red pepper flakes
     1 teaspoon crumbled oregano
     ¼ cup chopped parsley
     3 small fresh or canned hot
       chiles, seeded and minced
  2½ cups water

1. Mix flour, ½ teaspoon salt, and ¼ teaspoon pepper, and dredge lamb. In a heavy, stove-top casserole, 2½ quarts or larger, heat oil over high heat. Add half of the lamb cubes and brown, trickling in more oil as needed. Remove lamb with a slotted spoon and reserve. Brown remaining lamb.

2. Put onion in casserole and sauté over medium heat. Crush juniper berries in a mortar (or with a rolling pin) and stir into frying onions. Lower heat to medium and continue sautéing, stirring occasionally, until onions are wilted and transparent.

3. As onions fry, purée tomatillos in a blender or food processor, and cut the mild chiles in 1-inch dice. Add drained tomatillos and hominy, mild chiles, reserved meat, red peppers, oregano, parsley, hot chiles, and water to onions. Stir well, bring to a boil, lower heat, and cover. Simmer for about 1½ hours, until meat and peppers are tender. Skim any visible fat from the surface, season to taste with black pepper and salt.

Serves 6 to 8.

TUCSON CHIMICHANGAS WITH ALL THE TRIMMINGS

A *chimichanga* is Arizona's long, lusciously overstuffed version of a burrito that is deep-fried until crisp all over and garnished to the point of disguise with salsa, guacamole, sour cream, and a sort of undressed salad. One chimichanga per person is sufficient for all but the heartiest eaters. If desired, serve a small portion of Refried Beans (see page 97) as well.

  1½ cups shredded cooked turkey
       or chicken
  1¼ cups grated Monterey jack
       cheese
     1 can (4 oz) diced mild green
       chiles, drained and rinsed
     2 cups chopped (in ½-inch
       pieces) fresh tomatoes (about
       2 medium tomatoes)
     2 tablespoons minced fresh
       cilantro
     ½ teaspoon ground cumin
     ½ teaspoon crumbled dried
       oregano
     ½ teaspoon salt (or to taste)
     3 tablespoons bottled salsa
       jalapeña
     2 tablespoons vegetable oil
     2 medium cloves garlic, minced
     1 medium onion, minced
       (about 1¼ cups)
     6 to 8 large (10 to 12 in.) flour
       tortillas (see Note)
       Vegetable oil for deep-frying
       Salsa Roja (see page 95) or
       Salsa Verde (see page 95)
       Guacamole (see page 95)
       Approximately 2 cups sour
       cream, for garnish
     1 head lettuce, shredded, for
       garnish
     2 large fresh tomatoes, chopped,
       for garnish
     1 can (4 oz) sliced black olives,
       for garnish
     6 radishes, sliced, for garnish

1. In a large bowl combine turkey or chicken, cheese, chiles, the diced tomatoes, cilantro, cumin, oregano, salt, and *salsa jalapeña*.

2. In a small skillet heat oil. Add garlic and onion and sauté over medium heat until wilted (about 5 minutes), stirring occasionally. Stir into the chicken mixture.

3. Lay a tortilla flat on a work surface. In center of tortilla place a generous rectangle of the chicken mixture (3 to 3½ inches thick, about ½ inch deep), leaving about 2 inches of tortilla uncovered at each end of the rectangle. Fold over both ends of the tortilla, then fold over the sides. Secure well with toothpicks. Repeat the process until you have one rolled chimichanga for each diner.

4. Have salsa of choice, Guacamole, lettuce, the chopped tomatoes, olives, and radishes ready. In a large, deep, heavy skillet, heat an inch of oil until it reaches 350° F. (Oil will be rippling and fragrant. To test, drop in a small bread cube. It should brown in exactly one minute.) Using two long spatulas, gently place a chimichanga in the oil, seam side down. Add a second chimichanga and fry until lightly browned and crisp (about 1 minute), then carefully turn and fry the other side. (Do not be perturbed if a small part of the tortilla breaks off, and some oil penetrates the filling. Continue as if nothing had happened; it will still taste wonderful, and the hole will be covered with sauce and garnishes.) Drain chimichangas on paper towels as they are done, keep warm in a low oven, and continue frying until all the chimichangas are cooked.

5. To serve, place one chimichanga on a plate; remove toothpicks. Coat thinly with salsa and top with a dollop of Guacamole over one half and a dollop of sour cream over the other half. Alongside the chimichanga arrange a pile of lettuce topped with a scattering of sliced olives and radishes and chopped tomatoes.

Serves 6 to 8.

Note Purchase tortillas the same day that you make the chimichangas. If stale, they will crack and let out the filling. If tortillas are slightly brittle, soften them: Wrap them in twos or threes in dampened cloth napkins or dish towels; place in a preheated 350° F oven for 10 minutes.

REAL TEXAS CHILI

Chili originated in Mexico as *chile colorado de res*—meat with red chiles. Texans transformed this simple stew into the elaborate dish we know today. Many Texans are hunting enthusiasts and enjoy this dish with ground venison, but you can use beef with equally good results. Do let the chili stand several hours (preferably overnight) at room temperature in a cool place before serving, to mellow the flavor. Serve it over cooked rice if desired.

- 2 tablespoons bacon fat or oil
- 3 large sweet onions (Walla Walla, Texas sweeties, or red globe), coarsely chopped
- 3 garlic cloves, minced
- 1 medium green bell pepper, seeded and cut in ½-inch dice
- 3 jalapeño or serrano chiles, seeded and minced
- 1½ pounds coarsely ground venison or beef, "chili grind"
- 1½ pounds pork, finely chopped or coarsely ground
- 3½ cups peeled whole tomatoes or 1 can (28 oz)
- 1 can (12 oz) beer
- 1 ounce tequila (optional)
- 5 tablespoons Texas chili powder
- 2 tablespoons powdered chile, either ancho or pasilla or 2 additional tablespoons Texas chili powder
- 2 tablespoons powdered hot New Mexico chile or 1 teaspoon cayenne pepper
- 1 tablespoon cumin (reduce to 2 teaspoons if using Texas chili powder instead of powdered ancho or pasilla)
- 1 teaspoon crumbled dried oregano
- 2 teaspoons paprika
- 2 teaspoons sugar
  Salt, black pepper, and cayenne to taste
- 2 tablespoons masa harina (see Note)
- 3 tablespoons cider vinegar
- 2 cups grated Cheddar cheese
- 2 cups minced red onion
- 2 avocados, sliced just before serving (optional)
  Minced fresh jalapeño chiles, to taste (optional)
- 6 cups cooked rice (optional)
- 6 cups cooked beans (optional)

1. Heat bacon fat in a heavy 6-quart pot. Add the chopped onions and sauté until transparent. Add garlic, bell pepper, and jalapeños and sauté over high heat, stirring constantly, until onions start to brown.

2. Add venison and pork and brown over high heat, stirring frequently and breaking up clumps. When meat has lost its pink color, add tomatoes, beer, tequila (if used), chili powder, powdered chiles, cumin, oregano, paprika, and sugar. Bring to a boil, cover, lower heat, and simmer 1½ hours, or until meat is tender.

3. Taste carefully for seasonings and add salt, black pepper, and—a little at a time—cayenne. (Chili should be spicy but not necessarily blistering.)

4. Ladle off liquid fat from top of chili and discard it. In a medium-sized mixing bowl, stir *masa harina* with cider vinegar. Into this mixture pour a ladleful of liquid from chili. Blend together until masa dissolves into a paste. Stir masa mixture into chili, cover pot, and cook 30 minutes longer, stirring occasionally and breaking up tomatoes with spoon.

5. If possible, let chili sit, covered, at room temperature for at least 6 hours before refrigerating or reheating. To serve, reheat thoroughly. Place cheese, the minced onions, avocado (if used), and minced jalapeños (if used) in separate small bowls; serve with chili. If desired, serve chili over rice with beans as a side dish.

Serves 6 to 8.

Note Masa harina, available in large supermarkets and Latin groceries, is a finely ground cornmeal. In chili it is used both for thickening and for flavor. Masa harina is available in well-stocked supermarkets and in Latin groceries. Chili may be thickened without masa by uncovering it for the last 30 minutes so that it reduces slightly.

NEW MEXICO NOCHE BUENA FEAST

Chile and Cheese Soup

Guajolote Relleno (Turkey with corn bread and chorizo stuffing)

---

*Mole Poblano ''Gravy''
or American-Style
Turkey Gravy*

Nopalito Salad (Cactus-strip salad)

*Nieve de Tunas
(Prickly-pear snow)*

Red Wine

In Latin America and much of the Southwest, the Christmas feast is typically held on Noche Buena (Christmas Eve). This gala dinner reveals a blend of Mexican and North American cuisines. The menu is easy on the cook: The dessert is prepared a day or two ahead, the salad can be composed while the turkey roasts, and the soup takes only a half hour to complete. Even the turkey ''gravy'' requires no last-minute rush since it's based on bottled mole poblano paste (see page 87) and can be prepared whenever it's convenient, then reheated just before serving. If desired, a more conventional gravy can be used instead.

The spicy, chocolaty gravy and stuffing for New Mexico's savory version of turkey dinner complement "rabbit ear" nopal cactus salad and dessert.

CHILE AND CHEESE SOUP

This satiny, slightly spicy soup has a creamy golden broth decorated by a confetti of multicolored diced vegetables.

    4   tablespoons unsalted butter
    1   large yellow onion, minced fine
    1   small clove garlic, minced
    1   large carrot, peeled and cut in ¼-inch dice
    1   large, semimild thin-skinned chile (such as Anaheim, guero, or New Mexico mild), seeded and cut in ¼-inch dice (about ⅓ cup) (see Note)
    1   small bell pepper (preferably red or yellow), seeded and cut in ¼-inch dice
    3   fresh jalapeño chiles, seeded and minced fine (see Note)
    4   tablespoons flour
    3   cups chicken stock
    1   cup whole milk
    1   cup whipping cream
    1   cup grated Monterey jack cheese (about 3 oz)
    1   cup grated longhorn Cheddar cheese (about 3 oz)
        Salt and white pepper, to taste
        Paprika, for garnish

1. In a heavy 2½-quart saucepan over medium heat, melt butter. Add onion, garlic, carrot, semimild chile, and pepper. Lower heat and simmer until vegetables are crisp-tender (about 10 minutes). Stir in jalapeños.

2. Sprinkle flour over vegetables and cook over very low heat, stirring, about 3 minutes, to toast flour slightly.

3. Mix stock and milk; pour into pan in a thin stream, stirring constantly to blend smoothly. Increase heat to high and bring mixture to a boil, continuing to stir constantly. Lower heat and simmer until the mixture is slightly thickened, stirring occasionally (about 10 minutes).

4. Stir in cream, then cheeses, and continue stirring over very low heat until cheeses have melted. Add salt and pepper to taste. Soup may be covered and set aside for several hours or refrigerated for up to a week. To serve, reheat gently over low heat, stirring frequently (do not boil). When soup is hot, sprinkle surface with paprika and serve.

Makes about 8 cups, 8 servings.

Note If fresh, semimild chiles are unavailable, use ⅓ cup canned diced chiles, adding them to pan along with the jalapeños. If a milder soup is desired, use only one jalapeño.

GUAJOLOTE RELLENO
Turkey with mole-style corn bread and chorizo stuffing

This festive dish is a North American adaptation of the famous Mexican specialty, *mole poblano de guajolote* (turkey in chocolate sauce), with a rich, savory base of bitter chocolate and exotic spices (it is not at all sweet). Here, a simplified version of mole (pronounced *MO-lay)* sauce moistens the nut-studded stuffing. The roasting is completed by the old-fashioned brown-bag method, which requires minimal attention from the cook and will roast turkeys up to 21 pounds in precisely 3 hours. Leftover turkey is especially delicious in Tucson Chimichangas (see page 89), or simply reheated in additional mole sauce.

    1   cup shelled pine nuts or chopped almonds
    1   recipe Southern Corn Bread (see page 37)
    2   chorizos (about ½ lb total)
    ¼   pound lean pork, finely diced (meat from one loin pork chop)
    1   small semimild, thin-skinned chile (Anaheim, guero, or New Mexico mild) or bell pepper, diced
    2   cups seedless golden raisins
    ½   teaspoon salt
    2   teaspoons coriander seed, crushed or ground just before using
    1   teaspoon cinnamon
    ½   teaspoon ground cloves
    2   squares (1 oz each) bitter chocolate
    1   cup chicken stock
    1   turkey (12 lb)
    ½   cup butter, at room temperature

1. Scatter pine nuts on a baking sheet or pie pan. While corn bread bakes, place pan in oven and toast until nuts are lightly browned (about 10 minutes), shaking every few minutes to turn nuts. Remove when done, cool, and turn off oven to cool. Coarsely crumble cooled corn bread and place in a mixing bowl or pot with a 6-quart capacity. Add cooled nuts.

2. Strip chorizo out of casing and place sausage in a large skillet with pork. Fry chorizo and pork over medium heat until browned through, stirring frequently and breaking up clumps with a fork. Add chile and turn for a few seconds in the hot oil rendered by meats.

3. Add chorizo mixture to corn bread. Stir in raisins, salt, coriander, cinnamon, and cloves.

4. Break chocolate into small pieces, place in a small, heavy pot, and add chicken stock. Stir over low heat until chocolate melts. Pour chocolate mixture over corn bread mixture and toss to blend all ingredients. When it is cool enough to handle, stuff neck cavity and body cavity of turkey and truss tightly. (If using trussing pins, push baker's string through the holes of the pins, crisscross the string between the pins, and tie ends together so that string is taut and turkey is held together compactly.) If there is extra stuffing, bake it in a covered casserole after the turkey is done.

5. Lay a large, heavy-duty, brown-paper grocery bag (see Note) on a flat surface, opening facing you. Smear about half of the butter all over the bottom of the inside of the bag (reserving remaining butter). Turn the bag over and place it on the rack of a large roasting pan so that the buttered side of the inside is on top. Place a sheet of aluminum foil inside the bag, covering the bottom. Slide the turkey into the bag, breast side down, on top of the aluminum foil. *Or:* Place bag directly in pan, and put rack inside bag; place turkey on top of rack. (You may need a helper to hold the bag open.) Tightly close end of bag with a wire tie.

6. Place turkey in a cold oven and turn the heat to 500° F. Roast for precisely 1 hour, then turn heat down to 400° F. Roast 1 hour longer and turn heat down to 300° F. Roast just 1 hour longer and remove turkey from the oven, still in the bag in the roasting pan. Cooking time is a total of 3 hours, regardless of size of turkey. *Do not attempt to turn the bird,* or the bag will break and the drippings will pour out into the oven. The bag will look and smell charred as the oven reaches roasting temperature, but the buttering on top and drippings underneath will keep it from catching fire. This method leaves back, legs, and sides of the bird beautifully browned and succulent, and the breast meat moist and tender. (The breast skin, however, will partially dissolve.)

7. Very carefully, tear off and discard brown bag in pieces from the top and upper sides of turkey, leaving lower half of bag in place. The bottom of the bag will be full of drippings. Using a bulb baster, remove drippings to a medium bowl; if you have leftover stuffing, or plan to make American-style gravy, reserve drippings. Place turkey on a carving board, turning it breast side up. Strip off and discard remaining paper bag. (Discard any drippings left in the roasting pan since they have percolated through the bag.) Allow turkey to rest for about 20 minutes before carving. Serve the turkey with Mole Poblano "Gravy" or American-Style Turkey Gravy, as you prefer.

8. If you have leftover stuffing to bake, turn oven up to 425° F. Toss ½ cup of the reserved drippings with the leftover stuffing. Cover stuffing and bake about 20 to 30 minutes, while the turkey rests.

Serves at least 8, with leftovers.

<u>Note</u> Do not use a commercial turkey-cooking bag for this recipe, as such bags are unreliable at high temperatures. The paper grocery bag will be sterilized by the heat during the first hour of cooking.

MOLE POBLANO "GRAVY"

>   2 *tablespoons lard*
>   4 *ounces of mole poblano paste (any brand)*
>   1½ *to 2 cups chicken broth*

In a heavy, medium-sized saucepan over medium-low heat, melt the lard. Stir in mole poblano paste and let cook a few seconds, then stir in 1½ cups of chicken broth. Simmer over low heat until thickened, stirring constantly. If sauce thickens excessively (this will vary with the brand of mole poblano paste), stir in the additional ½ cup broth, and heat, stirring, until smooth. Sauce may be adjusted to taste with small amounts of shaved unsweetened chocolate, sugar, salt, hot pepper, ground coriander, cinnamon, or cloves.

Makes about 2 cups.

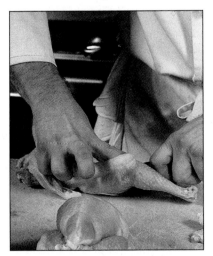

AMERICAN-STYLE TURKEY GRAVY

For those who prefer a sweeter, less spicy gravy, this traditional sauce will provide a flavorful accompaniment to any holiday turkey.

>   *Turkey neck and giblets, chopped*
>   1 *large onion, trimmed and quartered*
>   1 *carrot, coarsely chopped*
>   1 *stalk celery, coarsely chopped*
>   2 *tablespoons butter*
>   2 *tablespoons flour*
>   *About ½ cup (or more, if available) reserved turkey drippings*
>   *Salt, white pepper, and nutmeg, to taste*
>   *Freshly squeezed lemon juice, to taste (optional)*

1. While turkey roasts, place turkey neck and giblets in a heavy 1½-quart saucepan. Cover with about 3 cups cold water. Bring to a boil over high heat and skim off scum from the top. Add onion, carrot, and celery and return to a boil. Lower heat to a simmer and cook slowly for about 2 hours, until liquid has reduced to a rich broth. Strain and reserve.

2. When turkey has completed roasting, melt butter in a medium-sized, heavy pan. Add flour and stir over low heat until flour begins to turn golden (about 2 minutes). Pour in 1½ cups broth and the reserved drippings, stirring strongly until smooth. Stirring constantly, bring to a boil. Lower heat and simmer about 5 minutes longer to thicken, stirring occasionally. Season with salt, white pepper, and nutmeg. Squeeze in lemon juice by droplets, if desired.

Makes about 2 cups.

NOPALITO SALAD
Cactus-strip salad

This lively salad is based on poached strips of the nopal, a cactus, and jicama, a large, turniplike root vegetable with a slightly sweet, crunchy flavor. See page 87 for information on obtaining these ingredients.

½ small red onion
1 jar (12 to 14 oz) nopalitos tiernos en rajas (young nopal in strips)
1 or 2 canned or pickled jalapeño chiles, seeded and sliced (optional)
1 small or half a large jicama root
2 medium cucumbers, peeled
2 small green bell peppers, trimmed and seeded
2 small red bell peppers, trimmed and seeded
3 thick green onions
1 can (4 oz) sliced black olives
¼ cup minced parsley
2 heaping tablespoons minced cilantro
½ cup grated Monterey jack cheese or crumbled farmer cheese
2 firm, ripe avocados
1 jar (2 oz) sliced pimientos, drained and rinsed, for garnish

Dressing

½ cup peanut or olive oil
⅓ cup freshly squeezed lime juice (the juice of about 4 small limes)
3 medium cloves garlic, crushed
½ teaspoon sugar
¼ teaspoon ground cumin seeds
    Salt and freshly ground black pepper, to taste

1. Prepare Dressing and chill it for about an hour.

2. Slice onion into thin rings and place in a bowl of ice water. (This will take the bite out of the onions.)

3. Drain nopalitos and place in a large bowl. Nopalitos are usually packed with at least one jalapeño, along with other items such as onion slices and garlic. If a spicy salad is desired, halve the jalapeño, remove seeds, cut in strips, and mix with the nopalitos. Remove the other elements. If you prefer an extremely spicy salad, add one or both of the optional jalapeños.

4. Peel the jicama with a small sharp knife by inserting knife tip just under the beige skin and pulling off the peel in strips. Discard the tough flesh from the root end and top. Cut jicama into matchstick julienne strips (about ¼ inch by ¼ inch by 1½ inches) and add to nopalitos. Cut cucumber, green pepper, and red pepper in matchstick julienne, and add to nopal mixture. Finely mince green onions, including the crisp parts of the green tops, and add to the salad. Add olives, parsley, cilantro, and grated cheese.

5. Remove garlic from Dressing and discard. At the last moment, slice avocados and add to the salad. Immediately dress and toss the salad to keep avocado from darkening. Let salad chill in the refrigerator, marinating in the dressing.

6. To serve, decorate the top of the salad with pimiento slices. Drain onions and scatter on top.

Serves 8.

Dressing Whisk together oil and lime juice; stir in garlic, sugar, cumin, and salt and pepper.

Makes ¾ cup.

NIEVE DE TUNAS
Prickly-pear snow

Prickly pear (see page 87) tastes like a seedy watermelon. Southwesterners often turn the fruit into prickly-pear jam, which has an exquisite color and virtually no flavor. Prickly-pear syrup, however, is good as an ice-cream topping, in milk shakes, and in this light, refreshing "southwestern nouvelle cuisine" sorbet. Handle prickly pears with care! Even store-bought ones retain a few tiny spines that will stick to fingers.

½ cup sugar
1 cup water
6 prickly-pear fruits
1 tablespoon lime or lemon juice
2 egg whites
    Pinch cream of tartar
½ teaspoon orange-peel liqueur

1. Heat sugar and water together in a heavy, 2-quart saucepan over low heat, stirring occasionally until the sugar dissolves. Simmer the mixture for 10 minutes until it has reduced slightly and thickened but has not yet started to color.

2. Meanwhile, *wearing thick rubber or leather gloves*, halve the prickly pears and spoon out the pulp. (Discard the shells before removing gloves.) Add the prickly-pear pulp and lime juice to the reduced sugar mixture, and simmer until fruit is mushy (about 20 minutes).

3. Briefly purée the prickly-pear mixture in a food processor or blender. With a wooden spoon, push purée through a strainer into a bowl. Discard seeds left in the strainer. Pour syrupy purée into two pie pans and freeze until partly solid (2½ hours), stirring the purée after one hour and again 30 minutes later.

4. Beat egg whites with cream of tartar until they are stiff but not dry. Remove the frozen prickly-pear purée from the freezer and stir again (or purée again in the food processor if it has become too firm to stir). Blend in the orange liqueur, then fold the purée into the egg white. Place the sorbet in a serving bowl, cover with plastic wrap, and return to the freezer until it chills to the consistency of ice cream (in 3 to 4 hours). (Sorbet will keep frozen for 2 to 3 weeks.) Before serving, place in the refrigerator for 30 minutes to soften slightly.

Serves 6 to 8.

Variation Serve the syrup yielded at the end of step 3 over vanilla ice cream or fresh-fruit salad, or use it to lend a brilliant beet-red color to any fruit dessert.

SAUCES

Where there are tortillas, there must be Mexican-style sauces to moisten them. This group includes a fiery Salsa Roja from the desert states; a tangy, exotic Salsa Verde; a fresh and spicy Salsa Cruda; and a soothingly suave Guacamole to quench the fires.

SALSA ROJA
Red chile sauce

If you cannot obtain powdered chiles (see page 87), use a Texas brand of chile powder, omit cumin, and add a little cayenne. Sauce should be quite spicy.

- 2 tablespoons lard or peanut oil
- 1 medium clove garlic, peeled and finely minced
- 2 tablespoons powdered dried mild chile (ancho, pasilla, or California)
- 2 tablespoons powdered New Mexico hot chile
- 1½ cups chicken broth
- ¼ teaspoon crumbled dried oregano
- ⅛ teaspoon ground cumin
  Pinch each ground cloves and ground cinnamon
  Salt, to taste (¼ to ¾ teaspoon)
- 1 egg, beaten

1. Melt lard in a small (1- or 1½-quart), heavy saucepan. Add garlic and cook over a low flame until translucent (about a minute). Add chile powders and stir constantly over a low flame until they darken slightly (about 20 seconds), taking care not to scorch them. Pour in just enough broth to make a wet paste and continue stirring for a minute, until the chile odor mellows. Pour in remaining broth, and add oregano, cumin, cloves, cinnamon, and salt. Bring to a boil, lower heat, and simmer 5 minutes. Remove from heat.

2. To thicken and enrich the sauce, use a large serving spoon to remove some of the chile mixture from saucepan. Holding spoon about 6 inches above beaten egg (to allow liquid to cool slightly), pour liquid into the beaten egg. Immediately whisk them together energetically until they are blended. Pour egg mixture into the remaining sauce and whisk well.

Makes 1¾ cups, sufficient for 8 chimichangas or enchiladas.

SALSA CRUDA
Mexican-style chunky hot sauce

This fresh, spicy table sauce is also called *pico de gallo* (rooster's beak) or *salsa fresca* (uncooked sauce).

- 1 pound fresh ripe tomatoes, seeded and cut into ¼-inch dice (about 2 c)
- ⅓ cup finely minced sweet red onion or white of scallion
- 4 fresh jalapeño or serrano chiles, trimmed, seeded, and minced fine
- ¼ cup minced cilantro
- 1 small clove garlic, peeled and minced fine
  Juice of 1 lime
  Salt and pepper, to taste

Combine all ingredients in a small bowl. Taste for seasoning and correct if necessary. Let stand at room temperature about 30 minutes to develop flavors. Serve the same day, or tightly cover with plastic wrap and refrigerate for no more than 2 days.

Makes about 3 cups.

GUACAMOLE

- 3 ripe medium-sized avocados (preferably Hass variety)
- 1 ripe, medium tomato, seeded, juiced and finely diced (a scant cup)
- 2 heaping tablespoons minced cilantro
- 2 tablespoons onion or white of green onion, finely minced
- 2 tablespoons freshly squeezed lime or lemon juice, or more, to taste
- 1 or 2 small hot fresh chiles (jalapeño or serrano), finely minced or bottled Mexican-style hot salsa, to taste
  Salt and pepper, to taste

1. Cut avocados in half lengthwise. Remove pits and scoop out the pulp with a tablespoon. Mash pulp with a fork until it is fairly smooth. (If avocados are not quite ripe, mash at least the softest one with a fork, and briefly purée the others in a food processor or blender.)

2. Stir in tomato, cilantro, and onion. Blend in lime juice by tablespoons, tasting carefully. Stir in half the minced chile and taste for spiciness, adding the remainder if needed. Season carefully with salt and pepper. Serve immediately, or cover well with plastic wrap and refrigerate for no more than 30 minutes.

Serves 4 as side dish or 6 to 8 as chimichanga garnish.

SALSA VERDE
Green sauce

This sauce, made with tomatillos (see page 87), is used with Tucson Chimichangas (see page 89); you could also use it with cheese or poultry enchiladas.

- 2 cans (13 oz each) tomatillos, drained
- 2 cans (4 oz each) diced mild green chiles, drained
- 4 jalapeño chiles or 6 serrano chiles (fresh, canned, or pickled), trimmed, seeded, and coarsely chopped
- 3 tablespoons minced cilantro
- 1 large clove garlic
- 2 teaspoons sugar
- 2 tablespoons lard or cooking oil
- 1 cup chicken broth
- 4 tablespoons whipping cream or half-and-half
  Salt and black pepper, to taste

1. In a blender or food processor, purée tomatillos, mild chiles, hot chiles, cilantro, garlic, and sugar to form a thick, grainy liquid.

2. Heat lard in a large skillet, add purée, and fry over high heat for 2 to 3 minutes, stirring constantly. Add broth, lower heat, and simmer for another two minutes. Stir in cream and season carefully to taste.

Makes sauce for 8 chimichangas.

HOW TO ROAST AND PEEL CHILES

Fresh chiles often have tough, thick skins that must be removed. Wear rubber gloves if you are peeling many chiles or if you have sensitive skin.

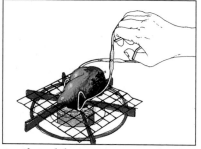

1. *Char chile over a gas or electric burner turned to highest heat and, if possible, covered with a metal screen. Turn frequently with tongs or cooking fork. Chile is done when skin is charred and blistered. Take care not to burn through to the flesh. Immediately place chile in a paper or thick plastic bag, close bag, and let steam 15 to 20 minutes.*

2. *Remove from bag and, under cold running water, slip off skin, starting from stem end. Use a small, sharp knife on any stubborn spots.*

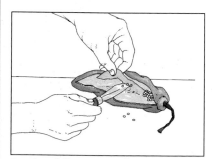

3. *Cut chile open and remove veins and seeds. Wash out the last of the seeds under running water.*

SOUPS, SIDE DISHES, AND VEGETABLES

"Never saw a man so tired he couldn't eat some beans," said the old prospector in *Treasure of the Sierra Madre*. Here are two classic southwestern bean dishes (a soup and a hearty vegetable course), along with dishes celebrating desert-country vegetation—luscious stuffed chiles and sensuous chayote squash.

CHILES EN NOGADA

This festive appetizer originated in Puebla, the walnut capital of Mexico, where it's eaten at the feast of St. Augustine (August 28) and on Mexico's Independence Day (September 15)—the colors mirror the green, white, and red of the Mexican flag. In Austin and San Antonio, however, Chiles en Nogada are eaten all year around. Combining sweetness, spiciness, and crunchiness, they are far easier to prepare than the standard version of *chiles rellenos*, which requires batter and frying.

> 6 large, fresh poblano chiles (see Note)
> 2 tablespoons lard or oil
> ½ pound ground pork
> ½ pound ground beef
> 1 small onion, minced
> 1 large clove garlic, minced
> 1 large tomato, peeled and chopped, or 1 can (8 oz) tomatoes, chopped
> 1 to 3 fresh or canned jalapeño chiles, trimmed, seeded, and minced
> ½ cup seedless raisins, soaked in hot tap water to cover
> 1 small apple, peeled, cored, and diced
> 1 small pear, peeled, cored, and diced
> 2½ teaspoons cinnamon
> ½ teaspoon ground cloves
>   Sugar
> 2 tablespoons vinegar
>   Salt and pepper, to taste
> ½ cup chopped blanched almonds or pine nuts
> 1 package (3 oz) Neufchâtel cheese or cream cheese
> 1 cup whipping cream
> ¾ cup blanched almonds
> ¾ cup chopped walnuts
> 2 tablespoons parsley
>   Seeds from 1 fresh pomegranate or 1 jar (2 oz) sliced pimientos, drained, for garnish

1. Roast, peel, and seed fresh chiles (see How to Roast and Peel Chiles at left); set aside.

2. In a large skillet over high heat, heat lard. Add pork and beef and sauté until browned, stirring and breaking up clumps.

3. Add onion, garlic, tomato, and jalapeños and continue to sauté until onions wilt (5 minutes). Stir in raisins, apple, pear, 2 teaspoons of cinnamon, cloves, 1 teaspoon sugar, vinegar, salt and pepper; sauté until fruits are soft and mixture thickens, about 7 minutes. Stir in nuts. Taste and add more sugar if desired. Keep warm until ready to serve.

4. Cut cheese into about 6 pieces, place in a small, heavy saucepan, and cover with about ⅓ cup of the cream. Melt cheese over low heat, stirring constantly, until mixture is smooth. In a food processor or blender, grind together almonds, walnuts, parsley, remaining cinnamon, and, if desired, ½ teaspoon sugar. Beat the remaining cream to soft peaks. Fold nut mixture into whipped cream, then add melted cheese mixture and fold in until blended.

5. Gently stuff poblano chiles with fruit mixture. (If some of the chiles split along the side despite your best efforts, lay them flat and spoon the meat mixture on top of them.) Spoon cheese sauce over chiles. Decorate with a scattering of pomegranate seeds or a cross of pimiento strips. Serve immediately.

Serves 6.

Note If poblano chiles are unavailable, substitute 12 large mild Anaheim chiles or 6 medium red or green bell peppers. If necessary, 2 cans (8 oz each) whole mild chiles may also be used, but there will be some loss of texture.

BLACK-BEAN SOUP

Rich and smoky, this soup can serve as a substantial first course or as a hearty main dish served with warmed corn tortillas, Navaho Fry Bread (see page 98), Southern Corn Bread (see page 37), or Texas Jalapeño-Cheese Corn Bread (see page 99). For this recipe the beans should not be pre-soaked, or the soup will be pale.

- 3 thick slices bacon (about 5 oz), chopped in ½-inch pieces
- 2 large onions, coarsely minced (about 3 cups)
- 4 large garlic cloves, minced fine (scant 2 tablespoons)
- 6 cups chicken broth
- 2 cups water
- ½ pound baked ham, cut in ½-inch dice
- 2 tablespoons ground cumin
- 2 tablespoons crumbled dried oregano
- 2 teaspoons crushed coriander seed
- 2 teaspoons crumbled dried thyme
- 3 whole cloves
- ½ teaspoon coarsely ground pepper
- 3 to 4 canned or pickled jalapeño chiles, seeded and minced
- 1 pound dried black turtle beans
  Salt, to taste

Garnishes

- 2 cups sour cream
- 2 large tomatoes, chopped
- ½ cup (approximately) minced green onions, white part only
  Grated Cheddar cheese, to taste
  Chopped avocado, to taste
  Salsa Cruda (see page 95) or bottled chunky hot sauce, to taste

1. In a large heavy pot, 3 quarts or larger, over medium heat, sauté bacon until it begins to brown. Add onions and garlic, decrease heat to medium-low, and sauté, stirring often, until onions are transparent (about 10 minutes).

2. Add broth, water, ham, cumin, oregano, coriander, thyme, cloves, pepper, and jalapeños. Stir in beans, bring to a boil, and lower heat to a simmer. Simmer, partly covered, until beans are tender (2½ to 3 hours), stirring occasionally. If too much liquid evaporates, add 1 additional cup water.

3. Using a slotted spoon, remove about half the beans and place in the bowl of a food processor fitted with metal blade or in a blender. (Work in two batches if necessary.) Purée them to a mush. Stir purée back into soup.

4. Reheat soup over low heat, stirring often, for about 10 minutes. Carefully taste for seasoning; add salt if necessary. To serve, ladle soup into deep bowls, and top each portion with a dollop of sour cream. Place small bowls of tomato, green onions, cheese, avocado, and salsa on the table, to be sprinkled on the soup as desired.

Serves 8 to 10 as first course, 5 to 6 as main dish.

FRIJOLES

Homemade beans do taste better than beans from a can, most notably in the case of southwestern indispensable, refried beans (see variation at right). Although pinto beans take a long time to cook, they need little attention until the end. Note that they have to soak overnight.

- 1 pound dry pinto beans
- 16 cups cold water
- 1 large onion, coarsely chopped (about 1½ cups)
- 1 tablespoon minced garlic (about 2 cloves)
- ¼ teaspoon crushed red pepper
- 3 tablespoons bacon fat or lard
- 1 medium onion, finely chopped (about 1 cup)
- 1 large tomato, peeled, seeded, and coarsely chopped (about 1 cup)
  Salt and black pepper, to taste

1. In a large pot soak beans overnight in 8 cups of cold water.

2. Drain and add 8 cups fresh water, the coarsely chopped onion, garlic, and red pepper. Bring to a boil, lower heat, cover, and simmer until beans are tender (about 90 minutes).

3. Heat bacon fat in a medium skillet over moderate heat, add the finely chopped onion, and sauté until wilted. Add tomato and sauté until it softens. Scoop ½ cup of the beans out of their liquid, place in a small bowl, and mash well with a fork. Add mashed beans to skillet and ladle in a little of their liquid (about ¼ cup). Stir mixture over low heat until it becomes a thick paste.

4. Spoon contents of skillet into bean pot. Simmer, stirring frequently, until liquid thickens (about 30 minutes). Season to taste with salt and pepper.

Serves 6 to 8.

Texas Jalapeño Pinto Beans
Complete steps 1 through 3. Spoon contents of skillet into bean pot and add canned or pickled jalapeño chiles to taste—up to an entire 4-ounce can for a very, very spicy dish. Continue with step 4.

Refried Beans Complete steps 1 and 2. Drain cooked beans, reserving liquid. Mash well with a fork or a potato masher (not a food processor). In a large, heavy skillet, heat 3 tablespoons of rendered bacon fat with 4 tablespoons of lard until it is aromatic and almost smoking. Very carefully add mashed beans (they will spatter) and lower heat. Cook over medium-low heat, stirring frequently, until fat is absorbed. Thin to desired consistency with some of the reserved cooking liquid, stirring it in by tablespoons. Add ¼ pound Monterey jack cheese, coarsely grated, and cook about 15 minutes longer, until cheese is completely absorbed. Season with salt and pepper to taste.

CHAYOTE IN CREAM-CHEESE SAUCE

This simple but luxurious recipe of Mexican origin can also be made with green patty-pan summer squash.

- 2 medium chayotes or 1 pound patty-pan squash
- 4 tablespoons unsalted butter
- 1 small onion, minced
- 1 package (3 oz) cream cheese or 3 ounces Neufchâtel cheese, at room temperature
- 1 cup sour cream or crème fraîche
- 4 tablespoons minced parsley
  Pinch of crushed coriander seed
  Pinch of dried tarragon (optional)
  Salt and freshly ground pepper, to taste

1. With a potato peeler, peel chayotes. Cut in ¼-inch-thick slices. Chop the central pit to the consistency of chopped nuts. (If using patty-pan squash, do not peel; instead, trim stem end and slice.)

2. In a large skillet over medium-low heat, melt butter. Add onion and sauté until it is wilted. Add chayote slices and chopped pit; sauté over low heat until tender (about 15 minutes), flipping slices occasionally with a spatula.

3. Meanwhile, mash cheese with a fork and blend with sour cream. Add half of the parsley, then add coriander and tarragon (if used); season with salt and pepper. When chayote is tender, pour cheese mixture over it in the skillet and heat very briefly over the lowest possible flame, stirring, until sauce reaches serving temperature (do not allow to boil, or sour cream will curdle). Garnish with remaining parsley and serve hot.

Serves 4.

BREADS

In the dry heat of the Southwest, few cooks will put up with the long kneading, long rising times, and long spells tending a hot oven that are all required by conventional yeast breads. Typical, instead, are the elaborate—but easy—spicy corn bread of the region and the light, savory stovetop fried breads borrowed from Mexican and Amerindian cuisines.

NAVAHO FRY BREAD

Navaho Fry Bread is both simple to make and addictive to eat. The bouncy, elastic dough is very forgiving and is even more easily handled when well chilled. Uncooked, the dough rounds look like tortillas, but before they are fried, a small hole is poked in the middle of each round to keep the center from puffing. Serve plain or substitute for tortillas; top them with Fajitas (see page 87), Zuni Lamb, Chile, and Hominy Stew (see page 89), Chiles En Nogada filling (see page 96), or a nacholike topping of warm Refried Beans (see page 97), grated cheese, and strips of canned jalapeños or canned mild chiles.

- 2 cups flour (more as needed)
- 1 tablespoon baking powder
- 1 teaspoon salt
- 1 tablespoon shortening or lard
- 1 cup boiling water
- 2 cups corn or peanut oil

1. Combine flour, baking powder, and salt. Add shortening and rub mixture between your fingers until shortening is well broken up. Pour the water into flour mixture and stir with a fork until mixture forms a ball. If the flour remains dry, add very hot tap water, ¼ cup at a time, and knead in with fingers. Should dough become too wet to form a ball, add flour by tablespoons. As soon as dough forms a firm ball, cover with plastic wrap and allow to rest at room temperature for 45 minutes, or refrigerate overnight or longer. (Dough will keep, chilled, for about a week. It may also be frozen for up to two months and defrosted in refrigerator when needed.)

2. Lightly flour a pastry board or a sheet of waxed paper. Take a lump of dough about the size of a lime or a plum and lightly sprinkle it with flour. Place dough on floured work surface and push it down with the heel of your hand so that it forms a slightly flattened round. Sprinkle flour on both sides of the round and swiftly roll out to a rough circle about 5 inches in diameter (like a small corn tortilla). As each circle is rolled out, place it on an individual sheet of lightly floured waxed paper until ready to fry. (A delay of up to an hour will make little or no difference.)

3. In a Dutch oven or heavy deep skillet, heat oil to 375° F. Just before frying poke a small hole in the center of each round of dough. Fry rounds, one by one, until they are browned, puffed, and crisped (about 2 minutes per side), turning with tongs halfway through cooking; regulate heat to maintain a temperature between 350° and 370° F. Remove from oil when done and drain on paper towels. Serve hot.

Makes eight to ten 5-inch fry-bread rounds.

SOPAIPILLAS
"Pillows"

These airy fried puffs, beloved of southwesterners, can be served for breakfast, or at dinner (in place of bread), or even for dessert. The dough is not hard to make or to roll; it's easier yet if the dough is chilled overnight.

- 2 cups flour
- ½ teaspoon salt
- 2 teaspoons baking powder
- 2 teaspoons sugar
- 2 tablespoons lard or shortening
- ½ scant cup (approximately) hot tap water
  Cooking oil
  Confectioners' sugar
- 1 cup (approximately) honey

1. Sift together flour, salt, baking powder, and sugar. With a pastry blender or your fingers, cut in lard to make an even, lumpy meal. Add water, stirring with a fork, until a dough is formed. Flour your hands and rapidly knead the dough about 12 times. If the dough sticks, sprinkle on more flour by tablespoons and knead it in until the dough is easily handled. If dough is too crumbly and dry to knead, add more hot water by tablespoons. After kneading, cover dough with plastic wrap and let stand at room temperature for about 30 minutes, or refrigerate overnight.

2. Heat oven to 325° F. Pour at least 1½ inches of oil into a deep skillet or Dutch oven and heat to 375° to 380° F. Meanwhile, flour a work surface and roll out dough in a rectangle about ¼ inch thick. Cut dough into 3-inch squares. Drop squares into hot oil, a few at a time, maintaining a temperature between 360° and 385° F. The squares will fall, then rise as they puff into "pillows." Push them down and turn often until they are golden. Remove with a slotted spoon, drain on paper towels, and keep warm in oven. Sprinkle with confectioners' sugar and serve with honey to spoon into the cavities.

Makes 16 puffs.

TEXAS JALAPEÑO-CHEESE CORN BREAD

This moist, multiflavored bread is a substantial side dish.

> 1½ cups yellow cornmeal
> 1½ tablespoons flour
> ½ teaspoon salt
> 2 tablespoons sugar
> 1 tablespoon baking powder
> ¾ cup minced onion
> 1¼ cups buttermilk
> 1 can (8 oz) creamed corn or 1 cup fresh corn scraped with its "cream" from the cob (see Corn Pudding, page 11)
> ½ cup melted butter
> 1 cup grated Cheddar cheese
> ½ pound chorizo, fried and chopped fine (optional)
> ¼ to ½ cup minced canned jalapeño chiles or 1 can (4 oz) diced mild chiles

1. Preheat oven to 400° F. Stir together cornmeal, flour, salt, sugar, and baking powder. Add onion, buttermilk, corn, and butter; mix rapidly until flour is well moistened. (Batter may be refrigerated overnight.)

2. Grease 8-inch square baking pan or 10-inch cast-iron skillet. Pour in half the batter. Sprinkle on half the cheese, chorizo (if used), jalapeños, then remaining cheese. Cover with remaining batter and bake until firm (45 to 50 minutes). If top is not browned, broil for 5 minutes. To serve, cut into 2-inch squares or pie-shaped wedges.

Makes 16 squares or 8 wedges.

Jalapeño Corn Muffins Preheat oven to 425° F. Mix cheese and chiles into batter; do not use chorizo. Pour into 12 to 16 greased muffin cups and bake 20 to 25 minutes.

Blue Corn Bread Preheat oven to 350° F. Use coarse-milled blue cornmeal; do not use chorizo. Bake for 1 hour.

Arizona's sopaipillas are heavenly squares of deep-fried dough. Served piping hot, these weightless "pillows" are ready to receive a spoonful of honey in their hollow centers.

TEXAS BARBECUE

*Barbecued Pork Ribs
and Sausages*

East Texas Caviar

Frijoles (see page 97)

*Elotes (Corn on the cob
with lime-chile butter)*

Jicama and Fruit Relish

Soft Rolls

Ice Creams of Choice

*Beer, Soft Drinks,
Lemonade*

---

*A full-blown Texas
ranch barbecue is
an all-day affair. A
typical menu
includes a selection
of meats ranging
from a 10-pound
beef brisket to pork
back ribs and
chickens on down to
sausages; corn on
the cob is roasted
along with the
barbecued meats.
The menu is
completed with
Frijoles, "caviar" (a
succulent salad
made from black-
eyed peas), and the
spicy-sweet relish.*

BARBECUED PORK RIBS AND SAUSAGES

Texas barbecue calls for a grill with a cover, and a supply of mesquite chips or mesquite charcoal, since the meats are slowly smoked, rather than just grilled. Texas barbecue is also distinguished by the use of two separate sauces. The meats are continually basted with a "moppin' sauce," which should not contain sugar or tomatoes—these would burn. (Leftover basting sauce may be refrigerated for several weeks or frozen indefinitely.) At serving the cooked meats are dabbed with a "soppin' sauce"— the familiar, sweet-sour tomatoey sauce we associate with Texas cooking. The following recipe is suited to a medium-sized barbecue grill and a medium-sized crowd.

> 6 pounds thick-cut pork country ribs or back ribs, in slabs
> 6 to 12 mixed sausages of choice (hot links, garlic sausage, kielbasa, chorizo, bratwurst, and/or knackwurst)

Basting ("Moppin'") Sauce

½ teaspoon salt
1 teaspoon pepper
4 tablespoons freshly squeezed lemon juice (2 lemons)
1 teaspoon garlic powder
2 teaspoons Texas chili powder
1½ teaspoons paprika
1 teaspoon Louisiana-style hot sauce
1 tablespoon Worcestershire sauce
2 cups beef stock
¼ cup bacon fat or butter
¼ cup vegetable oil

Texas-Style Barbecue ("Soppin'") Sauce

¼ cup butter
¼ cup peanut oil
½ cup minced onion
4 cloves garlic, peeled and minced
1 cup chicken stock
1½ cups ketchup
½ teaspoon Tabasco sauce
¼ cup molasses
¼ cup vinegar
¾ cup water
1 tablespoon lemon juice
1 tablespoon smoke flavoring
2 tablespoons Worcestershire sauce
3 tablespoons brown sugar
1 bay leaf, broken in half
1 teaspoon paprika
2 teaspoons dry mustard
⅛ teaspoon thyme
½ teaspoon cayenne pepper
1 teaspoon salt
½ teaspoon pepper

1. In a barbecue with a cover, prepare fire with mesquite charcoal briquettes, or use another type of briquettes with mesquite chips. Let burn down to glowing white coals (about 45 minutes to 1 hour).

2. Meanwhile, prepare Basting Sauce and Texas-Style Barbecue Sauce.

3. When charcoal is ready, push the briquettes to the edges of the barbecue. (If there is room in your barbecue, place a flameproof pot filled with hot water in the center of the coals.) Mop pork slabs on the bony side with Basting Sauce and place mopped side down about 8 inches above the coals in the center of the grill. Now moisten the upper side with the sauce. Cover the barbecue and smoke pork for about 2½ hours, basting every 15 minutes. Leave the bony side down until the last few minutes. If rack is closer than 8 inches to the coals, decrease cooking time to about 1 hour. Add a few fresh briquettes to the fire every 30 minutes. If using a circular grill with perforations in one side of the cover, rotate the perforations every 15 minutes to keep charcoal from going out.

4. When pork is nearly cooked, turn meaty side down and brown meat well. At the same time, add sausages to the grill, placing them directly over the coals, and grill, turning every few minutes, until done through (about 10 to 15 minutes). Cut pork slabs into serving portions and cover with Texas-Style Barbecue Sauce. Serve sausages along with the pork.

Serves 6 to 8.

Basting Sauce Mix ingredients together in a 1½-quart saucepan and heat until fat melts.

Makes 2¾ cups.

Texas-Style Barbecue Sauce

1. In a heavy saucepan over medium heat, melt butter and oil. Add onion and sauté until it is slightly caramelized, about 5 minutes. Add garlic and sauté another 2 minutes.

2. Add remaining ingredients, raise heat, and cook at a full boil for 10 minutes, stirring frequently.

3. Reduce heat, cover partially, and simmer for 1 hour, stirring occasionally. Sauce may be refrigerated for up to a week and reheated when needed.

Makes about 4 cups.

EAST TEXAS CAVIAR

No Texas barbecue would be complete without this "caviar" made from black-eyed peas. Actually it bears no conceivable resemblance to fish eggs: It's a simple salad with a clean, fresh taste and wonderful texture. It also goes well with hamburgers, or it can be served on toast as an hors d'oeuvre. (Texans are convinced that eating it on New Year's Day will bestow good luck for the rest of the year, just as residents of the Deep South insist on Hoppin' John.) Texas caviar must be mixed at least one day (preferably three days) before serving, to mellow the flavors, so plan accordingly.

> 2 cans (15 oz each) black-eyed peas (with or without jalapeños, depending on taste) or 4 cups cooked black-eyed peas, drained
> ½ cup very thinly sliced red onion
> ½ cup salad oil
> ¼ cup red wine vinegar
> 1 large clove garlic, minced
> Salt and black pepper, to taste
> ½ teaspoon Louisiana-style hot sauce, or to taste
> 1 heaping tablespoon minced cilantro or 2 tablespoons minced parsley
> Crackers or triangles of toast

1. At least one day before serving, drain black-eyed peas and rinse under cold water. Place in a large bowl.

2. Soak onion slices in ice water to cover for 30 to 45 minutes. Drain.

3. Thoroughly mix oil, vinegar, garlic, salt, pepper, hot sauce, and drained onion slices, carefully adjusting seasonings to taste. Pour over black-eyed peas and toss gently. Cover and let stand for 8 hours at room temperature (if serving the next day), then chill before serving, or refrigerate for 3 days, stirring daily.

4. Just before serving, place mixture in a serving bowl and stir in the cilantro or parsley. Accompany with crackers or toast triangles.

Serves 6 to 8.

Variations For extra spiciness, add 2 seeded, minced jalapeño chiles to the marinade. To vary flavor and texture, add 2 chopped hard-cooked eggs or a small minced tomato along with the cilantro.

ELOTES
Corn on the cob with lime-chile butter

In this dish, corn on the cob is roasted on the grill and seasoned with lime and chili powder. These sour and piquant flavors bring out the sweetness of the corn. Elotes can also be cooked indoors if the weather turns bad.

> Fresh ears of corn (about 2 per person), silk removed, husks left intact
> ¾ to 1 cup butter, at room temperature
> Generous ¼ cup freshly squeezed lime juice
> 2 to 3 tablespoons Texas chili powder or powdered hot chiles (such as New Mexico chile)
> Salt, to taste

1. *To cook corn outdoors:* Prepare fire in grill. Drench corn with water until husks can absorb no more; twist shut. If fire is very hot, wrap the ears in foil. Place corn on the grill and roast for about 20 minutes, turning frequently, until tender. Keep warm until ready to serve. *To cook corn indoors:* Preheat oven to 400° F. Remove husks and smear ears with a small amount of butter. Wrap each ear in aluminum foil and roast for 20 to 25 minutes, until tender.

2. As corn roasts, use a fork to beat together butter, lime juice, chili powder, and salt, adjusting proportions to taste. When ready to serve, remove husks and coat corn with the mixture.

Serves 6 to 8.

JICAMA AND FRUIT RELISH

An ideal accompaniment to a meat-heavy barbecue, this relish is a Texas-border version of an ancient Mexican hot-weather refresher—orange sections coated with hot pepper. The heat of the chiles is actually cooling. (Relish will keep in the refrigerator for a week, but the texture is best within two days.)

> 3 tablespoons freshly squeezed lime juice or lemon juice
> 4 tablespoons salad oil
> ¼ teaspoon brown sugar
> ⅛ teaspoon salt
> 1 small jicama root (about 8 oz)
> 2 large seedless oranges
> 1 large, tart-sweet apple (Granny Smith, Winesap)
> 1 small mango (optional)
> 1 tablespoon Texas chili powder
> 1 teaspoon cayenne pepper

1. Mix lime juice, oil, sugar, and salt. Set aside.

2. Insert a small, sharp knife just under the peel of the jicama and tear away the peel in sheets. Trim off the ends, and cut the remainder in ¼-inch dice. Place in a serving bowl.

3. Halve and peel oranges; cut in bite-size chunks. Peel and core apple and cut to match oranges. If you are using mango, peel and cut to match oranges. Add fruits to the jicama.

4. Sprinkle the jicama mixture with chili powder and cayenne. Immediately pour on the lime-juice mixture and toss. Chill until ready to serve.

Serves 6 to 8.

The Southwest's rakish Margarita Sorbet is a delightfully tart and tipsy refresher. Here, the snowy mound is made even more elegant with a colorful fresh-fruit garnish—the crunchy crimson pips of a fresh pomegranate.

DESSERTS

This array of sweets includes a creamy fruit pudding (Walaxshi), fried dumplings (Empanaditas Dulces), a nut-flavored Tex-Mex pudding (Flan de Almendras), and an "adult" sherbet (Margarita Sorbet).

EMPANADITAS DULCES DE HOJA
Fried dessert empanadas

Empanadas are turnovers popular throughout the Spanish-speaking world. They can be stuffed with meat or made into small dessert pastries called *empanaditas*.

- 1¼ cups flour
- ½ teaspoon salt
- ½ tablespoon baking powder
- ½ tablespoon sugar
- 5 tablespoons margarine or shortening (not butter) at room temperature (see Note)
- ½ cup hot water
  Cooking oil
  Confectioners' sugar

Filling Choices

Filling for Sweet-Potato Pie Variation (see page 33) or other pie filling of choice
Jam or preserves
Strips of cream cheese or Neufchâtel cheese, alternating with strips of canned guava or guava paste
Whipped cream cheese mixed with chopped nuts and chopped dried fruits, sweetened with confectioners' sugar, to taste

1. Mix flour, salt, baking powder, and sugar in a large bowl or in food processor fitted with metal blade. Cut in margarine. Pour in the hot water and quickly mix to make a sticky batter. Scoop batter into a plastic bag, seal the top, and bang it on the table a half dozen times. Refrigerate for an hour or two.

2. When dough is well chilled, thoroughly flour a work surface and your palms. Pinch off about a tablespoon of dough and roll it into a ball between your palms. Dip the ball in flour, place it on the work surface, and flatten it to a small circle with the heel of your hand. Roll it out to a circle approximately 4 inches across. Place about a tablespoon of filling just off-center, fold the circle in half, and crimp the edges to seal. Place empanaditas on a floured surface as they are completed.

3. In a small, deep pot, heat about 3 inches of cooking oil to 375° F. Fry empanaditas one at a time, pushing them gently down into oil after they rise to the top, until golden brown. With a slotted spoon, remove and drain on paper towels. Sprinkle with confectioners' sugar.

Makes about 15 empanaditas.

<u>Note</u> This extremely short version of the dough is rather sticky and elastic, resulting in a wonderfully light crust but requiring some skill to roll out. An easier but less spectacular version can be made by decreasing the margarine to 2 tablespoons.

WALAXSHI
Fruits in custard

Originally a Choctaw wedding dish, this Oklahoma dessert evolved into a combination of poached fruits and roasted nuts in a custard cream sauce. Walaxshi will keep, refrigerated, for a week; lightly stir custard and turn fruits every two days.

> 6 firm-ripe medium pears or peaches
> 1¼ cups sugar
> 2 cups red seedless grapes
> ¼ cup pine nuts
> ¼ cup pecans
> 2 eggs
> 1 pint extra-rich milk or 1¾ cup whole milk mixed with ¼ cup whipping cream
> ¼ teaspoon vanilla extract
> 2 tablespoons flour
> Pinch salt
> 1 tablespoon butter
> ⅛ to ¼ teaspoon nutmeg

1. Preheat oven to 325° F. Peel and core pears. (If using peaches, halve them and remove pits.) Place in a 2-quart saucepan; add ½ cup of sugar and water to cover fruit. Simmer over low heat until firm-tender (about 12 minutes). During the last 3 minutes, add grapes to the pot. Drain fruits and place them in a serving bowl.

2. Meanwhile, scatter pine nuts and pecans on a baking sheet and toast in the oven for 5 minutes, flipping occasionally, until lightly browned on both sides. Sprinkle the nuts over the poached fruits.

3. Beat eggs until pale and bubbly. Beat in milk and vanilla. Stir in flour, salt, and remaining ¾ cup of sugar. Pour into a heavy 1½-quart saucepan, add butter, and bring to a boil, beating constantly with a whisk. Remove from heat, stir in nutmeg to taste, and beat again, off heat, until smooth and thick. Pour custard over fruit mixture and refrigerate until chilled.

Serves 6.

FLAN DE ALMENDRAS
Fluffy almond custard

This light, silky custard isn't a true baked flan, but a stove-top cousin.

> ¾ cup blanched slivered almonds
> 1 can (14 oz) sweetened condensed milk
> 1½ tablespoons nut- or coffee-flavored liqueur or 1 teaspoon almond extract
> 4 egg whites
> Butter to grease pan

1. In blender, food processor, or with a rolling pin, grind ½ cup of almonds to a meal. Mix well with condensed milk and liqueur.

2. Beat egg whites to stiff peaks. Pour milk mixture into beaten egg whites and fold together gently but thoroughly, until all the liquid has been absorbed by eggs.

3. Heavily grease the top of a double boiler with butter, pour in milk mixture, and cover it. Bring about 3 inches of water to a gentle boil in the bottom of the double boiler (water level should be well below milk mixture in top half). Place top half over boiling water and regulate heat so that water remains at a gentle boil. Cook, covered, until mixture becomes tender-firm all the way through, and bottom and sides are lightly caramelized, about 1 to 1½ hours. (After the first 45 minutes, check every 10 minutes or so by inserting a small measuring spoon about halfway through center of mixture and removing a bit to taste. When mixture has thickened to a true custard, flan is ready.)

4. Let custard cool to room temperature, then chill if desired. Meanwhile, toast remaining almonds in a dry skillet, shaking frequently to lightly brown all sides. To serve, unmold custard onto a serving dish (briefly immerse the bottom of the bowl in hot water; then cover the top with the serving plate; flip both over together; and rap them sharply on a table). Stud the top of the custard with the toasted almond slivers.

Serves 4 to 6.

MARGARITA SORBET

In the dry heat of the southwestern summer, iced desserts—the lighter the better—are especially favored. This fluffy sorbet, based on the ingredients of the margarita cocktail, is tart enough to serve as a between-course refresher; otherwise, it's an adult dessert. For a gala presentation, surround each portion with chilled, sliced, ripe summer fruits.

> 1⅛ cups sugar
> 2 cups water
> ⅓ cup lime juice (from 3 to 4 juicy limes)
> 1 tablespoon lime pulp (scoop from juiced limes with a teaspoon)
> 2 tablespoons "gold" or añejo tequila
> 2 teaspoons triple sec (orange-peel liqueur)
> 2 egg whites

1. In a heavy 1½-quart saucepan, heat sugar and water over medium heat until sugar melts and mixture starts to bubble. Continue cooking 10 minutes longer, regulating heat so that mixture bubbles gently. Remove from heat and allow to cool slightly.

2. Stir lime juice, lime pulp, tequila, and liqueur into sugar mixture. Pour into a 2-quart freezerproof serving dish. Freeze until the mixture starts to set (about 1 hour). Remove from freezer and quickly but thoroughly stir with a fork. Return to freezer and chill until mixture forms a thick, grainy mush (about 2 more hours), stirring again every half hour or so to keep mixture from freezing solid.

3. Beat egg whites to soft (not stiff) peaks. Remove lime mixture from freezer and beat very rapidly to a fluff (using a fork or electric mixer). Immediately fold in egg whites. Return the mixture to the freezer and continue to chill for at least 1 more hour. This sorbet should be served directly from the freezer (it should not be softened in the refrigerator) since it melts rather quickly.

Serves 6 to 9.

A charcoal fire with chips of aromatic hardwood brings out the best in fresh Pacific salmon and oysters in their shells. Recipes start on page 122.

The Pacific States

The recipes of the Pacific States, a region that encourages innovation, reflect European, Latin American, and Asian influences as well as the wealth of fresh food available. Menus for two outstanding west-coast meals are presented in this chapter. A Seashore Barbecue (see page 122) features Alder-Grilled Salmon and Barbecued Oysters, and a Gold Miner's Brunch (see page 114) presents a hearty meal of Hangtown Fry, sausage, and Sourdough Pancakes With Wild Berry Syrup. Other Pacific States favorites included in this chapter are Hawaiian Lomi-Lomi Salmon (page 107), California Roll Sushi (page 109), and Crab Salad Louis (page 110).

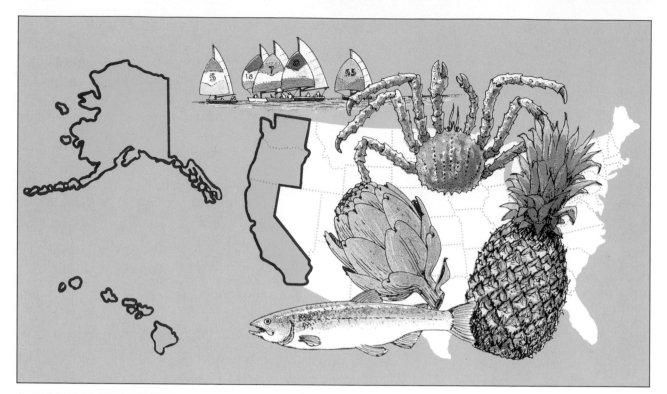

A REGION OF EXTREMES

The Pacific States—Alaska, Washington, Oregon, California, and Hawaii—make up a region of extremes. The geography ranges from tropical to high arctic, and the food of the area is just as varied.

In a sense the Pacific States are not old enough to have developed their own culinary classics. But this newness and lack of tradition is what gives the region its style. Energetic, eclectic, experimental, innovative—the people of the Pacific States are all of these, and the cooking of the region reflects the same qualities.

Still, there are certain foods and dishes so characteristic of the area that they can be called classics. They reflect the abundance and variety of foods produced, the unique mix of ethnic influences (chiefly European, Latin American, and Asian), and the freedom to rethink the food traditions of many cultures.

The Pacific States produce an incredible quantity and range of fresh fruits and vegetables. The varied climates of California, Oregon, and Washington accommodate everything from grains and potatoes to wine and table grapes, tree fruits, berries, and a year-round supply of lettuce and other fresh vegetables.

Tropical fruits and vegetables from Hawaii, Mexico, and the Caribbean—pineapples, coconuts, fresh ginger, mangoes, papayas, passion fruit, cherimoya, and guava—are more and more common in mainland markets and are becoming part of many cooks' everyday dishes.

Throughout the Pacific States, immigrant farmers have traditionally grown "foreign" produce for their own ethnic markets. Many of these crops, such as Chinese cabbage, bean sprouts, and cilantro, have become mainstream items used by other cooks as well. With each successive wave of immigrants, a whole new range of flavors becomes available to experimental cooks.

West-coast cooks also make excellent use of local seafood, from the salmon and crab of the colder northern Pacific and the clams, mussels, and oysters of the coastal bays to the tunas and other warm-water species of Mexican and Hawaiian waters.

Wild foods are also an important part of the food resources of the coastal region. Wild berries abound all along the coast, reaching the greatest profusion in Alaska. Knowledgeable mushroom hunters in the coastal forests can find chanterelles,

cèpes, morels, and other choice varieties including the matsutake prized by Japanese gourmets.

Although the culture of the Pacific-coast region is still basically Anglo-American, the melting pot has a stronger Oriental flavor there than elsewhere in the country, as well as a vibrant Latin American touch.

Traditional restaurant cookery in the early days was strictly European, particularly French and Italian, and this is still the style of the fanciest and oldest restaurants. Most of the founders of the California wine industry were immigrants from the wine-growing regions of Europe, and the wine-country cooking of Napa, Sonoma, and the other wine valleys has a distinctly Mediterranean touch.

As immigrants have arrived—from the Chinese railroad and mining laborers of the last century to today's refugees arriving daily from Southeast Asia and Central America—they have opened restaurants to serve their own communities.

To adventurous diners this has meant an endless variety of new tastes. The exotic quickly becomes familiar, and Pacific-states cooks are quick to incorporate ingredients, flavors, and dishes from foreign cuisines into their personal cooking styles.

APPETIZERS AND FIRST COURSES

For appetizers, Pacific-states food lovers—whether entertaining at home or dining out—look to their native seafoods and to such local produce specialties as artichokes. But these foods are not confined to the first course; more and more, a meal is likely to consist entirely of dishes that might be classified as appetizers or entrées.

OLYMPIA OYSTERS IN SAKE CUPS

Tiny Olympia oysters served in individual sake cups have been a favorite at San Francisco's Stanford Court Hotel since the hotel opened in 1969. They make an elegant hors d'oeuvre for cocktail parties, as long as you have plenty of cups or someone in the kitchen to wash and refill them!

1 tablespoon finely minced shallot
3 tablespoons wine vinegar (sherry, Champagne, or red)
Freshly ground pepper, to taste
2 dozen Olympia oysters, shucked, with their juices

Combine shallot, vinegar, and pepper; set aside 15 minutes to let flavors blend. Spoon each oyster into a chilled sake cup and add ¼ teaspoon sauce. Pass on trays; guests sip oyster and sauce directly from cup.

Serves 6 to 8.

LOMI-LOMI SALMON

Salmon are not found within thousands of miles of Hawaii. So how did this dish become a Hawaiian classic? It began with the salted salmon from the Northwest that the early American missionaries ate. Hawaiian cooks soaked the fish to remove the salt, then massaged it to a paste with the fingertips *(lomi* means massage), and seasoned it with tomatoes and onions. The modern version, made with fresh salmon, makes a refreshing appetizer. When sweet Maui onions are available, try them in place of green onions. Note that the dish must be started a day ahead.

1 pound fresh salmon fillet
Juice of 1 lemon
6 tablespoons kosher salt or coarse sea salt
1 pound ripe tomatoes, peeled, seeded, and chopped
2 green onions or 1 sweet yellow onion
Lettuce leaves, for dipping

1. Place salmon in a large glass or ceramic bowl. Sprinkle salmon with lemon juice and cover with salt. Cover and marinate in refrigerator overnight.

2. Drain salmon and rinse off salt. Cover with cold water and soak 2 hours, changing water 2 or 3 times. Drain well.

3. Pull salmon meat away from bones and skin by hand; discard skin and bones. Massage salmon with fingertips until thoroughly mashed. Add tomatoes and green onions and continue massaging until mixture is smooth. Chill 30 minutes before serving. Serve with lettuce leaves.

Serves 6 to 8.

OYSTERS KIRKPATRICK

One of the many creations of Chef Ernest Arbogast of the Palace Hotel in San Francisco, this dish was named after the hotel's general manager, Colonel John C. Kirkpatrick.

3 slices bacon
1 pound rock salt
1 dozen live oysters
2 tablespoons catsup or bottled chili sauce
Worcestershire sauce
Pepper, to taste
1 tablespoon butter (optional)
2 tablespoons grated Parmesan cheese

1. Blanch bacon in boiling water 30 seconds to remove excess salt; drain. Bake or fry until crisp. Crumble bacon and set aside.

2. Preheat oven to 450° F. Fill a shallow roasting pan, just large enough to hold the oysters, with rock salt to a depth of ¼ inch (to keep oysters upright during cooking).

3. With an oyster knife remove flatter top shells from oysters and cut loose from bottom shells (see Note). Nestle oysters into salt in roasting pan. To each oyster add a few bits of bacon, ½ teaspoon catsup, a dash of Worcestershire, a little pepper, and ¼ teaspoon butter (if desired). Top with Parmesan. Bake until oysters are just heated through, about 5 minutes.

Serves 2 to 4 as an appetizer.

<u>Note</u> For additional information on opening oysters, see page 10. For easier shucking, oysters may be baked first, just until shells begin to open, then shucked as in Barbecued Oysters (see page 123). However, this additional cooking time may make them a little tougher.

Step-by-Step

PREPARING WHOLE ARTICHOKES

Trim off thorny tips of outer leaves with scissors or a paring knife. Snap or cut off smallest, toughest leaves close to stem. Rub freshly cut parts with lemon to prevent discoloration. Slice stem off to form flat bottom. Set artichoke stem side down on a steamer above at least 1 inch of boiling water. Cover and steam until bases are tender (30 to 60 minutes, depending on size). Artichokes are now ready to eat, or for one of the following preparations:

Artichoke Cups *Use large artichokes. Carefully spread outer leaves to expose heart. Remove small heart leaves and scrape out fuzzy choke with a spoon. Fill hollow with a sauce for dipping outer leaves or a salad such as shrimp with herbed mayonnaise.*

Marinated Artichokes *Cut cooked artichokes into quarters or smaller wedges. Remove chokes and heart leaves. Trim tops of outer leaves down to entirely edible parts (pull off a leaf and test it). Marinate in a mixture of 3 parts olive oil, 2 parts water, 1 part vinegar or lemon juice, and salt and pepper to taste. Fresh or dried herbs, blanched whole garlic cloves, or red pepper flakes may be added to marinade. Store in refrigerator; it will keep for weeks in the marinade.*

Artichoke Bottoms *Use large artichokes. After steaming remove all leaves and scrape away choke, leaving a shallow cup that can be used to hold hot savory ingredients such as poached eggs or oysters. Leave artichokes slightly underdone if filled bottoms will be reheated with other ingredients.*

If you have a lot of leftover leaves from preparing artichoke cups or bottoms, make them into a cream soup. Simmer in chicken stock until quite tender, purée in a food processor or food mill, strain out fibers, add milk or cream, and thicken with a flour-and-butter roux.

ARTICHOKES WITH DIPPING SAUCES

Eating artichokes is an informal affair; there is no substitute for fingers. Pull off leaves one at a time, dip them into a sauce, and use your teeth to scrape off the "meat" on the inside at the base of each leaf. Discard the small, fibrous heart leaves and cut out the fuzzy choke. Eat the base with knife and fork, dipping chunks into the sauce. Provide a large bowl for the discarded leaves.

> 1 medium to large artichoke for each person
> 2 tablespoons dipping sauce for each person

Lemon Butter

> ¼ cup butter
> Juice of ½ lemon
> Pinch pepper or dash Louisiana-style hot sauce (optional)

Curry Mayonnaise

> 1 tablespoon vegetable oil
> ¼ teaspoon curry powder
> ¼ cup mayonnaise
> 1 teaspoon lemon juice

Herbed Vinaigrette

> Pinch salt and pepper
> 1 tablespoon tarragon-flavored wine vinegar
> 4 tablespoons olive oil
> 1 tablespoon minced fresh herbs (tarragon, basil, dill, or chervil)

Trim and steam artichokes (see Preparing Whole Artichokes at left). Serve warm, tepid, or cold, with dipping sauce of choice.

Lemon Butter Melt butter and add lemon juice and pepper. Pour into warm individual bowls.

Serves 2 to 3.

Curry Mayonnaise In a small skillet heat oil over low heat. Add curry powder and cook 2 to 3 minutes. Allow to cool, then stir into mayonnaise. Add lemon juice to taste. Flavor will improve if allowed to stand several hours.

Serves 2 to 3.

Herbed Vinaigrette Dissolve salt and pepper in vinegar. Whisk in oil and blend in herbs. Taste for seasoning and adjust to taste. This sauce does not keep well (the herbs can become bitter), so make it the same day it will be used.

Serves 2 to 3.

CALIFORNIA ROLL SUSHI

Sushi is a popular Japanese snack of vinegared rice combined with the finest of fresh ingredients, particularly raw or cooked seafood and vegetables. Japanese sushi chefs in California combined two local ingredients, crab and avocado, and the California roll (pictured at right) was born.

> ½ teaspoon wasabi powder
> (Japanese green horseradish)
> 1 avocado, ripe but still firm
> 1 recipe Sushi Rice (at right)
> 2 sheets nori (dried seaweed),
> 7 by 8 inches
> ½ cup cooked crabmeat

1. Combine wasabi with just enough water to form a loose paste and set aside. Split avocado, remove pit and peel, and cut flesh lengthwise into ¼-inch sticks.

2. Moisten hands with vinegar mixture (see Sushi Rice, at right). Dampen a bamboo sushi-rolling mat or a clean kitchen towel. Spread with a 7-inch square of rice, ¼ inch thick. Cut nori sheets in half into 4-by 7-inch pieces and lay one across rice 1 inch from near edge. Lift near edge of mat and roll inward about one third of way to far edge. Peel back mat and spread top of roll with a thin layer of wasabi paste. Lay avocado strips end to end along length of roll, then lay crab pieces alongside avocado. Cover again with mat and roll rice around filling into a firm cylinder, using towel or mat to maintain shape. Unwrap and slice into 1-inch-long sections and arrange on plates or serving tray cut side up. Repeat with remaining ingredients.

Makes 4 rolls, 4 appetizer servings.

MAKING SUSHI RICE

Making delicious sushi rice (as pictured above) is a quick and easy process. The secret is to cool the rice quickly by fanning it vigorously while combining the cooked rice and liquid mixture. Leftover sushi rice can be formed into small balls, rolled in dark sesame seeds, and served with soy sauce as an appetizer.

> 2 cups short-grain rice
> 2½ cups water
> ½ cup rice vinegar
> ¼ cup sugar
> 4 teaspoons salt

1. Wash rice several times by covering with cold water, swirling with the fingers, and draining off water. Repeat until water runs clear. Place rice in medium pot, cover with water, and let soak up to 1 hour. Cover pot and bring to a boil. When steam escapes quickly from around lid, reduce heat to low and simmer 20 minutes. Remove from heat and let stand 10 minutes longer.

2. While rice is cooking, combine vinegar, sugar, and salt in a small saucepan and cook until sugar dissolves. Cool.

3. Using a rice paddle or wooden spatula, scoop cooked rice into a large, shallow baking pan. Sprinkle evenly with half of vinegar mixture. Fold liquid in carefully without mashing grains. With a hand-held fan or folded newspaper, fan rice with other hand while folding in liquid. Continue fanning and folding until liquid is nearly all absorbed and rice glistens. Reserve remaining vinegar mixture for moistening your hands while forming sushi (see California Roll Sushi, at left).

Makes 4 cups.

SOUPS, SALADS, AND SIDE DISHES

In a typical Pacific-states meal, the soup may be anything from a simple broth with a few garden-fresh vegetables to a hearty meal-in-a-bowl seafood stew. Salads also range from a selection of greens with a simple vinaigrette to elaborate compositions that can stand alone for lunch or warm-weather supper. Here again seafood and fresh vegetables have a starring role.

STIR-FRIED VEGETABLES WITH ALMONDS

Chinese-style stir-frying has become a standard part of the repertoire of many west-coast cooks. This dish of assorted seasonal vegetables with almonds would go equally well with a Chinese or a Western menu. Use whatever vegetables are in season, with an eye to contrasting colors and textures. Green beans, carrots, cauliflower, and other firm vegetables may be blanched before stir-frying, but this isn't necessary with other quick-cooking vegetables such as snow peas, asparagus, and mushrooms.

> 1 stalk broccoli
> 2 tablespoons soy sauce
> 2 tablespoons water or dry white wine
> 1 teaspoon cornstarch
> 3 tablespoons peanut or other vegetable oil
> ¼ cup whole blanched almonds
> 1 teaspoon minced ginger
> 3 or 4 green onions, trimmed and cut into 2-inch lengths
> 1 red or green bell pepper, seeded and cut into 1-inch squares
> 1 stalk celery, diagonally sliced
> ½ cup sliced fresh mushrooms or 2 or 3 dried Chinese or Japanese black (shiitake) mushroom caps, soaked in water until soft and cut into strips

1. Trim base of broccoli stem. Starting at base, cut across stem into ⅛-inch slices, continuing until top comes apart into florets. Blanch in lightly salted boiling water for 30 seconds and transfer to a bowl of ice water to keep cold.

2. Combine soy sauce and the 3 tablespoons water; add cornstarch, stir to dissolve, and set aside.

3. Heat oil in a wok or large skillet over medium heat. Add almonds and cook, stirring constantly, until almonds begin to brown. Remove with a slotted spoon or Chinese skimmer and drain on paper towels.

4. Turn heat to medium-high. Add ginger to remaining oil, stir and cook a few seconds until fragrant, and add green onions, pepper, and celery. Cook 1 minute, stirring constantly. Drain broccoli and add to pan along with mushrooms and almonds. Stir-fry just until mushrooms soften. Stir cornstarch mixture and add to pan. Stir and cook until sauce thickens and becomes glossy. Transfer to a warm serving platter.

Serves 4 to 6 as a side dish.

CRAB SALAD LOUIS

To a generation or two of Californians, crab Louis (pronounced *Louie*) is a salad with a tomato-flavored mayonnaise dressing—a sort of Thousand Island without the islands. According to some historians, however, the original Louis dressing contained not a speck of mayonnaise. There is not even universal agreement on the origin of the name of the dressing; some attribute it to chef Louis Coutard, others to Italian restaurateur Louis Besozzi. Whoever invented it and whatever it contains, Crab Salad Louis has remained a San Francisco favorite. All versions have a few things in common—crab or other shellfish and sliced hard-cooked egg on a bed of lettuce, with a dressing containing bottled chili sauce. Other vegetables, such as cooked asparagus and fresh tomatoes, are often included. Two versions of the dressing follow.

> ½ head lettuce
> ½ cup cooked crabmeat
> 1 hard-cooked egg, sliced
> Freshly ground black pepper
> Chopped chives

Louis Dressing I

> 2 tablespoons white wine vinegar or lemon juice
> Pinch of salt and pepper
> ½ teaspoon dry mustard
> ¼ teaspoon paprika
> ½ teaspoon Worcestershire sauce
> ½ cup olive oil
> ¼ cup chili sauce
> 2 tablespoons chopped fresh herbs (parsley, chives, tarragon, or a blend)

Louis Dressing II

> ¼ teaspoon dry mustard
> 1 tablespoon lemon juice
> Dash of Worcestershire sauce
> ¼ cup olive oil
> ⅓ cup mayonnaise
> ⅓ cup chili sauce
> 1 tablespoon chopped fresh herbs (parsley, chives, tarragon, or a blend)

Line a large individual salad bowl or dinner plate with a few outside leaves of lettuce. Tear remaining lettuce and arrange in bowl; place crabmeat in center. Arrange egg slices around outside and sprinkle salad with pepper and chives. Just before serving, pour ¼ cup dressing over salad. Serve additional dressing on the side.

Serves 1 as a main course, 2 as a first course.

Louis Dressing I Combine vinegar, salt and pepper, mustard, paprika, and Worcestershire; beat with a wire whisk until dissolved. Beat in oil, then chili sauce and herbs. Chill well and stir before serving.

Makes 1 cup.

Louis Dressing II Combine mustard, lemon juice, and Worcestershire; beat to dissolve, then beat in oil. Add mayonnaise, chili sauce, and herbs; blend thoroughly. Chill before serving.

Makes 1 cup.

CIOPPINO

Northern California's own version of the typical Mediterranean fisherman's stew features the local Dungeness crab along with other shellfish and fish in a fragrant, tomato-flavored broth. For an authentic flavor, serve with San Francisco Sourdough French Bread (see page 113) and a dry white or red California wine.

- 1 to 2 pounds fish heads and bones (preferably rockfish, halibut, or other lean, white fish)
- 1 cleaned and cracked Dungeness crab (see Note) or 1 pound king crab legs
- 2 medium onions, sliced
- 8 sprigs parsley
- ½ teaspoon fennel or anise seed, cracked
- 12 peppercorns, cracked
- 1 cup dry white wine
- 4 cups water
- 3 tablespoons olive oil
- 3 cloves garlic, chopped
  Pinch red-pepper flakes
- 1 red or green bell pepper, seeded and diced
- 1 large can (28 oz) Italian-style tomatoes
- 2 tablespoons minced basil or ½ teaspoon dried oregano
  Salt and pepper, to taste
- 2 to 3 pounds assorted fish and shellfish (for example, clams or mussels, scrubbed; lean, white fish, in 1-inch cubes; shrimp, peeled and deveined; squid, cleaned and cut into rings)

1. Wash fish heads and bones well, removing any bits of blood or organs. Split heads and chop large sections of bone into smaller pieces. Place in a large saucepan or stockpot with crab shell, 1 onion, parsley, fennel seeds, peppercorns, wine, and the water. Bring to a boil, reduce heat, and simmer 30 to 45 minutes, skimming off any foam that rises to surface. Strain stock.

2. In a large soup kettle, heat olive oil over medium heat. Add garlic, remaining onion, pepper flakes, and

bell pepper; sauté until wilted. Add tomatoes, basil, reserved crab fat, and stock; bring to a boil and simmer until slightly thickened (30 minutes). Season with salt and pepper, allowing for salty clam juices.

3. Arrange fish and shellfish in order of cooking time. Add clams and uncooked crab 10 minutes before ready to serve; halibut, 8 minutes; shrimp, cooked crab, mussels, and rockfish or ocean perch, 5 minutes; and squid, 2 minutes. Serve hot in large soup plates.

Serves 4 to 6 as a main dish.

Note Some fishmongers will clean and crack crabs—either live or cooked—for you. For information on cleaning and cracking crabs yourself, see the California Culinary Academy book *Fish & Shellfish*. Whether you clean the crab yourself or have it done by the fishmonger, save the top shell for the stock and reserve the tasty fat from the corners of the shell for the tomato broth. Uncooked crab fat is olive green and turns pale yellow when cooked.

Experts may argue over who invented crab Louis and what makes an authentic Louis dressing, but the countless diners who order this salad regularly in California seafood restaurants probably don't care. Whether made with crab or shrimp, Louis salads are among the state's most popular dishes.

GEODUCK CHOWDER

Clamdiggers on northwestern bays generally find two types of clams: a small hard-shell one known as a butter clam and the foot-long, soft-shell geoduck (pronounced *gooey-duck*). The butter clams go into the steaming pot and the geoducks are made into chowder.

1 *live geoduck (2 to 3 lbs)*
6 *green onions, white parts sliced, green tops reserved*
3 *tablespoons butter*
3 *ounces bacon, diced and blanched 1 minute in boiling water*
1 *pound boiling potatoes, scrubbed and cut into ¼-inch dice*
1 *pint light cream or half-and-half*
Salt and white or cayenne pepper, to taste

1. Scrub outside of geoduck shell. Parboil clam for 1 minute, then transfer to cold water to stop cooking. Remove shell with a sharp knife, slit open brownish skin from neck, and peel away skin. Reserve shell and skin for stock . Cut away and discard dark entrails; all remaining cream-colored meat is edible. Chop meat by hand into pea-sized pieces or grind on coarsest setting of a meat grinder.

2. Place shell and skin in a large saucepan or stockpot with 6 cups water and tops of green onions. Bring to a boil, reduce heat, and simmer 20 minutes. Skim off any foam that rises to surface. Strain finished stock, discarding last cup or so to trap any sand or grit. Wash saucepan.

3. In saucepan over medium-low heat, melt butter. Add bacon and sliced green onions, and cook until onions soften (about 1 minute). Add chopped clam and stock. Bring to a boil, reduce heat, and simmer 10 minutes. Add potatoes and cook until tender (about 10 minutes).

4. Add cream, season with salt and pepper, and bring to serving temperature (but do not boil soup after adding cream). Serve immediately or keep warm until ready to serve.

Makes about 4 cups, serves 6 to 8.

112

COBB SALAD

This exuberant salad, the specialty of the late Brown Derby restaurant in Los Angeles, might be called Hollywood's answer to the chef's salad. This adaptation uses hand-torn greens rather than the chopped greens of the original, but it is still tossed at the table.

1 *clove garlic*
½ *teaspoon dry mustard*
Dash Worcestershire sauce
2 *tablespoons wine vinegar*
Juice of ½ lemon
⅓ *cup olive oil or vegetable oil or a blend*
Salt and pepper, to taste
Mixed salad greens (leaf and head lettuces, romaine, curly endive, and watercress), washed, dried, and torn into bite-sized pieces
1 *stalk celery, thinly sliced*
1 *ripe but firm avocado, peeled, pitted, and diced*
2 *medium tomatoes, peeled, seeded, and chopped*
1 *poached chicken breast, skinned, boned, and diced*
2 *hard-cooked eggs, diced*
4 *thick slices bacon, cooked crisp and diced*
⅓ *cup crumbled blue cheese*
Chopped chives, for garnish

1. *To prepare dressing:* Press or mash garlic into a small bowl. Add mustard, Worcestershire, vinegar, and lemon juice; blend with a fork. Stir in oil and season to taste with salt and pepper. Transfer dressing to a sauceboat.

2. Place greens and celery in a large, shallow salad bowl with 3 tablespoons dressing and toss to coat evenly (omit dressing if preparing ahead of time). Arrange avocado, tomatoes, chicken, eggs, bacon, and cheese in radiating wedges on top of salad. Sprinkle chives in a ring over all. Toss salad at table with half the remaining dressing and serve with more dressing on the side.

Serves 4 as a first course, 2 as a main course.

BREADS

For the most part, west-coast bakeries offer the same all-American breads and international specialties as those in other parts of the country. But there are a few baked goods that are characteristic of the region: the sourdough breads of San Francisco and Alaska and the cracker bread baked by Californians of Armenian descent.

SOURDOUGH BAKING

One of the enduring symbols of the old West is a bubbling crock of sourdough starter. In Conestoga wagons, homesteads, and miner's cabins, the starter was the main source of leavening for all baked goods. It was a treasured possession and one that had to be carefully protected.

A sourdough starter is a living culture of yeast cells and leavening bacteria. It must be replenished regularly by the addition of more flour. The easiest way to do this is the way the pioneers did daily: They mixed the starter with additional flour and water and the whole mixture fermented overnight. Some of it was ladled back into the crock to form the starter for the next day, and the rest was used for pancakes, breads, and other baked goods.

Now that reliable dry yeasts are available, cooks do not need to keep a starter alive in order to bake bread. However, the characteristic flavor of sourdough has remained popular. Although it is possible to make sourdough breads by using only the starter for leavening, this technique results in a dense bread. Most commercial sourdough is made with a combination of starter and another leavener, either yeast or baking soda.

San Francisco is famous for a particular style of sourdough French bread, one that cannot be exactly reproduced elsewhere. No one knows why. Whether it is the climate, the salt air from the Pacific, a secret process, or just the presence of a particular strain of yeast from a century of bread baking, the flavor of San Francisco sourdough is unique.

Another distinctive style of sourdough bread developed in Alaska. Here, the sour flavor is tamed by the addition of baking soda, which also adds leavening, and a little sugar. This is also the formula for sourdough pancakes, which are composed simply of starter with sugar, soda, salt, eggs, and oil added.

The easiest way to make a sourdough starter is from a commercial packaged mix, available in many fancy food shops and supermarkets. Of course, if you know someone who has a good starter, perhaps they will give you a cup or so. Once established, a starter can be kept alive indefinitely.

SOURDOUGH STARTER

If you are using a dry starter mix, prepare it according to package directions. Most starters require several days to establish, so plan ahead. Once you have an established starter— whether you began with dry mix or with a borrowed sponge—each time you bake with it, the first step is to combine the starter with flour and water and let the mixture ferment overnight. This procedure, which replenishes the basic starter and provides the additional quantity for baking, is given in the recipe below.

Sourdough starters should be stored only in glass, ceramic, or food-grade plastic containers. Never use metal containers, which might react chemically with the starter. Caps should also be nonreactive. A glass jar or ceramic crock with a clamp top and a rubber gasket is ideal. From time to time, when the starter is being replenished, the container should also be washed.

If the starter will not be used for more than a week, it should be replenished by the process given here, and the excess discarded.

> 1 cup sourdough starter
> Equal parts warm water
> (90° to 100° F) and flour
> (at least 1 cup each)

1. Combine starter and water in a large bowl. Stir in flour and beat to a smooth batter.

2. Cover bowl with plastic wrap and set aside in a warm (about 75° F) place. Let mixture stand until it is bubbly and sour, and a clear liquid begins to collect on surface (6 to 12 hours depending on liveliness of starter).

3. Stir starter and scoop out 1 cup of sponge and place it in storage container; refrigerate until next use.

SAN FRANCISCO SOURDOUGH FRENCH BREAD

Even if you do not live near the Golden Gate, you can make a delicious sourdough bread with the flavor of the classic San Francisco-style loaf. However, it takes time for the dough to get really sour. Try it on a weekend or some other time when you can let the dough ferment and rise at its own leisurely pace.

The traditional shapes for San Francisco sourdough bread are a long, oval French loaf and a 12-inch round, 3 to 4 inches thick.

> 1 cup sourdough starter
> 2½ cups warm water (90° to 100° F)
> 6½ to 7 cups bread flour
> 1 tablespoon salt
> Oil, for greasing
> 2 teaspoons (1 package) active dry yeast
> Cornmeal, for dusting
> 1 egg, beaten with ¼ cup milk or water (optional)

1. *Two nights ahead:* Follow the procedure under Sourdough Starter, left, adding the warm water and 2½ cups flour to the cup of starter. Mixture should sit 8 to 12 hours.

2. *Next day:* Return 1 cup sponge to storage container. To remaining sponge add salt and 2½ cups flour. Stir until dough is too stiff to work. Spread 1 cup flour on board, turn out dough onto board, and knead until smooth and resilient (8 to 10 minutes). Add more flour as necessary to keep dough from sticking; knead until flour is thoroughly incorporated.

3. Place dough ball in lightly oiled bowl and turn to oil all surfaces. Cover bowl with plastic wrap and let rise 4 to 6 hours in a warm place. Punch down dough, cover again, and refrigerate overnight.

4. *On day of baking:* Remove dough from refrigerator and allow to return to room temperature. In a large bowl warmed with hot water, dissolve yeast in ½ cup warm water (90° to 100° F). Add dough and knead to incorporate yeast mixture. Add ½ cup flour and knead in bowl until surface is not too sticky, then turn dough out onto a floured surface and knead until smooth, adding additional flour as needed.

5. Return dough to oiled bowl and let rise, covered, until doubled in bulk (about 1 hour). Punch down and allow to rise a second time if time allows; otherwise, proceed to form loaves.

6. Preheat oven to 350° F. Punch down dough after rising. Form into loaves and place on baking sheets dusted with cornmeal; allow room between loaves for rising. Cover with a towel and let dough rise until nearly doubled in bulk. If desired, brush tops lightly with egg wash. Slash tops with shallow cuts from a sharp knife (lengthwise or diagonal on long loaves, cross-hatched on round loaves). Bake on lowest shelf of oven until crust is golden brown and loaves sound hollow when tapped on bottom (about 1 hour). Cool on racks.

Makes two 16-inch loaves or 12-inch rounds or 4 baguettes.

Note For a more substantial crust, add moisture to the oven either by placing a pan of hot water on the oven floor for the first 15 minutes of baking (remove the pan to allow the bottoms of the loaves to bake fully) or by spraying the loaves halfway through baking with water from a spray bottle. The bread is also excellent baked on a tile surface such as unglazed quarry tiles or specially made pizza bricks.

ALASKAN SOURDOUGH BREAD

Baking soda is the key to Alaska-style sourdough bread. It sweetens the dough by counteracting some of the acidity in the starter; at the same time, it adds some leavening. This bread can be made into rolls but is more commonly baked in pans.

  1 cup sourdough starter
  3 cups warm water (90° to 100° F)
  6 to 7 cups bread flour
  1 teaspoon baking soda
  1 teaspoon salt
  2 tablespoons sugar
  ⅓ cup vegetable oil

1. *One day ahead:* Follow the procedure under Sourdough Starter, page 113, adding the warm water and 3 cups flour to the cup of starter.

2. *Next day:* Return 1 cup sponge to storage container. To remaining sponge, add baking soda, salt, sugar, and oil and stir in thoroughly. Add 3 cups flour, stir until dough is too stiff to work, then turn out onto a floured board. Knead until smooth and resilient (8 to 10 minutes) incorporating additional flour as necessary to keep dough from sticking.

3. Let dough rise in an oiled bowl, covered with a towel, until doubled in bulk. Punch down. Allow to rise a second time and punch down.

4. Preheat oven to 350°F. Form dough into loaves and place in greased 9- by 4-inch loaf pans. Cover with a towel and allow to rise to top of pans. Bake 1 hour. To test for doneness, remove a loaf from pan and tap bottom; it should be firm and sound hollow. Cool on wire racks.

Makes two 1½-pound loaves.

ARMENIAN CRACKER BREAD

Lahvosh, a thin, crisp bread, is a favorite among Americans of Armenian descent, thousands of whom live in and around Fresno, California. The commercial recipes are trade secrets, but home economist and prolific food writer Cynthia Scheer figured out this recipe.

  2 eggs
  1 cup milk
  4 to 4½ cups all-purpose flour
  1½ teaspoons each sugar and salt
  ¼ cup vegetable shortening
  4 teaspoons sesame seed

1. Preheat oven to 450° F. In a small bowl beat eggs and milk.

2. In a large bowl mix 4 cups of the flour with sugar and salt. Cut in shortening until mixture resembles coarse crumbs. Gradually blend in egg mixture, mixing until dough pulls away from sides of bowl.

3. On a floured board or pastry cloth knead dough lightly to form a smooth ball. Divide dough into 4 parts; wrap 3 of them in plastic wrap to keep them from drying out. Roll out and bake one portion at a time.

4. On the floured surface roll out a ball of dough to about ⅛ inch thick. Add flour as needed to prevent sticking. Reshape into a ball, then roll out again to a 14-inch circle.

5. Transfer carefully to a greased baking sheet or pizza pan. Brush lightly with water, then sprinkle with 1 teaspoon sesame seed.

6. Place a shallow pan of hot water on bottom rack of oven. Place baking sheet on rack above it and bake 3 minutes. Remove water, reduce heat to 300° F, and bake until bread is blistered, feels dry to the touch, and is lightly browned (12 to 15 minutes). Cool on a wire rack.

7. Repeat rolling and baking with remaining portions of dough.

8. When rounds of bread are crisp and cool, break into irregular pieces to serve.

Makes 4 cracker breads, each 13 to 14 inches in diameter.

A GOLD MINER'S BRUNCH

Hangtown Fry

Sautéed Sausage Rounds

Sourdough Pancakes with Wild Berry Syrup

San Francisco Sourdough French Bread or Alaskan Sourdough Bread (see page 113 and at left)

Coffee, Orange Juice, White Wine

This hearty brunch of gold rush–era favorites is ideal for a Sunday gathering of football fans. Hangtown Fry comes from California's Mother Lode; sourdough bread makes a tasty accompaniment. Sourdough pancakes derive from the other great gold rush—the Alaskan one. If game meats are sold in your area, look for sausages of venison or other game; otherwise use any unsmoked sausage.

A stack of Sourdough Pancakes served with Wild Berry Syrup, Hangtown Fry, sausages, and coffee adds up to a weekend brunch fit for a miner's appetite.

HANGTOWN FRY

Soon after the gold rush of 1849, the Sierra foothill town of Placerville, California, became a major center for transacting business and administering justice. Because of the latter the miners nicknamed it Hangtown. As the story goes, a miner who had struck it rich came to one of Placerville's hotels and asked for the most expensive breakfast in the house. The most precious delicacy on hand was fresh oysters, which the cook fried and combined with scrambled eggs. The dish was a success, and soon diners in San Francisco and elsewhere were enjoying Hangtown Fry.

> 1 *pint small shucked oysters, drained*
> ½ *to 1 teaspoon Worcestershire sauce*
> 1 *cup plain or seasoned bread crumbs*
> *Oil for deep-frying*
> 2 *tablespoons each butter and oil*
> 12 *eggs, beaten, at room temperature*
> *Salt and pepper, to taste*
> 1 *tablespoon minced chives (optional)*

1. Place oysters in a bowl and sprinkle with Worcestershire sauce. Roll oysters one at a time in bread crumbs, keeping one hand dry to handle them after coating. Shake off excess crumbs and set aside.

2. In a saucepan or deep skillet, heat 2 inches of oil to 375° F. Fry oysters a few at a time until golden brown, about 3 to 5 minutes each. Drain on paper towels and keep warm.

3. Heat 1 tablespoon each butter and oil in a large skillet over medium heat. Add half of beaten eggs. Cook 1 minute or until eggs on bottom begin to set, then stir once, gently. Continue cooking, stirring occasionally, until eggs are set in large curds but moist. Stir in half the oysters and season

with salt and pepper. Transfer to a warm serving platter. Garnish with chives (if desired). Repeat with remaining egg and oysters.

Serves 8.

SOURDOUGH PANCAKES

The easiest of all sourdough baked goods. Note that, as with other sourdough cooking, the sponge has to be prepared the day before.

> 1 *cup sourdough starter (see page 113)*
> 1 *cup warm water (90° to 100° F)*
> 1 *cup flour*
> 1 *tablespoon sugar*
> ¼ *teaspoon salt and baking soda*
> 1 *tablespoon oil or melted butter*
> 1 *egg, lightly beaten Butter*

1. *The night before:* Follow the procedure under Sourdough Starter, page 113, adding the warm water and flour to the cup of starter.

2. *On day of baking:* Return 1 cup of sponge to sourdough-starter storage container. To remaining sponge add sugar, salt, baking soda, oil, and egg; stir to combine.

3. Preheat a large lightly oiled griddle or heavy skillet until a drop of water dances on the surface. Pour 2 to 3 tablespoons batter per pancake onto griddle; cook until bubbles on top side burst and stay open. Flip with a spatula and cook until second side is golden brown. Serve with butter and Wild Berry Syrup.

Makes twenty-four 3-inch or sixteen 4-inch pancakes.

<u>Note</u> Pancakes can be cooked 15 to 20 minutes ahead and kept warm in a low oven.

WILD BERRY SYRUP

This is really more of a sauce than a syrup because the berries are not cooked. Use whatever berries are in season—blackberries, raspberries, blueberries, and huckleberries are among the many possibilities. Adjust the amount of sugar to taste and according to the sweetness of the berries. You might want to add a bit of lemon juice to blueberries or other low-acid varieties. For a more interesting texture, set aside ½ cup of berries and add to the strained syrup.

> ½ *cup sugar*
> ½ *cup water*
> 1 *pint fresh or frozen berries Lemon juice, to taste (optional)*

1. Make a simple syrup by combining sugar and water in a small saucepan and bringing to a boil. When sugar is dissolved, remove from heat and allow to cool.

2. Place berries in a blender or food processor. Turn on motor and pour in half the syrup. Blend to a smooth purée. Strain through a fine wire strainer over whole berries in bowl. (This can also be done with a food mill.) Adjust flavor to taste with more syrup or lemon juice. Store leftover sauce in refrigerator. It will keep for 2 or 3 days.

Makes about 1½ cups.

116

MAIN DISHES

Favorite entrées of Pacific-states cooks and diners are as diverse as their ethnic backgrounds. Entrées may recall the cooking of the early Mexican *ranchos*, classical French restaurants, or informal Italian cafés; or they may show a growing familiarity with the other countries and cuisines of the Pacific Rim. But main dishes are all based on the abundant food resources of the region.

JOE'S SPECIAL

San Francisco has had a number of restaurants named Joe's, all claiming to be the "original" Joe's and all featuring some variation of the following recipe. According to local legend, the dish was concocted when a hungry patron arrived at the end of a particularly busy night. About all the cook had left was eggs, spinach, and sausage (hamburger in some versions of the story) . . . and Joe's Special was born.

- *¼ pound mild Italian sausage or ground beef*
- *2 tablespoons olive oil*
- *1 small onion, sliced*
- *2 cloves garlic, minced*
- *1 bunch spinach (about 1½ cups), washed, trimmed, and shredded*
- *4 eggs, lightly beaten, at room temperature*
  Salt and pepper, to taste

1. Remove casing from sausage and slice or crumble. Heat olive oil in a large skillet over medium heat. Add sausage and sauté until meat loses the raw color. Pour off all but 2 tablespoons of fat; add onion and garlic, and cook gently until onion begins to turn brown.

2. Reduce heat to medium-low. Add spinach, eggs, and salt and pepper (season more heavily if using beef, less with sausage). Cook, stirring frequently, until eggs are nearly set. Serve on warm plates.

Serves 2.

MESQUITE-GRILLED SAND DABS

Two of San Francisco's oldest and best-loved restaurants are the Tadich Grill and Sam's Grill. Both were started just after the Gold Rush by immigrants from the Dalmatian coast of Yugoslavia, who brought with them the technique of grilling fish over charcoal. When mesquite-charcoal grilling became suddenly popular in the 1970s, it was no surprise to their regular customers, who had been enjoying grilled fish for years. The high heat of the charcoal fire produces a crisp skin and seals in the moisture of the fish. Sand dabs and rex sole, two small species of flounder, are popular grilled this way, but any small flatfish will do. Serve with French fries and a vegetable.

- *⅔ to 1 pound whole sand dabs or rex sole per person (see Note)*

1. If desired, trim fins and tails from fish. Be sure belly cavity is clean; rinse fish well, including belly cavity.

2. Prepare a very hot charcoal fire, preferably with mesquite or other natural hardwood charcoal. Arrange coals so that there are hotter and cooler parts of the fire. Oil grill and preheat thoroughly.

3. Place fish dark-skin side down on hottest part of fire. Cook until skin is well marked and fish can be easily lifted off grill with tongs or spatula (3 to 5 minutes). Do not overcook. Turn and transfer to cooler part of fire for a few minutes of cooking on other side.

Note Allow ⅔ pound per person if fish is sold pan dressed. If it is not available in this form, allow 1 pound per person. Prepare whole fish for cooking by cutting off heads and bellies with one diagonal cut from behind head to vent.

ENCHILADAS VERDES DE MARISCOS
Seafood enchiladas with green sauce

- *2 tablespoons oil*
- *2 tablespoons minced garlic*
- *3 green onions, minced*
- *1 or 2 fresh or canned Anaheim chiles, finely chopped*
- *1 can (12 oz) tomatillos (see page 87), puréed in a blender or food processor*
  Salt, to taste
- *2 cups cooked shellfish (shrimp, crabmeat, scallops, or a combination)*
- *¼ cup chopped cilantro*
- *8 corn tortillas*
- *½ cup sour cream*
- *½ cup grated jack or Swiss cheese*

1. Preheat oven to 400° F. Heat oil in a large skillet over moderate heat. Add garlic, green onions, and chiles; cook until soft but not browned. Stir in tomatillo purée and cook 10 minutes over low heat, adding a little water if the sauce starts to dry out. Add salt.

2. Combine shellfish and cilantro in a small bowl and moisten with a little of the sauce. Moisten bottom of a shallow 8- by 13-inch baking dish with about ¼ cup of the sauce.

3. Dip a tortilla into simmering sauce until soft and pliable (about 30 seconds); transfer to prepared baking dish. Place ¼ cup seafood mixture across center of tortilla and roll it into a cylinder. Repeat with remaining tortillas, fitting them snugly side by side in baking dish.

4. Pour remaining sauce over enchiladas, top each one with a spoonful of sour cream, and sprinkle cheese over top. Bake 10 minutes and serve with sauce from baking pan.

Makes 8 enchiladas, 4 main-course or 8 first-course servings.

Golden chanterelles are a favorite quarry of west-coast mushroom hunters; they may also be found in produce markets in fall and winter. Here they give their delicate but distinctive flavor to a creamy pasta dish.

FETTUCCINE WITH CHANTERELLES AND CREAM

Much of the cooking of west-coast restaurants combines classic European techniques and locally available ingredients. This delicious pasta dish, equally at home in a traditional or a contemporary menu, is a perfect example. It is so rich it is best served in small portions as a first course. Follow it with a piece of grilled or poached fish, a steamed vegetable, and a salad for a memorable meal. Other wild mushrooms—including hedgehog, oyster, and morel—are also delicious this way.

½ *pound fresh chanterelles or other wild mushrooms*
2 *cups unsalted chicken stock*
1 *tablespoon* each *butter and oil*
2 *tablespoons minced shallot or green onions*
¼ *cup dry white wine*
1½ *cups whipping cream*
1 *tablespoon chopped parsley*
1 *pound fettuccine or other fresh egg noodles*
 Salt and pepper, to taste

1. Brush dirt and debris off tops and undersides of mushrooms. If necessary, use a dampened towel to dab away any dirty spots, but avoid washing if at all possible. Discard any damp, spongy parts that have darkened. Any especially dirty stems or caps may be peeled; add peelings to stock. Slice vertically through caps and stems into T-shaped pieces about ¼ inch thick.

2. In a small saucepan bring stock and trimmings to a boil. Cook over medium-high heat until reduced to about ½ cup. Strain out trimmings and discard. (Stock may be prepared to this point several hours ahead; refrigerate until ready to continue.)

3. Have a large pot of boiling salted water ready to cook pasta. In a large skillet (or a wok) heat butter and oil over medium-high heat almost to smoking point. Add mushrooms and shallot and cook, stirring, until mushrooms begin to render liquid. Add wine and cook over high heat until liquid is mostly evaporated. Add reduced stock and cream and bring to a boil.

4. When sauce has reduced by one third, start cooking fettuccine. Continue reducing sauce to one half original volume and season with salt and pepper. Drain cooked pasta thoroughly, add to skillet, add parsley, and toss to coat evenly with sauce. If sauce is too thin, reduce further. Serve on warm plates.

Serves 4 as a main course, 8 as a first course.

Note It is difficult to give precise cooking times for this dish because fresh pasta can vary in cooking time from 30 seconds to several minutes depending on the composition of the dough and the degree of dryness. Ideally, pasta and sauce should be ready at the same time. Once cooked, however, the pasta cannot wait for the sauce, so if in doubt err on the side of keeping the sauce waiting for the pasta.

SANTA MARIA BARBECUED BEEF

The Santa Maria Valley on California's central coast has a tradition of outdoor barbecues going back to the early Spanish *rancheros*. Valley cooks have evolved a particular style—simply seasoned slabs of beef cooked over oak fires and served with a fresh tomato salsa and barbecue beans. A 3-inch-thick top sirloin steak is the preferred cut of beef used, but the whole triangle tip and other small roasts from the sirloin tip are also suitable. Serve the barbecued beef with either Frijoles or Texas Jalapeño Pinto Beans (see page 97).

1 large sirloin steak or small roast (about 3 lbs)
1 teaspoon each *salt* and *garlic salt*
½ teaspoon *pepper*
1 cup Salsa Cruda (see page 95)

1. Trim meat of excess fat and tough membranes. If using a sirloin-tip roast, remove strings and butterfly (cut across grain almost through, then open like a book). Overall thickness should be 2½ to 3 inches. Combine salt, garlic salt, and pepper and rub generously all over meat. Set aside to season at room temperature for up to 2 hours, or longer in the refrigerator.

2. Two to 3 hours ahead of serving, build a fire of oak or other hardwood and allow fire to burn down to red-hot coals. *Or:* Build a charcoal fire 1½ hours ahead and, when most of the charcoal is burning, add small chunks of oak. Sear meat over hottest part of fire, then move to a slightly cooler part and cook to taste. Total cooking time depends on size of meat, heat of fire, and type of grill (open or covered); thinner cuts over a hot fire may be medium-rare in 8 to 10 minutes per side, but with a slower fire or a larger piece of meat allow 15 to 20 minutes per side.

3. Carve thin slices of meat on a cutting board with grooves to catch juices. Transfer slices to a warm platter and moisten with juices. Garnish with salsa; serve immediately.

Serves 6.

BONELESS TROUT TERIYAKI

In teriyaki dishes, meats or fish are grilled, broiled, or cooked in a skillet, then coated with a sweetened soy-sauce glaze. A Japanese-style of cooking, teriyaki has been popular for many years in Hawaii and is now common on the mainland as well. Chicken, beef, and rich fish such as salmon or tuna are especially good.

4 boneless whole trout or farm-raised baby salmon (6 to 8 oz each)
2 tablespoons sake

Teriyaki Sauce

6 tablespoons Japanese-style soy sauce
4 tablespoons sake
2 tablespoons sugar
2 tablespoons finely grated ginger with juice

1. Remove trout from refrigerator 30 minutes before cooking. Prepare Teriyaki Sauce. Combine 2 tablespoons sauce with sake and rub on fish inside and out. Place 6 tablespoons sauce in a small saucepan, bring to a boil, then simmer until it is reduced by half.

2. *Broiler method:* Preheat broiler. Open fish and place skin side down; broil 1 to 2 inches from flame until done (about 4 minutes). Brush with reduced sauce and serve. *Outdoor grill method:* Open fish and cook skin side up on a well-oiled, preheated grill over a charcoal or gas fire. Turn onto platter when done and brush with reduced sauce.

Serves 4.

Teriyaki Sauce Combine ingredients in a small saucepan. Bring to a boil, stirring to dissolve sugar. Strain sauce through a fine sieve, pressing with a spoon to squeeze juice out of ginger shreds. Sauce will keep several weeks in a jar in refrigerator.

Makes ½ cup.

CHICKEN TETRAZZINI

San Francisco has always been an opera-loving town. This dish of chicken, mushrooms, and pasta in cream sauce was named in honor of soprano Luisa Tetrazzini, a local favorite from the time of her San Francisco debut at the Tivoli Opera House in 1904.

    1   stewing chicken (about 5 lb),
        whole or cut up
    1   onion, quartered
   12   peppercorns, cracked
        Bouquet garni (celery, pars-
        ley, and bay leaf tied in a
        bundle or wrapped in
        cheesecloth)
    1   teaspoon salt
    6   tablespoons butter or chicken
        fat
    ½   pound mushrooms, sliced
    3   tablespoons dry sherry
    ⅓   cup flour
    ⅛   teaspoon cayenne pepper
        Salt and white pepper, to taste
    1   cup whipping cream, at room
        temperature
    ½   pound spaghetti or other
        dried pasta
    ¼   cup grated Parmesan cheese
    ¼   cup sliced almonds, toasted,
        for garnish (optional)

1. Place chicken in a pot just large enough to hold it. Add onion, peppercorns, bouquet garni, water to cover, and the 1 teaspoon salt. Bring to a boil, reduce heat, cover, and simmer until chicken is tender (about 1½ hours). Strain stock and reserve. Let chicken cool enough to handle, then remove meat and shred by hand. Discard skin and bones.

2. Melt 2 tablespoons of the butter in a medium skillet over medium heat. Add mushrooms and sauté until they begin to soften. Add sherry. Cook until mushrooms are tender; set aside. Melt remaining butter in a large saucepan over medium heat; stir in flour. Cook until lightly colored. Stirring constantly, add 2 cups of the reserved stock. Bring to a boil and cook until lightly thickened and smooth. Add cayenne. Season with salt and pepper, reduce heat, and add cream. Add chicken and mushrooms; keep warm but do not let sauce boil.

120

3. Preheat oven to 375° F. Cook spaghetti in boiling salted water until just done; drain. Moisten with ½ cup sauce. Spread half of spaghetti in a buttered casserole dish. Top with half of chicken mixture. Repeat with another layer of spaghetti and another of chicken. Top with cheese and bake until top is browned (about 15 minutes). Garnish with toasted almonds, if desired.

Serves 6 to 8.

GRILLED ALBACORE WITH TORTILLAS AND SALSA

Albacore, a small, pale-fleshed tuna, is caught in late summer and fall from California to Washington by both commercial and sport fishermen. Most of the commercial catch formerly went to canneries, but more and more is being sold as fresh or frozen fillet. To many, there is no better way to enjoy fresh albacore than straight from the charcoal grill, folded in a warm tortilla.

   1½   to 2 pounds albacore fillet
         or steaks
         Olive oil
         Freshly ground pepper
         Fresh oregano or marjoram
         (optional)
    1   dozen corn tortillas
    1   cup Salsa Cruda (see page 95)
         or Salsa Verde (see page 95)

1. Cut albacore into 1-inch cubes. Thread on skewers, 3 or 4 cubes per skewer. Drizzle with olive oil; sprinkle with pepper and oregano (if used). Marinate in refrigerator 1 to 4 hours, turning occasionally.

2. Build a hot charcoal fire and let it burn down to a glowing red. Remove fish from refrigerator at least 30 minutes before grilling. Heat tortillas and transfer to a basket lined with a towel to keep warm. Grill fish over hottest part of fire until just done (3 to 5 minutes per side). To serve, wrap a skewer of fish inside a tortilla, garnish with salsa, and pull out skewer.

Serves 4 to 6.

DESSERTS

In many homes, dessert can be just a piece of ripe seasonal fruit, perhaps accompanied by cheese. But there are times when a more elaborate dessert is in order. Here is a small sampling of desserts created from locally available ingredients, plus a classic after-dinner drink that can serve as a liquid dessert.

TROPICAL FRUIT SALAD WITH COCONUT MILK

Making a fruit salad is not so much a matter of following a recipe as choosing and combining the best fruits the market has to offer at the moment. Tropical fruits (which make particularly good fruit salads) are becoming more widely available, not just from Hawaii but also from Mexico and the Caribbean. To provide additional colors and flavors, add watermelon or honeydew, kiwifruit, or strawberries. The pineapple boat described in step 1 makes an attractive presentation. Here are a few tips for choosing tropical fruits.

Pineapples Look for plump, firm fruit beginning to turn golden and a fresh, ripe aroma. Avoid any with soft spots, browning skin, or a sourish, fermented aroma.

Mangoes Choose firm fruit with skin that is more yellow or red than green; avoid those with soft or black spots. Allow to soften a day or two at room temperature, then refrigerate or use promptly.

Papayas Ripe fruit should have smooth, unblemished yellow or orange skin over flesh that is just slightly soft like a ripe peach. Handle carefully—they bruise easily.

    1   large pineapple
    1   large mango
    1   large papaya
    1   firm but ripe banana
    2   or 3 tangerines, peeled and
        separated into sections
    ½   cup thin coconut milk
        (see Note)
        Fresh lime juice, to taste

ALDER-GRILLED SALMON

Red alder provides the favorite wood for grilling seafoods in the Northwest. If you have a ready supply, you can build a fire entirely of this hardwood and let it burn down to glowing coals. An easier way is to add chunks of alder or other aromatic hardwoods (available in cookware and specialty-food stores) to a charcoal fire. No sauce is necessary, but you can melt butter with a squeeze of lemon juice in a pan on the grill's edge. For an authentic northwestern flavor, serve with a Washington State Riesling or an Oregon Chardonnay.

> 6 salmon steaks, 1 inch thick, or 2 to 3 pounds fillet
> Vegetable oil
> Salt and pepper
> Lemon wedges

1. Prepare a hot charcoal fire in an open or covered grill. When charcoal is mostly lit, add alder or other hardwood chunks. Let fire burn until charcoal is covered with a light gray ash. Oil grill and preheat thoroughly.

2. Meanwhile, prepare salmon. If using a large piece of fillet, slice diagonally into pieces of even size and thickness. Skin may be left on or removed according to taste. Rub salmon lightly with oil and sprinkle with salt and pepper. Refrigerate fish if necessary, but remove from refrigerator 30 minutes before grilling.

3. Place salmon on grill, starting fillets bone side down on hottest part of fire. Cook until edges are turning opaque (4 to 6 minutes). Turn with a long-bladed spatula and cook until a skewer easily penetrates the thickest part (3 to 4 minutes). Serve immediately with lemon wedges.

Serves 6.

Variation If you prefer a smokier flavor and have a covered grill, build a smaller fire off-center in the grill and let it burn down farther. Add the hardwood chunks just before cooking fish, and place it to the side rather than directly over fire. Cover and cook longer, 15 to 20 minutes total depending on the heat of the fire.

BARBECUED OYSTERS

Around Tomales Bay in Northern California and many other oyster-raising bays of the Northwest, oysters grilled in the shell are a popular appetizer. Some prefer to season them with a tomato-based sauce, others enjoy a garlic butter like the one below. If you are skilled with an oyster knife and you prefer your oysters less cooked, shuck them first, add the sauce, and cook them just once on the half shell.

> ¼ pound butter, softened
> 4 cloves garlic, minced or pressed
> Juice and grated peel of ½ lemon
> Pepper, to taste
> 2 dozen small or medium oysters, in the shell

1. *One day ahead:* In a medium bowl, combine butter, garlic, lemon peel and juice, and pepper; beat until light and thoroughly mixed. Form into a thin log on a sheet of waxed paper, roll in paper, and wrap tightly in plastic wrap. Refrigerate until 1 hour before using.

2. Build a hot charcoal fire and let it burn down to red-hot coals. Place unopened oysters on grill, deeper shell down. As soon as shells begin to open, remove top shell with an oyster knife (use an oven mitt to protect your oyster-holding hand), and cut oyster free from bottom shell (see page 10). Place a pat of garlic butter in shell and return oyster to fire. Serve as soon as juices are bubbly and butter is melted.

Serves 6 as a first course.

MIXED VEGETABLES VINAIGRETTE

Use whatever vegetables are in season for this salad; the ones listed below make a summertime version. Earlier in the year a similar salad might feature artichoke hearts or asparagus. In fall and winter use cool-season vegetables such as broccoli, cauliflower, and celery root.

> 1 pound slender green beans
> 2 large red or yellow bell peppers
> 1 medium cucumber, peeled, seeded, and thickly sliced
> ½ teaspoon salt
> 1 head escarole or red-leaf lettuce
> 1 pint cherry or yellow-pear tomatoes
> 2 teaspoons each Dijon mustard and wine vinegar
> 6 tablespoons olive oil
> Salt and pepper, to taste
> Basil leaves and flowers, for garnish

1. *The day before:* Trim green beans and cut into 2-inch lengths. Immerse in rapidly boiling salted water until tender but still bright green and a little crunchy. Drain, rinse immediately in cold water to stop cooking, and refrigerate. Roast and peel peppers (see page 96). Working over a bowl to catch juices, cut peppers into strips, discarding seeds and ribs. Refrigerate peppers with their juices.

2. *On picnic day:* Toss cucumber slices with salt, place in a colander, and allow to drain 15 minutes. Wash escarole, tear into bite-sized pieces, and dry thoroughly. In a large salad bowl combine greens with beans, peppers, cucumbers, and tomatoes; reserve pepper juices for dressing. Cover tightly with plastic wrap above dampened paper towel.

3. In a small jar combine mustard, vinegar, olive oil, and reserved pepper juices. Stir or shake to combine. Taste for seasoning and, if necessary, add salt and pepper. Just before serving, pour dressing over salad and toss to coat vegetables evenly. Garnish with basil leaves and flowers.

Serves 6.

INDEX

Note: Page numbers in italics refer to illustrations separated from recipe text.

A

Acorn Squash, Stuffed, 58
African influence
  in Louisiana cooking, 66
  in southern cooking, 26, 30,
    32–33, 36
Alaska, sourdough baking in, 113
Alaskan Sourdough Bread, 114
Albacore, Grilled, With Tortillas and
  Salsa, 120
Alcoholic beverages
  Irish Coffee, 121
  liquor-laced coffees, 121
  in southern cooking, 26
  in southwestern cooking, 86
Almonds
  Chiles en Nogada, 96
  Flan de Almendras, 103
  Stir-Fried Vegetables With, 110
Amana Colonies
  Red Marble Cake, 58, *59*, 60
  Radish Salad, 58
Anadama Bread, 16
Andouille, 67
  Chicken, Andouille, and Tasso
    Jambalaya, *64*, 83
  Creole Baked Eggs With Andouille,
    Ham, and Asparagus, 76
  in Oyster and Eggplant Casserole, 71
  in Pork Chops With Oyster
    Stuffing, 76
  in Red Beans and Rice, 74–75
  in Seafood Filé Gumbo, *64*, 83
  in Stuffed Mirliton, 72
Appetizers or first courses
  See also Soups
  Artichokes With Dipping Sauces,
    108–9
  Barbecued Oysters, *104*, 123
  California Roll Sushi, 109
  Chiles en Nogada, 96
  Crabmeat Ravigote, 70
  East Texas Caviar, *84*, 101
  Fettuccine With Chanterelles and
    Cream, 118–19
  Lomi-Lomi Salmon, 107
  as main courses, 107
  Olympia Oysters in Sake Cups, 107
  Oysters Kirkpatrick, 107
  Oysters "Rockefeller," 68, *69*
  Raw Oysters With Cocktail
    Sauce, *64*, 82
  Shrimp Rémoulade, 68–69
Apple(s)
  Dumplings With Nutmeg Sauce, *4*, 15
  in Jicama and Fruit Relish, *84*, 101
  Mom's Green-Apple Pie, 63
  Ozark Pudding, 41
  Pandowdy, 20
  Sautéed, *44*, 47
  Tangy Apple Butter, 50
Armenian Cracker Bread, 114
Artichokes
  With Dipping Sauces, 108–9
  Oyster and Artichoke Soup, 68
  preparing, 108
Asian influence, 106, 119
Asparagus, Creole Baked Eggs With
  Andouille, Ham, and, 76
Avocados, 86
  Guacamole, 95

B

Bacon
  in Cobb Salad, 112

in Geoduck Chowder, 112
in southern cooking, 26, 29
  Country-Style Greens, *24*, 33
  Hoppin' John, 35
  Lowlands Okra Pilau, 36
  Okra and Tomato Stew, 36
  Shrimp Okra Pilau, 36
Bananas
  Foster, *80*, 81
  in Tropical Fruit Salad With Coconut
    Milk, 120–21
Barbecued Beef, Santa Maria, 119
Barbecued Oysters, *104*, 123
Barbecued Pork Ribs and Sausages, *84*,
  100–101
Basting ("Moppin' ") Sauce, 100, 101
Beans
  Black-Bean Soup, 97
  Boston Baked, 21, *23*
  East Texas Caviar, *84*, 101
  Frijoles, *84*, 97
  Hoppin' John, 35
  Idaho White-Bean Soup, 49
  Red Beans and Rice, 74–75
  Refried, 97
  Succotash, 11
  Texas Jalapeño Pinto, 97
Beef
  Broiled Porterhouse Steak With
    Savory Butter, 53
  Chicken-Fried Steak, 29
  Chiles en Nogada, 96
  Corned Beef Hash, 8
  Country-Fried Steak, 29
  Fajitas, 87
  Grillades, 78
  Joe's Special, 117
  New England Boiled Dinner, *4*, 14
  Pookie's Liver and Onions, 32
  Real Texas Chili, 90
  Red-Flannel Hash, 8
  Ropa Vieja, 31
  Santa Maria Barbecued Beef, 119
  Texas Chuck-wagon Country-Fried
    Steak, 29
  Upper Peninsula Pasties, 50–51
  Winter Vegetable-Beef Soup, 48–49
Beets, in Red-Flannel Hash, 8
Berries
  Berry Gratiné, 82
  Blueberry Slump, 20
  in Pacific States cooking, 106
  Plump Blueberry Muffins, 56
  Wild Berry Syrup, *115*, 116
  Wild Blackberry Pie, 122
Beverages. *See* Alcoholic beverages
Biscuit Crust, for Georgia Peach
  Cobbler, 43
Biscuit Dough, for Apple Dumplings
  With Nutmeg Sauce, 15
Biscuits
  Buttery Baking Powder, 56
  Georgia Drop, 37
Biscuit-Topped Chicken Potpie, 54
Biscuit Topping, for Apple
  Pandowdy, 20
Bisque, Crayfish, 70
Black-Bean Soup, 97
Blackberries. *See* Berries
Black-eyed peas
  East Texas Caviar, *84*, 101
  Hoppin' John, 35
Blueberries. *See* Berries
Blue Corn Bread, 99. *See also*
  Cornmeal, blue
Boiled Dinner, New England, *4*, 14
Boiled Seafood Dinner, 78, *79*
Boston Baked Beans, 21, *23*
Boston Brown Bread, 22, *23*

Boston Cream Pie, 22, *23*
Bourbon, 26, 81
Bratwurst, Grilled Polish Sausage
  and, *59*, 60
Bread Pudding With Bourbon Sauce,
  80, 81
Bread(s)
  Alaskan Sourdough, 114
  Anadama, 16
  Armenian Cracker, 114
  Blue Corn, 99
  Boston Brown, 22, *23*
  Buttery Baking Powder Biscuits, 56
  Georgia Drop Biscuits, 37
  Gingerbread, 16
  Hush Puppies, 38
  Jalapeño Corn Muffins, 99
  Johnnycake, 17
  main-dish, Chicago-Style Deep-Dish
    Pizza, 54–55, *55*
  Navaho Fry, 98
  Oatmeal Gems, 16
  Parker House Rolls, *4*, 14–15
  Plump Blueberry Muffins, 56
  Sally Lunn, Georgia Style, 37
  San Francisco Sourdough
    French, 113
  Seeded Parker House Rolls, 14–15
  Sopaipillas, 98–99
  Sourdough Pancakes, *115*, 116
  Sourdough Starter, 113
  Southern Corn, *36*, 37
  Sticky Cinnamon Buns, *44*, 48
  Texas Jalapeño-Cheese Corn, 99
  Virginia Spoon, 38
Breakfast or brunch dishes
  Baked Garlic Grits, 34–35
  Cajun Home-Fried Potatoes, 71
  Corned Beef Hash, 8
  Corn Oysters, 11
  Cream-Basted Fried Eggs, *44*, 47
  Fried Scrapple, *44*, 47
  Hangtown Fry, *115*, 116
  Johnnycake, 17
  Kedgeree, 7
  Maple-Glazed Sweet Potatoes, 10
  Sautéed Apples, *44*, 47
  Scalloped Codfish, 7
  Sourdough Pancakes, *115*, 116
  Virginia Spoon Bread, 38
  Wild Berry Syrup, *115*, 116
Brown Bread, Boston, 6, 21, *23*
Buns, Sticky Cinnamon, *44*, 48
Burned-Sugar Cake, Aunt Lou's 61
Buttermilk, in southern cooking, 26
Buttermilk-Battered Fried Chicken With
  Honey-Pecan Glaze, 39
Butter(s)
  compound, for oysters, 68, *69*
  Creole, for Baked Fish, 73
  Lemon, for artichokes, 108
  lime-chile, for Elotes, *84*, 101
  Savory, for broiled steak, 53
  Tangy Apple, 50
Buying special ingredients. *See* Mail-
  order sources

C

Cabbage
  Creole Slaw, *64*, 82–83
  Crispy Coleslaw, *59*, 60
Cajun cooking, 66
Cajun Home-Fried Potatoes, 71
Cakes
  Aunt Lou's Burned-Sugar, 61
  Boston Cream Pie, 22, *23*
  coffee, Parker House dough as, 14
  Election, 19

Gingerbread, 16
  Lane, 43
  Mississippi Mud, 41
  Norwegian Chocolate, 62–63
  Red Marble, *59*, 60
  Sally Lunn, Georgia Style, 37
  "tipsy," 26
  Mississippi Mud Cake, 41
  Washington Pie, 22
Candies, Pralines, *80*, 81
Canning pickles or relishes
  Cranberry Chutney, 13
  Mustard Pickles, 12
  Watermelon Pickles, 12
Caramelized Maple Dumplings, *18*, 19
Caribbean influence, 31, 106
Catfish, in southern cooking, 26
  Pan-Fried, 27
Cayenne pepper, 67
Central American influence, 106
Chanterelles, 106
  and Cream, Fettuccine With, 118–19
Chaurice, 67
  in Grillades, 78
  in Pork Chops With Oyster
    Stuffing, 76
  in Red Beans and Rice, 74–75
Chayote, 67, 86, 87
  in Cream-Cheese Sauce, 98
  Stuffed Mirliton, 72
Cheese
  Chicago-Style Deep-Dish Pizza,
    54–55
  Chile and Cheese Soup, *91*, 92
  Chiles en Nogada, 96
  Cobb Salad, 112
  Jalapeño Corn Muffins, 99
  Oyster and Eggplant Casserole, 71
  Stuffed Acorn Squash, 58
  Texas Jalapeño-Cheese Corn
    Bread, 99
  Tucson Chimichangas With All the
    Trimmings, 88, 89
  Twice-Baked Potatoes With
    Wisconsin Cheddar Cheese, 57
Cherokee Green Onions and Eggs, 88
Cherries, Michigan Sour-Cherry Pie, 62
Chicago-Style Deep-Dish Pizza, 54–55
Chicken
  Basic Southern-Fried, 39, *40*
  Biscuit-Topped Chicken Potpie, 54
  Buttermilk-Battered Fried Chicken
    With Honey-Pecan Glaze, 39
  Chicken, Andouille, and Tasso
    Jambalaya, *64*, 83
  Cobb Salad, 112
  deep-red brown roux for, 77
  Étouffée, 73
  Maryland Oven-Fried, 39
  Oyster Stuffing for, 76
  Roast, With Minnesota Wild-Rice
    Stuffing, 52–53
  in southern cooking, 26
  Tetrazzini, 120
  Tucson Chimichangas With All the
    Trimmings, 88, 89
Chicken-Fried Steak, 29
Chiles, 86, 87
  See also Chile sauces
  Blue Corn Bread, 99
  Chile and Cheese Soup, *91*, 92
  in East Texas Caviar, *84*, 101
  in Enchiladas Verdes de
    Mariscos, 117
  Jalapeño Corn Muffins, 99
  en Nogada, 96

124

mail-order source for, 87
peeling and roasting, 96
Texas Jalapeño-Cheese Corn
　　Bread, 99
Chile sauces
　Guacamole, 95
　Salsa Cruda, 95
　Salsa Roja (Red chile sauce), 95
　Salsa Verde (Green sauce), 95
Chili, Real Texas, 90
Chili powder, 86
Chimichangas, Tucson, With All the
　Trimmings, 88, 89
Chinese influence, 106
　Stir-Fried Vegetables With
　　Almonds, 110
Chocolate, in mole poblano, 87
Chocolate Cake, Norwegian, 62–63
Chocolate Frosting, for Boston Cream
　Pie, 22
Chorizo, in southwestern cooking, 87
　Barbecued Pork Ribs and Sausages,
　　84, 100–101
　Guajolote Relleno, 91, 92–93
　Texas Jalapeño-Cheese Corn
　　Bread, 99
Chowder(s)
　Clam, 21, 23
　Fish, 9
　Geoduck, 112
Chutney, Cranberry, 13
Cider-Baked Country Ham, 28–29
Cider-Glazed Pork Loin Roast, 52, 53
Cilantro, 86, 87, 106
Cinnamon Buns, Sticky, 44, 48
Cinnamon rolls, Parker House Rolls
　as, 14–15
Cioppino, 111
Clam(s)
　Chowder, 21, 23
　in Cioppino, 111
　Fritters, 10
　Geoduck Chowder, 112
　opening, 10
　Pie, 7
Cobbler, Georgia Peach, 43
Cobb Salad, 112
Coconut milk, 121
　Tropical Fruit Salad With, 120–21
Coconuts, in Pacific States cooking, 106
Cod
　Baked Fish With Creole Butter in
　　Foil Packages, 73
　Fish Chowder, 9
　Kedgeree, 7
　Scalloped Codfish, 7
Coffee, Irish, 121, 121
Collard greens. See Greens
Cookies
　Ipperwash Beach Sand Tarts, 61
　Sour-Cream Sugar, 62
Corn, 6, 26
　Elotes, 84, 101
　Maquechoux, 71
　Oysters, 11
　Pudding, 11
　Succotash, 11
　Sweet-Sour Corn Relish, 50
Corn bread. See Cornmeal, in breads
Corned beef
　Corned Beef Hash, 8
　New England Boiled Dinner, 4, 14
　Red-Flannel Hash, 8
Corn flour, yellow, 67
　in Louisiana Seafood Fry, 75
Cornmeal
　blue, 86, 87
　　Blue Corn Bread, 99

　in breads
　　Anadama Bread, 16
　　Blue Corn Bread, 99
　　Boston Brown Bread, 22, 23
　　Hush Puppies, 38
　　Johnnycake, 17
　　Southern Corn Bread, 36, 37
　　Texas Jalapeño-Cheese Corn
　　　Bread, 99
　　Virginia Spoon Bread, 38
　　in Fried Scrapple, 44, 47
　　in Indian Pudding, 19
　　in Lemon Chess Pie, 42
　　in Pan-Fried Catfish, 27
Corn scrapers, 11
Country-Fried Steak, 29
Country-Style Greens, 24, 33
Crab
　California Roll Sushi, 109
　blue, 67
　　Boiled Seafood Dinner, 78, 79
　　Crabmeat Ravigote, 70
　　Maryland Crab Cakes, 27
　　Seafood Filé Gumbo, 64, 83
　Cioppino, 111
　Enchiladas Verdes de Mariscos, 117
　Salad Louis, 110, 111
Crab, Shrimp, or Crayfish Boil, 67
Cracker Bread, Armenian, 114
Cranberry beans, in Succotash, 11
Cranberry Chutney, 13
Crayfish, in Louisiana cooking, 67
　Boiled Seafood Dinner, 78, 79
　Crayfish Bisque, 70
　Louisiana Seafood Fry, 75
　Stuffed Crayfish Heads, 70
Creole Baked Eggs With Andouille,
　Ham, and Asparagus, 76
Creole Butter, for Baked Fish, 73
Creole cooking, 66
Creole Slaw, 64, 82–83
Creole Tartar Sauce, 75
Cuban Shredded Beef (Ropa Vieja), 31
Curried dishes, from India trade, 6
Curry Mayonnaise, for artichokes, 108
Custard
　Flan de Almendras, 103
　fruits in (Walaxshi), 103

D

Desserts
　See also Cakes; Cookies; Dumplings;
　　Pies or tarts; Puddings
　Apple Pandowdy, 20
　Bananas Foster, 80, 81
　Berry Gratiné, 82
　Blueberry Slump, 20
　Empanaditas Dulces de Hoja, 102
　Flan de Almendras, 103
　Georgia Peach Cobbler, 43
　Gingerbread, 16
　Macadamia-Ginger Ice Cream, 122
　Margarita Sorbet, 102, 103
　Nieve de Tunas, 91, 94
　Pralines, 80, 81
　Tropical Fruit Salad With Coconut
　　Milk, 120–21
　Walaxshi (Fruits in custard), 103
Dressing(s)
　for Creole Slaw, 82, 83
　Louis, 110, 111
　for Nopalito Salad, 91, 94
Dumplings
　Apple, with Nutmeg Sauce, 4, 15
　Caramelized Maple, 18, 19

E

East Texas Caviar, 84, 101
Eggplant, Oyster and Eggplant
　Casserole, 71
Eggs
　Cherokee Green Onions and, 88
　in Cobb Salad, 112
　in Crab Salad Louis, 110, 111
　Cream-Basted Fried, 44, 47
　Creole Baked Eggs With Andouille,
　　Ham, and Asparagus, 76
　Hangtown Fry, 115, 116
　Joe's Special, 117
Election Cake, 19
Elotes, 84, 101
Empanadas, described, 102
Empanaditas Dulces de Hoja, 102
Enchiladas Verdes de Mariscos, 117
English influence
　in heartland cooking, 50–51
　in New England cooking, 7
Étouffée, 67
　Chicken, 73
European influence, 106

F

Fajitas, 87
Fats
　bacon or ham grease, 29
　for pie crusts, 63
Fettuccine With Chanterelles and
　Cream, 118–19
Filé powder, 66, 67
First courses. See Appetizers or first
　courses; Soups
Fish
　See also specific kinds
　Baked Fish With Creole Butter in Foil
　　Packages, 73
　cakes, as "standing dish," 6
　Chowder, 9
　　as "standing dish," 6
　Cioppino, 111
　grilled
　　Alder-Grilled Salmon, 104, 123
　　Grilled Albacore With Tortillas
　　　and Salsa, 120
　　Mesquite-Grilled Sand Dabs, 117
　Kedgeree, 7
　in Louisiana cooking, 66
　in New England cooking, 6
　in Pacific States cooking, 106
　in southern cooking, 26
　teriyaki, 119
Flan de Almendras, 103
Food-processor doughs
　Flaky Pastry, 63
　Pizza Dough, 54, 55
French bread, San Francisco
　Sourdough, 113
French influence
　in Louisiana cooking, 66, 77
　in Pacific States cooking, 106
　in southern cooking, 39, 41
Fritters
　Clam, 10
　Corn Oysters, 11
Frostings
　Burned-Sugar, 61
　Chocolate, 22
　Fudge, 62, 63
Fruits
　See also specific fruits
　Jicama and Fruit Relish, 84, 101
　Ozark Pudding, 41
　in southern cooking, 26
　Tropical Fruit Salad With Coconut
　　Milk, 120–21
　Walaxshi (Fruits in custard), 103

Frying
　seafood, techniques, 75
　in southern cooking, 26

G

Game, 26. See also Rabbit
Geoduck Chowder, 112
Georgia Drop Biscuits, 37
Georgia Peach Cobbler, 43
Georgia Rabbit and Oyster Gumbo, 30
　light-brown roux for, 77
German influence
　in heartland cooking, 57, 58, 68
　in Louisiana cooking, 66
　in southern cooking, 39, 40
　in southwestern cooking, 86
Ginger, 6, 16, 106
　Gingerbread, 16
　Macadamia-Ginger Ice Cream, 122
Goulash, Pork, and Sauerkraut, 51
Grapes, in Walaxshi, 103
Gravy
　American-Style Turkey, 93
　Cream, for fried chicken, 39
　Mole Poblano, 91, 93
　Red-Eye, 29
Greens, in southern cooking, 26
　Country-Style Greens, 24, 33
Green tomatoes
　Fried, 58
　Green-Tomato Pie, 18
Grillades, 77, 78
Grilled fish
　Alder-Grilled Salmon, 104, 123
　Grilled Albacore With Tortillas and
　　Salsa, 120
　Mesquite-Grilled Sand Dabs, 117
Grilled Polish Sausage and Bratwurst,
　59, 60
Grits, Baked Garlic, 34–35
Guacamole, 95
Guajolote Relleno, 91, 92–93
Gumbo, 30, 66, 67
　brown roux for, 77
　Georgia Rabbit and Oyster, 30
　Seafood Filé, 64, 83
Gumbo filé, described, 67

H

Halibut
　Baked Fish With Creole Butter in
　　Foil Packages, 73
　in Cioppino, 111
　Kedgeree, 7
Ham, 26, 28
　buying and storing, 28
　Cider-Baked Country, 28–29
　Country Ham Slices With Red-Eye
　　Gravy, 29
　Creole Baked Eggs With Andouille,
　　Ham, and Asparagus, 76
　fat, cooking with, 29
　in Idaho White-Bean Soup, 49
Hangtown Fry, 115, 116
Hash, Corned Beef or Red-Flannel, 8
Hawaiian influence, 106, 107, 119,
　120–21, 122
Holiday dishes
　Chiles en Nogada, 96
　East Texas Caviar, 84, 101
　Hoppin' John, 35
Holiday menus
　Fourth of July Picnic in the Park, 58,
　　59, 60
　New Mexico Noche Buena Feast, 90,
　　91, 92–94

Hominy
    Baked Garlic Grits, 34–35
    Zuni Lamb, Chile, and Hominy
        Stew, 89
Hoppin' John, 35
Horseradish Sauce, 14
Hot peppers, 26. *See also* Chiles
Hot sauces
    Louisiana-style, described, 67
    Salsa Cruda, 95
    Salsa Roja (Red chile sauce), 95
Hungarian influence, in heartland
    cooking, 51
Hush Puppies, 38
    Pan-Fried Catfish and, 27

I

Ice Cream, Macadamia-Ginger, 122
Idaho White-Bean Soup, 49
India trade, 6
    Kedgeree, 7
Indian Pudding, 6, 19
Ipperwash Beach Sand Tarts, 61
Irish Coffee, 121, *121*
Italian influence
    in Louisiana cooking, 66
    in New England cooking, 6
    in Pacific States cooking, 106
Italian sausage
    in Chicago-Style Deep-Dish
        Pizza, 54–55
    in Joe's Special, 117

J, K

Jalapeño chiles, 86
    Blue Corn Bread, 99
    in East Texas Caviar, *84*, 101
    Jalapeño Corn Muffins, 99
    Texas Jalapeño-Cheese Corn
        Bread, 99
Jambalaya, 67
    Chicken, Andouille, and Tasso,
        64, 83
Japanese influence, 119
Jicama, in southwestern cooking, 87
    Jicama and Fruit Relish, *84*, 101
Joe's Special, 117
Johnnycake, 17
Kedgeree, 7
Key-Lime Pie, 42

L

Lagniappe, in Louisiana cooking, 66
Lahvosh, 114
Lamb, in southwestern cooking, 86
    Zuni Lamb, Chile, and Hominy
        Stew, 89
Lane Cake, 43
Lard
    for pie crusts, 63
    in southern cooking, 26
Latin American influence, 31, 106
Leeks Braised With Tasso, 71
Lemon Butter, for artichokes, 108
Lemon Chess Pie, 42
Lima beans, in Succotash, 11
Limes, 86
    Lime-chile butter, for Elotes, *84*, 101
    Margarita Sorbet, *102*, 103
Liver, Pookie's Liver and Onions, 32
Lomi-Lomi Salmon, 107
Louisiana Seafood Fry, 75
Louisiana-style hot sauce, described, 67
Lowlands Okra Pilau, 36

M

Macadamia-Ginger Ice Cream, 122
Mail-order sources
    for Louisiana ingredients, 67

for southwestern ingredients, 87
for Virginia hams, 28
Mangoes, 106, 120
    in Jicama and Fruit Relish, *84*, 101
    in Tropical Fruit Salad With Coconut
        Milk, 120–21
Maple sugar or syrup, 6
Margarita Sorbet, *102*, 103
Marinated artichokes, preparing, 108
Maryland Crab Cakes, 27
Maryland Oven-Fried Chicken, 39
Masa harina, described, 90
Matsutake, 106
Mayonnaise, Curry, for artichokes, 108
Mediterranean influence, 106
Menus
    Backyard Seafood Dinner, 78, *79*
    Boston Dinner, 20–22, *23*
    Church-Social, 38–39, *40*, 41
    Family Supper, *4*, 14–15
    A Gold Miner's Brunch, 114,
        115, 116
    Fais Dodo, *64*, 82–83
    Fourth of July Picnic in the Park,
        58, *59*, 60
    New Mexico Noche Buena Feast,
        90, *91*, 92–94
    A Seashore Barbecue, *104*, 122–23
    Soul Food Dinner, *24*, 32–33
    Sunday Breakfast, *44*, 47–48
    Texas Barbecue, *84*, 100–101
Mexican influence, in Pacific States
        cooking, 106, 120–21
    in southwestern cooking, 86
Michigan Sour-Cherry Pie, 62
Mirepoix, in Louisiana cooking, 66
Mirliton. *See* Chayote
Mississippi Mud Cake, 41
Mole poblano paste, 87
Mole Poblano "Gravy," *91*, 93
Morel(s), 106
    in Fettuccine With Chanterelles and
        Cream, 118–19
    Soup, 49
Muffins
    Jalapeño Corn, 99
    Oatmeal Gems, 16
    Plump Blueberry, 56
Mulberries. *See* Berries
Mushrooms, 106
    Fettuccine With Chanterelles and
        Cream, 118–19
    Morel Soup, 49
Mussels
    in Cioppino, 111
    opening, 10
Mustard Greens, Country-Style, *24*, 33
Mustard Pickles, 12

N

Native American influence
    in Louisiana cooking, 66
    in New England cooking, 6
    in southern cooking, 34
    in southwestern cooking, 86
Navaho Fry Bread, 98
New England Boiled Dinner, *4*, 14
New England influence, in heartland
        cooking, 46
Nieve de Tunas, *91*, 94
Nopal cactus, 86
Nopalitos, 87
    Nopalito Salad, *91*, 94
Norwegian Chocolate Cake, 62–63
Nutmeg Sauce, Apple Dumplings
        With, *4*, 15
Nuts, Chiles en Nogada, 96

O

Oatmeal Gems, 16
Okra, 26, 36, 67
    Georgia Rabbit and Oyster
        Gumbo, 30
    Lowlands Okra Pilau, 36
    Shrimp Okra Pilau, 36
    and Tomato Stew, *35*, 36
Oranges, in Jicama and Fruit
        Relish, *84*, 101
Oriental influence, 106, 119
Oyster(s), 8, 67
    and Artichoke Soup, 68
    Barbecued, *104*, 123
    Georgia Rabbit and Oyster
        Gumbo, 30
    Hangtown Fry, *115*, 116
    Kirkpatrick, 107
    Louisiana Seafood Fry, 75
    Olympia Oysters in Sake Cups, 107
    opening, 10
    in Pork Chops With Oyster
        Stuffing, 76
    Raw, with Cocktail Sauce, *64*, 82
    "Rockefeller," 68, *69*
    Scalloped, 8
    Seafood Filé Gumbo, *64*, 83

P, Q

Pancakes
    Johnnycake, 17
    Sourdough, with Wild Berry Syrup,
        115, 116
Pan-Fried Catfish, 27
Pan-Fried Trout, Ernest Hemingway's
        Way, 51
Papayas, 106, 120
    in Tropical Fruit Salad With Coconut
        Milk, 120–21
Parker House Rolls, *4*, 14–15
Parsnip Stew, 8
Pasta
    Chicken Tetrazzini, 120
    Fettuccine With Chanterelles and
        Cream, 118–19
Pasties, Upper Peninsula, 50–51
Pastry
    Empanaditas Dulces de Hoja, 102
    Flaky, 63
    for Ipperwash Beach Sand Tarts, 61
    Pasty, 51
Peaches
    Georgia Peach Cobbler, 43
    Walaxshi (Fruits in custard), 103
Pears, in Walaxshi, 103
Pecans, in southern cooking, 26
    Pecan Pie, *40*, 41
Pennsylvania Dutch cooking, 50
Pepper, in Louisiana cooking, 67
Peppers, hot, 26. *See also* Chiles
Pickles
    Mustard, 12
    Watermelon, 12
Pie crusts. *See* Pastry
Pies or tarts
    Boston Cream Pie, 22, *23*
    Empanaditas Dulces de Hoja, 102
    Green-Tomato, 18
    Ipperwash Beach Sand Tarts, 61
    Key-Lime, 42
    Lemon Chess, 42
    main-dish
        Biscuit-Topped Chicken pot-
            pie, 54
        Chicago-Style Deep-Dish
            Pizza, 54–55
        Clam, 7
        Upper Peninsula Pasties, 50–51
    Michigan Sour-Cherry, 62
    Mom's Green-Apple, 63

Pecan, *40*, 41
    Sweet-Potato, 33
    Washington, 22
    Wild Blackberry, 122
Pilaus, 36
Pineapples, 106, 120
    in Tropical Fruit Salad With Coconut
        Milk, 120–21
Pine nuts, 87
    in Walaxshi (Fruits in custard), 103
Pinto beans, Frijoles, *84*, 97
Pizza, Chicago-Style Deep-Dish, 54–55
Polish influence, 86
Polish sausage, in Grilled Polish
        Sausage and Bratwurst, *59*, 60
Pone, Yam, 34
Pork
    See also Sausage; Salt pork
    Barbecued Pork Ribs and Sausages,
        84, 100–101
    Chiles en Nogada, 96
    Chops, with Oyster Stuffing, 76
    Cider-Glazed Pork Loin Roast, *52*, 53
    Fried Scrapple, *44*, 47
    in heartland cooking, 50
    in Real Texas Chili, 90
    roast, Oyster Stuffing for, 76
    and Sauerkraut Goulash, 51
    Smothered Pork Chops, *24*, 32
    in southern cooking, 26
Portuguese influence, 6
Potatoes
    See also Sweet potatoes
    Cajun Home-Fried, 71
    Church-Social Potato Salad, 39, *40*
    Down-Home Mashed, *24*, 33
    German Potato Salad, *59*, 60
    Swedish Mashed Potatoes and
        Rutabaga, 57
    Twice-Baked Potatoes With
        Wisconsin Cheddar Cheese, 57
Pralines, 80, 81
Prickly pears, 86, 87
    Nieve de Tunas, *91*, 94
Puddings
    Baked Rice, 18
    Bread, With Bourbon Sauce, 80, 81
    Corn, 11
    Indian, 19
    Ozark, 41
    Raisin Rice, 18

R

Rabbit, 26
    cutting up, 31
    Georgia Rabbit and Oyster
        Gumbo, 30
Radish Salad, Amana Colonies, 58
Raisin Rice Pudding, 18
Raspberries. *See* Berries
Raw Oysters With Cocktail
        Sauce, *64*, 82
Red Beans and Rice, 74–75
Redfish, in Louisiana cooking, 67
    Baked Fish With Creole Butter in
        Foil Packages, 73
Red-Flannel Hash, 8
Red Marble Cake, *59*, 60
Red snapper. *See* Snapper
Refried beans, 97
Relishes
    Cranberry Chutney, 13
    Jicama and Fruit, *84*, 101
    Mustard Pickles, 12
    Sweet-Sour Corn, 50
    Tangy Apple Butter, 50
    Watermelon Pickles, 12
Rettigsalat, 58
Rex sole, mesquite-grilled, 117

Rice, 26
  Baked Rice Pudding, 18
  California Roll Sushi, 109
  Chicken, Andouille, and Tasso
    Jambalaya, *64*, 83
  Raisin Rice Pudding, 18
  Red Beans and, 74–75
  Seafood Filé Gumbo, *64*, 83
  Wild-Rice Stuffing, for Roast
    Chicken, 52–53
Rock cod. *See* Cod
Rockfish, in Cioppino, 111
Rolls. *See* Breads
Ropa Vieja, 31
Rotmus, 57
Roux, in Louisiana cooking, 66, 67
  techniques, 77
Rutabaga, Swedish Mashed Potatoes
  and, 57

S

Salad(s)
  Amana Colonies Radish, 58
  Church-Social Potato, 39, *40*
  Cobb, 112
  Crab Salad Louis, 110, *111*
  Creole Slaw, *64*, 82–83
  Crispy Coleslaw, *59*, 60
  East Texas Caviar, *84*, 101
  German Potato, *59*, 60
  Mixed Vegetables Vinaigrette, 123
  Nopalito, *91*, 94
  Tropical Fruit Salad With Coconut
    Milk, 120–21
  Wilted Green Salad With Sweet-Sour
    Dressing, 57
Sally Lunn, Georgia Style, 37
Salmon
  Alder-Grilled, *104*, 123
  Kedgeree, 7
  Lomi-Lomi, 107
  Teriyaki, 119
Salsa
  Cruda, 95
  Fresca. *See* Salsa Cruda
  Grilled Albacore With Tortillas
    and, 120
  Roja (Red chile sauce), 95
  Verde (Green sauce), 95
Salt cod, cooking, 6
  Scalloped Codfish, 7
Salt pork
  in Boston Baked Beans, 21, *23*
  in Clam Chowder, 21, *23*
  in Fish Chowder, 9
  in Parsnip Stew, 8
Sand Dabs, Mesquite-Grilled, 117
Sand Tarts, Ipperwash Beach, 61
San Francisco, sourdough baking
  in, 112
  San Francisco Sourdough French
    Bread, 113
Sauce(s)
  See also Butters; Gravy; Salsa
  Basting ("Moppin'") Sauce,
    100, 101
  Creole Tartar, for Louisiana Seafood
    Fry, 75
  Curry Mayonnaise, for
    artichokes, 108
  dessert
    Bourbon Sauce, for Bread
      Pudding, 81
    Nutmeg Sauce, for Apple
      Dumplings, 15
    Prickly-pear syrup, 94
  dipping, for artichokes, 108–9
  Guacamole, 95
  Horseradish, 14

Louis Dressing, 110
Mole Poblano "Gravy," *91*, 93
Rémoulade, 68–69
roux, 66, 67
  techniques, 77
Tartar, 27
  Creole, 75
Teriyaki, 119
Texas-Style Barbecue ("Soppin'")
  Sauce, 100, 101
Tomato
  for Creole Baked Eggs With
    Andouille, Ham, and
    Asparagus, 76
  Fresh, for Chicago-Style Deep-
    Dish Pizza, 54–55
Wild Berry Syrup, *115*, 116
Sausage(s)
  See also Andouille; Chaurice;
    Chorizo; Italian sausage
  Barbecued Pork Ribs and, *84*,
    100–101
  Louisiana, mail-order sources for, 67
  Polish, in Grilled Polish Sausage and
    Bratwurst, *59*, 60
  in Red Beans and Rice, 74, 74–75
  in Stuffed Acorn Squash, 58
Scalloped Codfish, 7
Scalloped Oysters, 8
Scallops, in Enchiladas Verdes de
  Mariscos, 117
Scandinavian influence, 50–51, 57,
  62–63
Scrapple, Fried, *44*, 47
Sea bass
  Baked Fish With Creole Butter in
    Foil Packages, 73
  Fish Chowder, 9
Shellfish
  See also specific kinds
  Boiled Seafood Dinner, 78, *79*
  Cioppino, 111
  Enchiladas Verdes de Mariscos, 117
  in Louisiana cooking, 66
  opening bivalves, 10
  in Pacific States cooking, 106
  Seafood Filé Gumbo, *64*, 83
  seafood gumbo, light-brown roux
    for, 77
  in southern cooking, 26
Shrimp
  in Boiled Seafood Dinner, 78, *79*
  in Cioppino, 111
  in Enchiladas Verdes de Mariscos
    (Seafood enchiladas with green
    sauce), 117
  in Louisiana cooking, 67
  in Louisiana Seafood Fry, 75
  Rémoulade, 68–69
  in Seafood Filé Gumbo, *64*, 83
  Shrimp Okra Pilau, 36
  in Stuffed Mirliton, 72, *72*
Side dishes
  See also Beans; Potatoes; Rice
  Baked Garlic Grits, 34–35
  Oyster and Eggplant Casserole, 71
  Virginia Spoon Bread, 38
Smithfield hams, 28
Smothered Pork Chops, *24*, 32
Snapper
  Baked Fish With Creole Butter in
    Foil Packages, 73
  in Fish Chowder, 9
Sopaipillas, 98–99
Sorbet
  Margarita, *102*, 103
  Nieve de Tunas, *91*, 94

Soup(s)
  from artichoke leaves, 108
  Black-Bean, 97
  Chile and Cheese, *91*, 92
  Cioppino, 111
  Crayfish Bisque, 70
  Fish Chowder, 9
  Geoduck Chowder, 112
  Idaho White-Bean, 49
  Morel, 49
  Oyster and Artichoke, 68
  Virginia Cream of Peanut, 34
  Winter Vegetable-Beef, 48–49
Sourdough baking, 112–13
  Alaskan Sourdough Bread, 114
  San Francisco Sourdough French
    Bread, 113
Sourdough Pancakes, *115*, 116
Sourdough Starter, 113
Southeast Asian influence, 106
Southern-Fried Chicken, 39, *40*
Spanish influence, 66, 76
Spoon Bread, Virginia, 38
Squash
  See also Chayote
  Acorn, Stuffed, 58
  patty-pan, in Cream-Cheese
    Sauce, 98
Squid, in Cioppino, 111
"Standing dishes," 6
Stews
  Cioppino, 111
  Fish Chowder, 9
  gumbo, described, 67
  Okra and Tomato, *35*, 36
  Parsnip, 8
  Zuni Lamb, Chile, and Hominy, 89
Stir-Fried Vegetables With Almonds,
  110
Strawberries. *See* Berries
Stuffing(s)
  Oyster, for Pork Chops, 76
  Wild-Rice, for Roast Chicken, 52–53
Succotash, 6, 11
Sushi, California Roll, 109
Sweet potatoes
  Maple-Glazed, 10
  in southern cooking, 26
  Sweet-Potato Pie, 33
  Yam Pone, 34
Syrup, Wild Berry, *115*, 116

T

Tangerines, in Tropical Fruit Salad With
  Coconut Milk, 120–21
Tartar Sauce, 27
  Creole, 75
Tarts. *See* Pies or tarts
Tasso, 67
  in Chicken Étouffée, 73
  in Grillades, 78
  Leeks Braised with, 71
  in Oyster and Eggplant Casserole, 71
  in Red Beans and Rice, 74–75
Techniques
  artichoke preparation, 108
  canning pickles or relishes, 12, 13
  chiles, peeling and roasting, 96
  coconut milk, 121
  cutting up a rabbit, 31
  food-processor doughs
    Flaky Pastry, 63
    Pizza Dough, 54, 55
  frying seafood, 75
  liquor-laced coffee drinks, 121
  roux, 77
  shellfish, opening bivalves, 10
  sushi rice, 109
  tortillas, softening, 89
  turkey, roasting in bag, 92–93

Tequila, 86
  in Margarita Sorbet, *102*, 103
Teriyaki Sauce, 119
Tetrazzini, Chicken, 120
Texas Barbecue, *84*, 100–101
Texas Chuck-wagon Country-Fried
  Steak, 29
Texas-Style Barbecue ("Soppin'")
  Sauce, 100, 101
Thanksgiving, original, 6
"Tipsy" cakes, 26
  Mississippi Mud Cake, 41
Tomatillos, 86, 87
  in Enchiladas Verdes de
    Mariscos, 117
  in Salsa Verde (Green sauce), 95
Tomatoes
  Fresh Tomato Sauce, for Chicago-
    Style Deep-Dish Pizza, 54–55
  Fried Green, 58
  Green-Tomato Pie, 18
  in Salsa Cruda, 95
  in southern cooking, 26
  Tomato Sauce, for Creole Baked
    Eggs With Andouille, Ham, and
    Asparagus, 76
Tortillas, softening, 89
Triple sec, 86
  in Margarita Sorbet, *102*, 103
Trout
  Baked Fish With Creole Butter in
    Foil Packages, 73
  Boneless Trout Teriyaki, 119
  Pan-Fried, Ernest Hemingway's
    Way, 51
Tucson Chimichangas With All the
  Trimmings, *88*, 89
Tuna
  Grilled Albacore With Tortillas and
    Salsa, 120
  Kedgeree, 7
Turbot, in Kedgeree, 7
Turkey
  gravies for, *91*, 93
  Guajolote Relleno, *91*, 92–93
  Oyster Stuffing for, 76
  roasting in brown paper bag, 92–93
  Tucson Chimichangas With All the
    Trimmings, *88*, 89
Turnip greens. *See* Greens
Turnovers, Empanaditas Dulces de Hoja
  (Fried dessert empanadas), 102

U, V

Upper Peninsula Pasties, 50–51
Vegetable pear. *See* Chayote
Vegetables
  See also Salad(s); *specific kinds*
  Country-Style Greens, *24*, 33
  Mixed Vegetables Vinaigrette, 123
  Stir-Fried Vegetables With
    Almonds, 110
  Succotash, 11
  Winter Vegetable-Beef Soup, 48–49
Vinaigrette, Herbed, for artichokes,
  108, 109
Vinaigrette, Mixed Vegetables, 123
Virginia Cream of Peanut Soup, 34
Virginia Spoon Bread, 38

W, X, Y, Z

Washington Pie, 22
Watermelon Pickles, 12
Whiskey, 26
  in Irish Coffee, 121
Wild-Rice Stuffing, 52–53
Yams. *See* Sweet potatoes
Yellow corn flour, 67
  in Louisiana Seafood Fry, 75

Special Thanks

From Bruce Aidells to:
Steve Armbruster
Carole Brendlinger
Regina Charboneau
Linda Gottschalk
Michael Wild

From John Phillip Carroll to:
Marion Cunningham
Sandra Griswold
Wayne Strei

From Sandra Cook to:
Helen Casartelli
Porter's Produce, San Francisco

From Jay Harlow to:
James Barrett
Buena Vista Cafe, San Francisco
Tori Bunting
Jim Dodge
Peggy Lyons
Jan Nix
Elaine Ratner
Cynthia Scheer
Stanford Court Hotel, San Francisco

From Cynthia Scheer to:
Sara Gafken
Patricia Pearson
Malcolm Rusk
John W. Smith
Vicki Vandamme
Windy City Pizza, Belmont, CA

From Naomi Wise and
 Michael Goodwin to:
Les Blank
Raul and Pilar Loaiza
Tom Miller
Ann Savoy
Carol Sutton and Mama
Martha Ture
Dolores "Pookie" Turner

U.S. MEASURE AND METRIC MEASURE CONVERSION CHART

Formulas for Exact Measures

Rounded Measures for Quick Reference

	Symbol	When you know:	Multiply by:	To find:			
Mass (Weight)	oz	ounces	28.35	grams	1 oz		= 30 g
	lb	pounds	0.45	kilograms	4 oz		= 115 g
	g	grams	0.035	ounces	8 oz		= 225 g
	kg	kilograms	2.2	pounds	16 oz	= 1 lb	= 450 g
					32 oz	= 2 lb	= 900 g
					36 oz	= 2¼ lb	= 1,000 g (1 kg)
Volume	tsp	teaspoons	5.0	milliliters	¼ tsp	= 1/24 oz	= 1 ml
	tbsp	tablespoons	15.0	milliliters	½ tsp	= 1/12 oz	= 2 ml
	fl oz	fluid ounces	29.57	milliliters	1 tsp	= 1/6 oz	= 5 ml
	c	cups	0.24	liters	1 tbsp	= ½ oz	= 15 ml
	pt	pints	0.47	liters	1 c	= 8 oz	= 250 ml
	qt	quarts	0.95	liters	2 c (1 pt)	= 16 oz	= 500 ml
	gal	gallons	3.785	liters	4 c (1 qt)	= 32 oz	= 1 l.
	ml	milliliters	0.034	fluid ounces	4 qt (1 gal)	= 128 oz	= 3¾ l.
Temperature	°F	Fahrenheit	5/9 (after subtracting 32)	Celsius	32° F	= 0° C	
					68° F	= 20° C	
	°C	Celsius	9/5 (then add 32)	Fahrenheit	212° F	= 100° C	